FROM HI

TO ST

EDUCATION AND THE AMERICAN MISSIONARY ASSOCIATION IN THE UWHARRIE "BACK COUNTRY" OF RANDOLPH COUNTY, NORTH CAROLINA

BY MARGO LEE WILLIAMS

Published by Backintyme Publishing

Crofton, Kentucky, U.S.A.

Backintyme Publishing

1341 Grapevine Rd.

Crofton, KY 42117

270-985-8568

Website: http://backintyme.biz

Email:backintyme@mehrapublishing.com

Printed in the United States of America

April 2016

Title ID: 5996076
ISBN-13: 978-0939479092
Library of Congress Control Number: 9780939479092

From Hill Town to Strieby

Education and the American Missionary Association in the Uwharrie "Back Country" of Randolph County, North Carolina

Margo Lee Williams

Foreword by Marvin T. Jones

To Edna
From NC to Arkansas –
Kindred spirits
Margo Lee Williams
2 Sept 2016

Dedicated to

The Rev. Islay Walden
Who loved God, Family,
Community and Education

Table of Contents

Table of Illustrations

Foreword

A lot of people contact me in hopes of finding any information about their ancestors who lived in my native rural community, in northeastern North Carolina. I wish for all of them and others that there will be more community histories like the one Margo Lee Williams presents here for Strieby.

Rare is a history of a rural African American community that is well researched, that stresses family, church, and education as Ms. Williams has done for her ancestral home of Strieby, forested under the Uwharrie Mountains in the North Carolina piedmont of Randolph County. The root of this research is Ms. Williams' award-winning biography of one of the Hilltown/Strieby community's progenitors, Miles Lassiter.

Hilltown/Strieby was a community that transitioned from slavery to freedom. In Williams' book we get to see the growth of a black community from antebellum free people of color and enslaved people to all being free with the chance for family-building, worship, education, landownership, and attainment of fuller rights for all.

Hilltown/Strieby and its early African American families must have been encouraged by, and perhaps participated in, the anti-Confederate resistance that was rife in Randolph County during the Civil War. In addition, Strieby is only a couple of counties west of the largest surrender of the Civil War, that of Joseph Johnston's army to William T. Sherman's Military Division of the Mississippi. This was days after Robert E. Lee's surrender to Ulysses S Grant. Notably, one of the Hilltown couples, Calvin Hill and his wife Elizabeth, gave names of Sherman and Grant to two of their sons.

Ms. Williams took well-spent time to profile the non-military forces of good that also benefitted Hilltown/Strieby: the Quakers, Howard University, a Rutgers professor, a New Jersey seminary, the American Missionary Association, and a northern church. A community should always acknowledge and remember its allies.

From the opportunities offered by emancipation, came the story of a remarkable ex-enslaved man, Rev. Islay Walden, highlighted by Williams. Despite near-blindness and illiteracy, Walden used his labor and poetic talents to sojourn by foot to the north. He returned to Hilltown an ordained Congregationalist pastor to found a school and a church that serves the community today. Walden was a true example of a nation-building man.

Rev. Islay Walden and his neighbors, of course, did not succeed alone. Before he marshaled his community to found its church and school, it is worthwhile to note that in addition to the Northern-led military victories that led to full emancipation, Walden's northern-acquired education assisted him to bring - probably by train given his successes up North - a new level of education and worship to Hilltown.

It was significant that Islay Walden brought a northern education to Hilltown, now Strieby. Walden also brought northern assistance in the form of the American Missionary Association. It must be remembered that thousands of African American communities quickly founded churches and schools during and after the Civil War. Those supported by missionary societies were also provided opportunities for their students to acquire higher education elsewhere. It is here that we learn how the AMA fostered schools for African Americans in the south when no other routes were open.

Rev. Islay Walden only lived for four years after his return to Hilltown. Besides his church, school, and institutional support, in his short time, Walden opened a post office in the now-named Strieby. This was an achievement made by few people of color. Perhaps his last gift to Strieby was to provide a successor. He was joined in Strieby by his northern-educated wife. Eleanora Farmer Walden followed in the tradition of educated northern women of color who were educational missionaries in the south. She contributed greatly as a teacher and as Strieby's the second postmaster.

Through Williams' diligent research, one can see where the impact of Mrs. Walden's teaching shows in World War I draft records, twenty-five years after her death. Others came forth to add more school buildings to the Strieby community. A Walden cousin, himself educated at Hampton, takes his ax and leads men into the woods to chop trees for the second school house. Three years earlier in Tuskegee, Alabama, Booker T. Washington would begin his first school structures this way.
Ms. Williams goes on to weigh the progress of the Strieby students against the racial disparities of public school support of African Americans in North Carolina. These

are detailed in the areas of spending, teacher education, buildings, attendance, school year length and books per student. Yet, there is the crucial point where Strieby School begins to produce benefits to the wider world: it is the step taken when one of its early students graduates and immediately proceeds to teach in another rural community.

Another result of Strieby natives pressing their presence on the outer world is the case of Strieby graduate and teacher Vella Lassiter. Eighteen years before Rosa Parks, Ms. Lassiter was forced off of a bus and injured. Aided by her cousin and fellow descendant of Miles Lassiter, lawyer T.F. Sanders, Ms. Lassiter successfully won damages against the bus company. The North Carolina Supreme Court upheld the verdict. This is one of many instances where some of Strieby's leaders were the descendants of the community's founders. This is brought out more when Ms. Williams adds extensive family genealogy pages that spans over 200 years. It is among these pages you learn of Sherman Hill and Ulysses Grant Hill.

All communities of color should have a book like this - one that develops its pre-Civil War history, then takes us through the gains made during Reconstruction and beyond, followed by extensive genealogical information. As of this date, there are thousands of descendants who can benefit from Margo Williams' work.

At a time when many Americans are in debt, underemployed, restricted from economic stability, victims of predatory capitalism, and subject to increased violence and racism, we need to turn to narratives of past and present self-determination. Strieby and its people offer powerful examples for the future.

Marvin T. Jones

Executive Director, *Chowan Discovery Group, Inc.*

Figure 1: Strieby Church Road at corner with High Pine Church Road. Strieby Church is up the road to the left of view. Photo by Margo Lee Williams, 2014.

Introduction

When I went to North Carolina for the first time in 1982, one of the places I was taken to see soon after arriving at the home of my cousin, Kate Lassiter Jones, in the Lassiter Mill area of New Hope Township, Randolph County, was Strieby Church, rebuilt just a few years before. I quickly learned of its significance as a church in the community and to our family, but I didn't know of its wider significance. Even after visiting the Randolph Room at the Randolph County Historical Society Library and learning that the founding pastor, the Rev. Islay Walden was also a recognized 19th century poet, I did not understand, nor did anyone suggest his significance as an educator, or that of the school to a rural and somewhat isolated African American community, or the place of both in the history of African American education in post-Civil War, Reconstruction-era North Carolina.

Probably one of the most important, if not the most important, liberties gained with emancipation was the freedom to be able to learn to read. Few things were valued more than the opportunity to get an education. The Freedmen's Bureau helped support schools, but missionary organizations also tried to bring education to former slaves. One of the most active organizations to do so was the American Missionary Association. Strieby School in Randolph County, North Carolina was one of their schools.

Strieby Church and School became a spiritual, cultural and educational center for the people living in the heart of the Uwharrie Mountains and Forest (Union Township), the "back country," as well as those from the neighboring Lassiter Mill community, on the Uwharrie River (New Hope Township), in Southwestern Randolph County. Unlike some of the other AMA churches and schools, Strieby was not founded by a northern missionary. Strieby was founded by a member of the local community. The Reverend (Alfred) Islay Walden had grown up an illiterate slave in Randolph County. When he returned to Randolph County after finishing his education as a teacher and minister, he returned to live with his sister and her family in Randolph County. He was one of Randolph County's own and it was very likely one of the most (if not the most) important elements in the success of Strieby Church and School.

When Walden left Randolph County around 1867-8 in search of medical assistance and an education, who would have guessed that 5-6 years later he would not only have learned to read and write, but also published a collection of poems? How inspiring that by the time 10 years had elapsed since leaving Randolph County in search of an education, he had graduated from Howard University's Normal program, graduated from New Brunswick Theological Seminary, and published a second collection of poems.

Walden was ambitious and industrious. Walden already had great experience and success as a grass roots organizer, running a successful mission school in New Brunswick, New Jersey, where he met his wife, Eleanora, also a teacher. With his wife, he was well on his way to seeing Strieby grow to include a secondary school. He even helped the community acquire its own Post Office, naming it "Strieby," but by 1884, just four years after he began his missionary work in Hill Town, he was dead. Surely no one could have been surprised if the school and church had faltered, but they did not. Despite his untimely death his wife and other community members carried on his dream and mission.

Strieby School is closed now, but Strieby Church continues to inspire the descendants of those early community members. Strieby Church continues to draw descendants back each year to discover their roots, be inspired to follow their dreams, and encourage their children to follow theirs, and Strieby Cemetery is still the final resting place chosen by many of those same descendants. In fact, before this manuscript could be published, the last surviving student of Strieby School, Aveus Lassiter Edmondson, died 19 October 2014, and was buried in Strieby Cemetery, 25 October 2014.
Much of Parts I, II, and III presented here were part of the author's historical presentation given to the Randolph County Historic Landmark Preservation Commission on 23 September 2014.[1] At that time they officially recognized Strieby's importance to the cultural heritage of Randolph County and the story of its African American community.[2] After a slide presentation to the Commission, combined with oral testimony by the author and descendants Elbert Lassiter Jr. and Jerry Laughlin, the Commission designated

---

[1] Williams, 2014. *See also:* Williams, 2015.
[2] HLPC, 2014a.

the Strieby site as a Cultural Heritage Site.[3] In Randolph County, Cultural Heritage Sites are recognized for their historic cultural significance regardless of any structures existing or no longer existing. The news was received enthusiastically by the community.[4] Fortunately, I was able to tell Aveus (who, sadly, would die a few weeks later) in person of this successful designation right away. In response she exclaimed "good!"

Part IV presents information on the families and cemetery at Strieby. Four generation genealogies of both the Hill family and Lassiter family are provided. These genealogies by extension include information on the other families that intermarried with these family members, some of whom were also part of the Strieby community. It also includes information on family members who moved away seeking their fortunes elsewhere in the country, including Arkansas, Illinois, Indiana, Massachusetts, Michigan, Missouri, New York, Ohio, and elsewhere. Also included in Part IV, along with names on the tombstones in Strieby Cemetery, are the names of those Hill and Lassiter family members buried in the cemetery without

---

[3] HLPC, 2014b.

[4] Penkava, 2014; Walker,

tombstones discovered from death certificates. This presentation of the Strieby story ends in Part V with a brief discussion of Strieby's current place in the community's life.

Recounting a community's history is in reality a community endeavor. In acknowledging those who so graciously and eagerly shared information about the history of Strieby church, school and community, there is a great fear that someone will be overlooked. If I have done so, I am profoundly apologetic, but appreciative of any information and encouragement you provided.

To those whom I harassed unmercifully for information, I am eternally grateful for your patience and support, including family and community members: the late Aveus Lassiter Edmondson, the late Evie Ruth Hill Grady, the late Harriet Glee Hill Jackson, the late Kate Lassiter Jones, the late Harold Lassiter, the late Vella Lassiter, the late Ruth Lassiter Laughlin, the late Margaret Lee Williams, as well as Martha Brooks, Patrice Lassiter Bryant, Roz Covington, Clyde Foust, Shirley Birkhead Green, Christine Hill, London Hill, Ruth M. Howard, Richard Jackson, Juanita Kessler, Nancy Barry Kline, Elbert Lassiter Jr., the Rev. Winston Lassiter, Jerry Laughlin,

Tiffany Pettiford, the Rev. Eric Ratliff Sr., Thomas Rush, Sharon Shanks, Tina Walden Spruill, Lettice McRae Tate, Daniel Thornburg, Patsy Waggoner, and Charleen Walker-Horton. In addition, not only am I immensely appreciative of those named herein, but also of those chance encounters with individuals who made passing comments, providing snippets of information, but to whom I may have never been introduced. I also wish to thank those non-community members who have been particularly supportive and encouraging, especially Randall Brown, Archivist, Elon University; Roland Barksdale-Hall, former editor of the *Journal of the Afro-American Historical and Genealogical Society*; Earl Ijames, Curator, North Carolina Museum of History; Paul Johnson, author and editor; Ann O'Bryan, Librarian, IUPUI Library; Carol Kostakos Petranek, Co-Director, Washington D.C. Temple Family History Center; and my dear mentor and friend, Marvin T. Jones, Executive Director, Chowan Discovery Group, Inc., whose suggestions and encouragement have been invaluable. Of course, I must thank my publisher, Stacy R. Webb, for all her patience and assistance with the publication process. Finally, any errors of fact must be laid ultimately at my feet, but I am always willing and anxious to acquire the correct information and documentation for future editions or other publications.

Margo Lee Williams

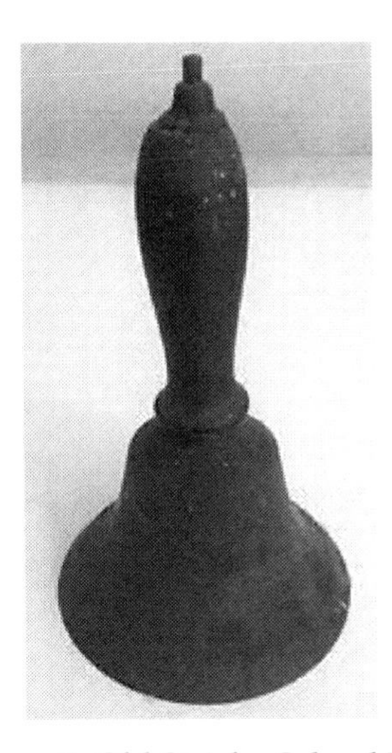

Figure 2: Old Strieby School Bell.

Prayer for the School

Jesus my Saviour, and my King,
Oh, grant this school a song to sing
That we together here may meet,
And bow and worship at thy feet.
And when we shall have left this place,
Then give us of thy richest grace,
And lead each one unto this home,
That we may praise thee on thy throne!
And if we here shall meet no more,
Then let us meet on Canaan's shore,
Where we may walk the streets around,
And wear a robe and starry crown.

The Rev. Islay Walden
From: ***Miscellaneous Poems***

PART ONE:

HILL TOWN and LASSITER MILL

Figure 3: Headed up Strieby Church Road towards the church. Photo by Margo Lee Williams, 2014.

Figure 4: Priscilla (Mahockly) Hill, "Granny Prissy." Photo courtesy of London Hill

The Hills and Hill Town

The central family, around whom the community of Hill Town grew, in what became Union Township, was that of Edward "Ned" Hill and his wife, Priscilla Mahockly, affectionately known as "Uncle Ned" and "Granny Prissy." Ned was reportedly a free man of color; however, he does not show up as a head of household prior to 1850. Priscilla on the other hand reportedly had a slave background, but may have been freed around 1830, when she and Ned began having children. Some descendants have said she was from Maryland, but from 1850 to 1910, in every census, she says she was born in North Carolina. [5]

It is thought by descendants that Ned had a relationship with a white "Hill" family. The only Hill family in both 1830 and 1840 that had free people of color in the household (though not named of course) was the Samuel Hill family.[6] Samuel Hill was a prominent, local,

---

[5]1850 US Federal Census; Census Place: Southern Division, Randolph, North Carolina; Roll: M432_641; Page: 133B; Image: 273. *Ancestry.com*. Priscilla Hill, age 50. *See also*: 1860; Census Place: Western Division, Randolph, North Carolina; Roll: M653_910; Page: 212; Image: 428; Family History Library Film: 803910. *Ancestry.com*. Prisci Hill, age 43 [*sic*]. *See also*: 1870; Census Place: Union, Randolph, North Carolina; Roll: M593_1156; Page: 506B; Image: 466; Family History Library Film: 552655. *Ancestry.com*. Priscilla Hill, age 45 [*sic*]. *See also*: 1880; Census Place: Union, Randolph, North Carolina; Roll: 978; Family History Film: 1254978; Page: 195B; Enumeration District: 224; Image: 0682. *Ancestry.com*. Priscilla Hill, age 65. *See also*: 1900; Census Place: Union, Randolph, North Carolina; Roll: 1213; Page: 6B; Enumeration District: 0099; FHL microfilm: 1241213. *Ancestry.com*. Priscilla Hill, age 95. *See also*: 1910; Census Place: Union, Randolph, North Carolina; Roll: T624_1128; Page: 2A; Enumeration District: 0100; FHL microfilm: 1375141. *Ancestry.com*. Priscilla Hill, age 106.

[6]1830; Census Place: Regiment 1, Randolph, North Carolina; Series: M19; Roll: 125; Page: 23; Family History Library Film: 0018091. *Ancestry.com*. Samuel Hill, 4 Free Persons of Color.

Quaker lawyer and abolitionist. He and his family were members of the Uwharrie Friends Meeting, a preparative meeting for Back Creek Monthly Meeting. Uwharrie Meeting was located in the Southwestern section of the county in what would become New Hope Township, next to what would become Union Township where Hill Town was located. By comparing ages of members of Ned's household in 1850 and that of the 1830 household of Samuel Hill, it would appear that the people of color in Samuel's household could very likely be Ned, Priscilla, and children, Nathan and Charity Hill. However, the 1840 census seems to indicate there might be 2 families of color living in the house, Ned's and one other.[7] Thus, it would appear that sometime before 1830, Edward "Ned" Hill became a free man of color, possibly even born free, living in the Southern District of Randolph County, most likely in the Uwharrie Mountain neighborhood he lived most of the rest of his life. It was during this time, 1842, that he entered a deed of trust. One of the trustees on this deed

---

[7]1840; Census Place: South Division, Randolph, North Carolina; Roll: 369; Page: 77; Image: 160; Family History Library Film: 0018097. *Ancestry.com.* Samuel Hill, 8 Free Persons of Color.

was Healy Phillips Lassiter, wife of Miles Lassiter, an African American Quaker who was also a member of Uwharrie Meeting (1842 Deed of trust).[8] Healy and Miles lived in the Lassiter Mill area of what would become New Hope Township about 2-3 miles from what would become "Hill Town."[9]

Ned and Priscilla had several children listed in the 1850 census: Charity, Calvin, Thany, Emsley, Mary and Sally. They lived next to Zeno Mose and his family, as well as Moses Winslow. Ned is listed as a laborer. According to the census, neither Ned or Priscilla, nor eldest daughter, Charity could read or write.[10]

There were other free people of color in the immediate area. It is difficult, however, to determine the boundaries of the various communities, because the census in 1850 only divides the county into North and South. On, the other hand, the 1860 census divides the county into

---

[8] Edward Hill to Samuel Hill, et al., 1842, Deed Book 25:1.

[9] 1850 US Federal Census; Census Place: Southern Division, Randolph, North Carolina; Roll: M432_641; Page: 136A; Image: 278. *Ancestry.com.* Miles Lassiter, age 73.

[10] 1850 US Federal Census; Census Place: Southern Division, Randolph, North Carolina; Roll: M432_641; Page: 133B; Image: 273. *Ancestry.com.* Edward Hill, age 30 [*sic*].

East and West. Nevertheless, it is possible to begin to identify the discrete communities. Among the families of color living within a few pages (5) of Ned in 1850 were the families of: Henley, Toney, Winslow, Mose, Phillips, Lassiter, Smith, Wallace, Baswell, and Williams. In fact within what appears to be only a few miles there were 92 free people of color counted. Some of them were living in the homes of known Quakers. Others, like Miles Lassiter and Ned Hill, were living independently with their own families [See *1850 Census, Free Families of Color*].

1850 census Randolph County -- Southern Section: Free Families of Color					
Dwelling #	Name	Color	# in house	Occupation	Comments
770	Andrew Phillips	B	1		Home of Thomas Low
770	Margaret Phillips	B	1		Home of Thomas Low
772	Edward Hill	B	8	Laborer	
773	Zeno Mose	B	9		
777	Thomas Henley	M	1		Home of Polly Henley
783	Henry B Smith	M	6		
785	Jesse Winslow	M	1		Home of Louise Hill
785	Henry Winslow	M	7		
789	Jesse Wallace	B	1		Home of Henry Henley
789	Lucy Wallace	B	1		Home of Henry Henley
792	Charles Toney	B	6	Chairmaker	
794	Caleb Winslow	B	3		
795	Reuben Baswell	B	1		Home of Aaron Hill
796	Luzena Winslow	B	1		Home of Franklin Gardner
802	Tony Henley	B	4	Laborer	
804	Jack Lassiter	[ ]	4		**Not listed as a person of color**
808	Miles Lassiter	B	8		Abigail Lassiter listed as farmer
813	Willie Lassiter	B	4	Painter	
822	Martin Horner	M	1		Home of Nathan Poston (sp?)
826	Laura Williams	M	1		Home of William Burney
841	Allen Floyd	M	1		
842	Lewis Phillips	M	1		Home of Eleazar Winslow
842	Green Henley	B	1		Home of Eleazar Winslow
842	Cynthia Phillips	M	1		Home of Eleazar Winslow
843	Ferebee Winslow	B	1		Home of Anna Henley
845	Emory Henley	M	1		Home of David Henley
848	Tamar Phillips	M	5		
852	Nathan Phillips	B	7	Miller	
854	James Walker	B	5		
	Total		**92**		

Figure 5: 1850 Census, Southern Division Randolph County -- Free Families of Color

By 1860, the community of free people of color seems to have dwindled. The community only had 9 intact families and 4 individuals living in white homes, for a total of 54 members. Ned and Priscilla's family had grown however. Calvin was now married with a child. Ned and

Calvin were listed as Farm Laborers.[11] Again living nearby were: the Anthony Henley family, the Colier Lassiter family, the Calvin Dunson family, Macam Polk (sometimes spelled Pope), Jack Lassiter and wife Charity, Thomas Conrad [sp] family, Nathan Hill (presumed oldest son of Ned and Priscilla) family, Micajah Cotton family, and Jack Henley with 2 apparent siblings living in the home of William Burney [See *1860 Census, Free Families of Color*].

1860 US Census Randolph County NC - Western Division: Free People of Color						
Dwelling #		Name	Color	# in home	Occupation	Comments
1072		Jack Henley	M	3	Farm Laborer	Home of William Burney
1075		Micajah Cotton	M	6	Farm Laborer	Wife: Harriett Polk
1094		Ed Hill	B	7	Farm Laborer	
1095		Calvin Hill	M	3	Farm Laborer	Son of Ed "Ned" Hill
1096		Anthony Henley	B	6	Farm Laborer	
1096	[sic]	Cal Lassiter	B	6	Farm Laborer	Wife: Katherine Polk
1097		Jack Lassiter	B	2	Farm Laborer	Uncle of Cal Lassiter
1098		Calvin Dunson	B	6	Blacksmith	Wife: Nancy Lassiter
1099		Macam Polk	M	1	Farm Laborer	Home of Winslow Thornburg
1103		Thomas Conrad	M	8	Farm Laborer	
1114		Nathan Hill	B	6	Farm Laborer	Son of Ned Hill/Wife: Sarah Lassiter
			Total	54		

Figure 6: 1860 Census, Western Division, Randolph County - Free Families of Color

[11] 1860; Census Place: Western Division, Randolph, North Carolina; Roll: M653_910; Page: 212; Image: 428; Family History Library Film: 803910. *Ancestry.com*. Ed Hill, age 50.

Birth of Hill Town

With the end of the Civil War, there were more families of color with the ability to choose where they wished to live. While, on the one hand, the Uwharrie River and its streams which included the Lassiter's Mill area of New Hope Township seemed to be a magnet for many of these families, on the other hand, the adjacent Uwharrie mountain area of Union Township, that would become known first as Hill Town, and then Strieby, seemed to attract very few. According to the census, by 1870, in all of New Hope Township there were a total of 201 people of color. By contrast, in Union Township, there were 4 families and 5 individuals living and working in white homes, for a total of 26 people of color [See Figure:*1870 Census*]. Economically, despite the fact that in the Uwharrie there was an active gold mine, as well as a federal distillery and sawmills for the dense pine forests, most families in either area seemed to be either farmers, or farm laborers.

1870 US Census Randolph County-Union Township : People of Color					
Dwelling #	Name	Color	# in home	Occupation	Comments
3	Allen Black	B	1	Farm Laborer	In Home of Addison Spencer
26	Julia Gatlin	B	1	Domestic Servant	In Home of Marmaduke Williams
36	Rhoda Moffitt	B	1	Cook	In Home of John Lucas
63	Anderson Smitherman	B	3	Farm Laborer	Son-in-law of Nancy Lassiter Dunson
64	Harrison Bingham	M	1	Farm Laborer	In Home of Lewis Bingham
75	Ned Hill	B	5	Farm Laborer	
76	Calvin Hill	M	8	Farm Laborer	Son of Ned Hill
116	Henry Brown	M	1	Farm Laborer	In Home of Calvin Shaw
117	Benjamin Luther	B	5	Farm Laborer	Wife: Bethany Hill
		Total	26		

1870 US Census Randolph County-New Hope Township-Lassiter's Mill: People of Color					
Dwelling #	Name	Color	# in home	Occupation	Comments
3	Samuel Brown	M	1	Day Laborer	Home of Micajah Lassiter
6	Adam Cogings	B	1	At Home	Child in home of H C Lassiter
10	Peter Bell	M	6	Farmer	
11	Amos Carter	M	6	Farmer	
15	Tomie Briles	B	1	Day Laborer	Home of Daniel Miller
17	Samuel Capell	B	1	Day Laborer	Home of Stimpson Keerns
18	David Barringer	B	1	At Home	Child in Home of T N Ingram
20	C A Fenelton	M	1	Farmer	Home of John L Riley
22	Angeline Fenelton	M	2	Keeping House	
24	Jesse Ingram	B	4	Day Laborer	
30	Giles Ingram	B	1	Day Laborer	Home of Wilson Russell
40	T Bryant	B	4	Farmer	Wife Nancy Jane Lassiter
44	Margaret Brown	B	2	Keeping House	
47	Calvin Harriss	B	1	At Home	Child in Home of JMC Russell
48	Fannie Raise	B	2	Keeping House	
64	Joseph Bell	B	3	Farmer	
68	John Kearns	B	1	Tanner	Home of W F Lassiter
70	Sarah Calico	M	4	Keeping House	
73	Adam Harriss	M	1	At Home	Child in Home of Henry Lassiter
79	Reuben Butler	B	4	Day Laborer	Wife: Charity Cotton
80	Calvin Dunson	B	8	Blacksmith	Wife: Nancy Lassiter
83	Seth Cranford	B	1	Farmer	
85	Robert Harris	B	1	Farm Hand	Home of Richard Graves
86	George Smitherman	B	1	Farmer	Home of Martin Luther
96	Mark Stokes	B	5	Farmer	
122	Isabella Dorsett	B	1	No occupation	Child in home of Virgil Dorsett
143	Seth Cranford	B	1	Farmer	
151	Sidney Ledbetter	B	13	Farmer	
153	Caroline Hopkins	B	4	Keeping House	
155	Charlotte Davis	B	9	Keeping House	
169	Sam Henley	B	2	At Home	Home of William Burney
169	Bob Baldwin	B	1	At Home	Home of William Burney
169	Lucy Burney	B	3	At Home	Home of William Burney
169	Bettie Ledbetter	B	1	Keeping House	Home of William Burney
170	Lucy Sanders	B	1	At Home	Home of M M Hopkins
190	Collier Lassiter	B	10	Farmer	Wife: Katherine Polk
191	Amos Brown	B	2	Farmer	
193	Loren Graves	B	8	Farmer	
194	Steven Lewis	B	2	Farm hand	
196	Ann Loftin	B	7	Housekeeper	
199	Harkless Bingam	B	7	Farm hand	
201	Spencer Cameron	B	2	Farmer	
201	John Brown	B	4	Farmer	In Home in Spencer Cameron
202	Gadison Garner	B	3	Farmer	
204	Amos Brown	B	4	Farmer	
205	Rebecca Winslow	B	3	Keeping House	
206	Micajah Cotton	B	8	Farmer	Wife: Harriett Polk
207	Joe Steed	M	7	Farmer	
208	Josiah Callicut	B	7	Farmer	
209	Abram Sanders	B	6	Farm hand	
210	Isham Sanders	B	5	Farm hand	
211	Nathan Hill	B	9	Farm hand	Wife: Sarah Lassiter/Son of Ned Hill
212	Thomas Revels	B	7	Farm hand	
213	Maranda Alexander	M	1	At home	In Home of William Scarlett
		Total	201		

Figure 7: 1870 Randolph County, Union and New Hope Townships: Families of Color

By 1880, however, the Uwharrie community in Union township had grown significantly to 10 families, for a total of 60 people. By this time, several of Ned and Priscilla's children had married and their families settled in the community. Because of the large number of Hill family members now living in the community, it began to be known as "Hill Town." The community also included a young minister and teacher, the Rev. Islay Walden, who had been educated at Howard University and the New Brunswick Theological Seminary (New Jersey). He was a former Randolph County slave who had returned to bring both the gospel and education to the community. Walden would also serve those living in the nearby Lassiter Mill area in New Hope Township. That community included another 9 families and one individual in a white home for an additional 60 people. Thus, altogether, the community that would be served by this minister and teacher comprised about 120 people [*See: Figure: 1880 Census below*].

1880 US Census Randolph County - Union Township: Families of Color								
Dwelling #	Name	Color	# in home	Occup	can't read	can't write	In School	Comments
15	Thomas Potter	B	3	Farmer	2	2	0	Wife: Mary Jane Hill
16	Edmund Cranford	B	4	Farmer	1	2	0	Wife: Sarah "Sally" Hill
17	Calvin Hill	B	10	Farmer	6	7	2	Son of Ned Hill
18	Benjamin Luther	B	8	Cooper	2	2	2	Wife: Bethany Hill
19	Priscilla Hill	B	4	House	0	0	0	Widow of Ned Hill
20	Nathan Hill	B	10	Farmer	2	6	4	Son of Ned Hill/Wife:Sarah Lassiter
21	Emsley Hill	B	7	Farmer	0	1	0	Son of Ned Hill
21	Mary Tony	B	1	Farm Lab	0	0	0	Boarder-Unemployed 10 mos
21	Islay Walden	B	1	Minister	0	0	0	Boarder:Bro-in-law-Emsley Hill
27	Henry Sanders	B	3	Farmer	0	0	0	Wife: Julia Lassiter
28	Samuel Sanders	B	9	Farmer	4	6	5	May be Father of Henry Sanders
	Total		60		17	26	13	71.7 % total literacy

1880 US Census Randolph County - New Hope Township: Families of Color								
Dwelling #	Name	Color	# in home	Occup	can't read	can't write	In School	Comments
1	Calier Lassiter	B	6	Farmer	1	1	3	
1	Mary Polk	W	1	At home	1	1	0	home of Calier Lassiter/Mother-in-law
2	Nancy Dunson	B	6	House	1	1	0	Sister of Calier Lassiter
7	Wiley Hill	B	1	Servant	0	0	0	Home of Fredric Garner/Son of Nathan Hill
9	Spencer Cameron	B	4	None	0	0	0	2 grandsons are farm workers
11	Antone Davis	B	9	Farmer	4	5	0	Lydia Hearn, mother-in-law; Nancy Davis, mother
12	William Davis	B	10	Farmer	5	5	0	Probable brother of Antone Davis
13	Garretson Garner	B	6	Farm Wrk	3	4	0	
18	Ande Smitherman	B	6	Laborer	0	1	0	Son-in-law of Nancy Lassiter Dunson
20	Harriett Cotton	B	9	House	1	4	0	Widow: Micajah/Probable sister of Kate Polk Lassiter
29	Adline Davis	B	2	Servant	0	1	0	
	Total		60		16	23	3	73.3% overall literacy

The following families are in New Hope Township but not near Lassiter's Mill or Strieby								
Dwelling #	Name	Color	# in home	Occup	Can't read	can't write	In School	Comments
44	Candis Burney	B	3	Servant	3	3	0	Home of Nancy Burney
46	James Haywood	B	5	Laborer	5	5	0	
61	Raner Dorsett	B	4	Servant	2	2	0	
64	Brock Kearns	B	7	Farmer	2	4	4	
65	Brazilla Ingram	B	3	Farmer	0	1	0	
67	Kate Stokes	B	1	Servant	0	0	0	In home of Nixon Ingram
69	Jiles Ingram	B	1	Serv/Lab	0	0	0	In Home of Manley Riley
71	Clinton Ingram	B	3	Farmer	0	0	0	
73	John Kearns	B	5	Farmer	0	2	0	
76	Jesse Ingram	B	4	Farmer	3	3	1	
86	Randel Ingram	Mu	3	Farmer	2	2	0	
87	Charley Cross	Mu	5	Farmer	1	1	0	
95	Calvun Taylor	B	2	Farmer	2	2	0	
96	Edmon Reves	B	2	Farmer	1	1	1	
97	Wilborn Taylor	B	4	Farmer	2	2	0	
97	Harriett Cotton	Mu	2	Home	1	1	0	in home of Wilborn Taylor
99	Mariah Russell	B	1	Servant	1	1	0	In home of Dovie Varner
109	Julius Hill	B	1	Laborer	0	1	0	In home of Sandy Lassiter
110	Charity Butler	B	7	House	5	5	0	
116	Frank Stafford	B	1	Servant	0	0	0	In home of Calvin Hancock
132	Fannie Birkhead	B	2	House	2	2	0	
134	Marc Stokes	B	4	Farmer	4	4	0	
136	William Stokes	B	6	Farmer	2	2	0	
168	Steven Lewis	B	2	Laborer	2	2	0	
186	George Steed	B	7	Farmer	4	4	2	
202	Jeremiah Davis	B	3	Farmer	3	3	0	
202	Eva Davis	B	2	Farmer	1	1	1	
	Total		90		48	54	9	89.5% overall literacy

Figure 8: 1880 Randolph County, Union and New Hope Townships: Families of Color

Figure 9: Arthur Haze Hill, great grandson, standing next to Priscilla "Granny Prissy" Hill's Tombstone. Strieby Church Cemetery. Photo courtesy of Richard Jackson.

Figure 10: Lassiter Mill.
Photo by Margo Lee Williams, 1982.

The Lassiter Mill Community

The second community to be served by Strieby Church and school founded by the Rev. Islay Walden was the Lassiter Mill community. The original Lassiter's Mill stood on the west side of the Uwharrie River and was apparently built before 1779, when the county was founded, since it reportedly appeared on a map at that time. Additionally, while the book, *Farmer*, said that the Lassiters didn't purchase their land on the Uwharrie until

1782, the "widow" Sarah Lassiter was already listed on the 1779 tax list for Randolph County.[12]

Lassiter's Mill was a water-powered grist mill, where Randolph County residents brought their corn and wheat to be ground for making bread. Many older living descendants can remember their families taking the grain to the mill for grinding. Around the time of the Civil War the Mill was run by brothers, S.T. and Clark Loflin. At some time prior to 1925 it was sold to a Frank Woolery, who then sold it to S.T. Loflin's son, Colonel Loflin. Colonel Loflin moved and rebuilt the mill on the east side of the Uwharrie River. During that time, the Mill was called "Loflin's Mill." In 1964, the Mill, now being called "River Side Mill," was owned by Jake Thornburg, who operated the mill three days a week.[13] However, all living community descendants with whom this writer has spoken call it "Lassiter's Mill" or "Lassiter Mill." The Mill stood on the east side of the river until it was irreparably damaged by storms in the summer of 2011. A decision was made not to reconstruct the mill, but rather to gather

---

[12] Hammond and Cranford, 1981, p. 143.

[13] Randolph Report, 1964, p. E2.

together the remaining timbers, place them in a pit, burn them as a funeral pyre, and bury the ashes next to the Uwharrie River on which it stood for over 200 hundred years.[14]

Miles Lassiter

Several of the families of color in the Lassiter Mill community of New Hope Township that were early members of Walden's church in Hill Town, were descendants of Miles Lassiter, born a slave circa 1777, and his wife Healy Phillips Lassiter, a free woman of color. Miles had been the property of Ezekiel (called "Josiah," in most published references) and Sarah Lassiter who lived in the Lassiter Mill area of New Hope Township, south of Asheboro, in Randolph County. Ezekiel Lassiter died about 1779 leaving Miles under the control of the widow, Sarah, for her lifetime, but the legal restrictions of his servitude were not strictly enforced, what some would call a "nominal slave."[15]

---

[14] Told to the Author by Patsy Cranford Waggoner, 9 December 2011.
[15] Williams, 2011.

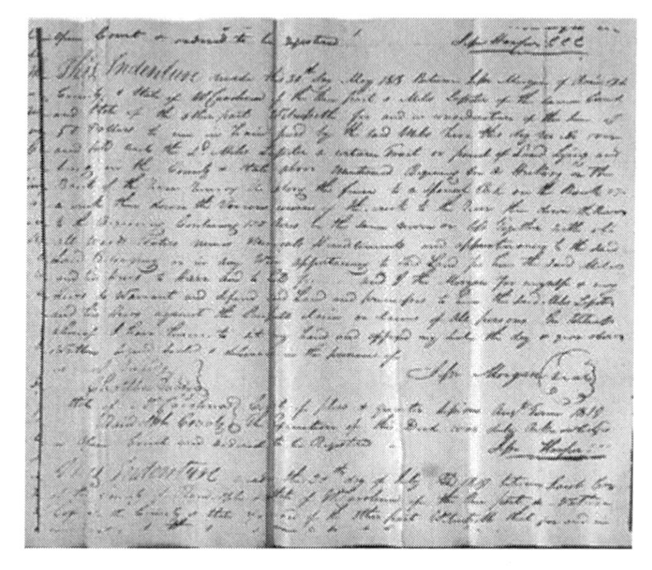

Figure 11: Miless Lassiter's 1815 Deed of Purchase for 100 Acres

The earliest record for Miles identified him in the 1807 court minutes being named to a road maintenance crew. However, it did not indicate that he was a person of color. By 1815 Miles had bought 100 acres of land, again with no reference to his color. In 1826, however, with Sarah Lassiter as co-signer, he sold the land to a local Quaker (Society of Friends) farmer, Henry Newby. Again, there was no reference to his color. In 1832, Newby apparently returned the land to Miles (though no deed of transfer has been located to date), before he and his family migrated to Indiana, accompanied by Miles' oldest son, Emsley.[16]

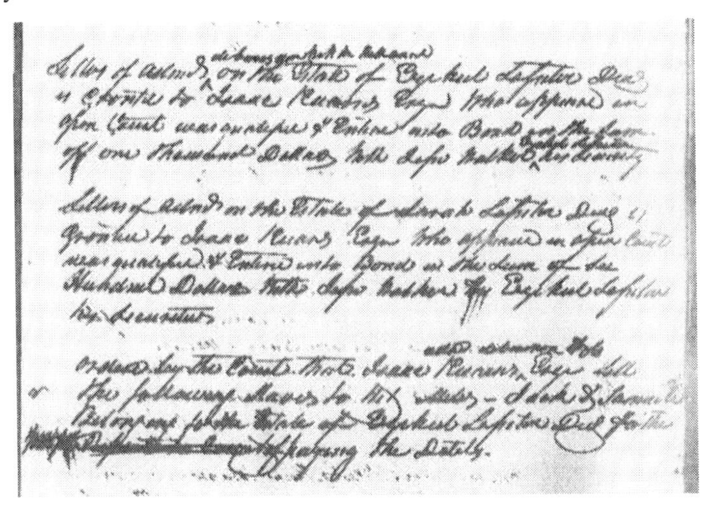

Figure 12: Letters of Administration for the Estates of Ezekiel and Sarah Lassiter, 1840.

In 1830, Miles is identified as a free head-of-household in the US census. During these years, according to his obituary in *Friends' Review*, he was Sarah Lassiter's business manager, a man with strong business acumen and someone who had helped her to expand her property and other financial holdings, indicating he was at least semi-literate.[17] In fact, the 1850 census confirmed that he

[16] Newby, 1916.

[17] *Friends Review,* 1850, iii:700.

could read and write.[18] This was not necessarily unusual since Miles lived a "quasi" free life and local Quakers (Friends) were known to teach Free People of Color to read and write in their schools.

It was only in 1840 that he was identified in court records as a slave when, on Sarah's death, he was sold as part of a delayed probate of Ezekiel's estate. This was because Miles was technically part of Ezekiel's estate, not Sarah's. Miles was much older by this time and partially disabled from a fall from a horse, thus no one at the sale wished to purchase him. This was fortuitous, however, because it provided an opportunity for his wife, Healy Phillips, a free woman of color described as "industrious," to purchase him for a nominal fee.[19]

Miles was found for the last time in the US census in 1850, as a free head-of-household, with family members, including a brother, Samuel, and several of his seven

---

[18]1850 US Federal Census; Census Place: Southern Division, Randolph, North Carolina; Roll: M432_641; Page: 136A; Image: 278. *Ancestry.com.* Miles Lassiter, age 73.

[19] Letters of Administration and Order to sell slaves, Ezekiel Lassiter & Sarah Lassiter, February 1840.FHL #019652 or #0470211. *See also*: Final Distribution of Estate of Sarah Lassiter and Ezekiel Lassiter, 1840, Will Book 7:406. FHL #0019643. *See also*: *Friends Review*, 1850, iii:700.

children. He was recorded as having property worth $500.[20] However, his household did not include Healy who had died about 1845.[21]

In March 1845, Miles took the *extraordinary* step of requesting membership in the Back Creek Friends Meeting. Even more extraordinary, he was accepted and became a member three months later in June 1845, with no evidence of discord over his application and acceptance.[22] This was remarkable. Henry Cadbury in his 1936 three part article on "Negro" Friends, in the *Journal of Negro History*, noted that although African Americans in North Carolina attended Friends' meetings, there had only been one other person of color accepted as a full member and that had been over 45 years earlier.[23] Thus, Miles was the *only* African American member of a Friends Meeting in North Carolina at that time. Indeed, there would not be another until after the Civil War, despite the strong involvement of the Society of Friends in abolition efforts,

---

[20]1850; Census Place: Southern Division, Randolph, North Carolina; Roll: M432_641; Page: 136A; Image: 278. *Ancestry.com*. Miles Lassiter, age 73.
[21]*The Genealogical Journal*, 1981, V(1): 38-42, "The Willie Lassiter Petition."
[22]U.S., Quaker Meeting Records, 1681-1994 [Database on-line]. *Ancestry.com*. Minutes of Back Creek Monthly Meeting, 25 March 1845 & 25 June 1845, Miles Lassiter.
[23] Cadbury, 1936, Miles Lassiter.

including the Underground Railroad. Cadbury, in his section on Miles, quoted the editor of *Friends Review* who was reflecting on this paradox at the time of Miles' death: "Is the religious of Friends unsuited to the coloured race? Or are they kept at a distance by our neglect or repulsive conduct?"[24] It is noteworthy, however, that Back Creek Meeting Minutes indicate that Miles was a well-respected member of the local preparative meeting to which he belonged, (Uwharrie Meeting), since he was appointed to one of its committees to oversee and address issues of behavior and character.[25]

---

[24] Cadbury, 1936, Miles Lassiter.
[25]U.S., Quaker Meeting Records, 1681-1994 [Database on-line]. *Ancestry.com*. Minutes of Back Creek Monthly Meeting, 31 Jan 1849 & 28 March 1849, Miles Lassiter.

700 FRIENDS' REVIEW.

Figure 13: Miles Lassiter Obituary, Friends Review, 1850

On 22 June 1850, Miles died after suffering for several days following an apparent heart attack, according to the obituary which appeared in *Friends Review*.[26] At the time of his death he owned 400 acres of land in the Lassiter Mill

[26]*Friends Review* 1850, iii:700.

community (New Hope Township) of Randolph County, between Black Mountain Road and High Pine Church Road. Much of the land is still in the possession of descendants. Miles was buried in the Uwharrie Friends Cemetery, on Lassiter Mill Road, south of present-day Science Hill Friends Meeting.[27]

Figure 14: Uwharrie Friends Cemetery, Lassiter Mill Road. Photo by Margo Lee Williams, 2011.

[27]*For more information on* Miles, *see* Williams, 2011.

Figure 15: Current Home Place on Lassiter Mill Road, Designed and Built by Colon Lassiter, Great Grandson of Miles Lassiter. The Late Margaret Lee Williams, a Great-Great-Great Granddaughter, in the foreground.
Photo by Margo Lee Williams, 1982.

Figure 16 Katherine (Polk) Lassiter, "Granny Kate," 1832-1906. Photo courtesy of Patrice Lassiter Bryant

Colier Lassiter

After the death of Miles in 1850, his son Colier/Calier seemed to become the head of the extended family, taking responsibility for the homestead (later known as the "Colier Lassiter Tract"). Colier was the second oldest son. The oldest son, Emsley, had moved west to Indiana with the Quaker migration in 1832, as mentioned above.

Colier's name first appeared in county records in 1840, when he bought the freedom of his uncle, Jack Lassiter from the estate of Ezekiel Lassiter, husband of the "Widow" Sarah Lassiter.[28] In 1850, his name, along with those of his sisters (Abigail, Nancy, and Jane) appeared in the census listed in the household of Miles Lassiter.[29] Nearby was another brother, Wiley Lassiter and his family. In the 1860, 1870, and 1880 censuses, respectively, Colier's name appeared as the head of his own household. In 1848, an unrecorded deed, in the possession of the late Harold Lassiter, indicated that he bought land adjacent to his mother from William Lassiter, one of Sarah Lassiter's descendants. The land was described as

> being...on the Est side of the Uharie River beginning at a rock in the middle of the River then East with Thornburgs line to Healy Phillips corner then South with said Phillipses line to a gum then west to a rock in the middle of the River then up the middle of the River to the beginning, half a acre more or less...[30]

---

[28] Final Distribution of the Estate of Ezekiel Lassiter, 1840, Will Book 7:406. FHL #0019643.

[29] 1850 US Federal Census; Census Place: Southern Division, Randolph, North Carolina; Roll: M432_641; Page: 136A; Image: 278. *Ancestry.com.* Miles Lassiter, age 73.

[30] Harold Lassiter papers.

The first recorded deed on the inherited land (recorded in 1855) was the 1851 deed wherein Nancy, Susannah, Emsley, and Wiley sold him all rights to 400 acres.[31] In 1855 he took his first deed of trust on 300 acres, subsequent to the filing of his mother's probate, with whom the land apparently originated.[32] In 1874, he and his wife, Katherine (Polk), called "Granny Kate," sold one acre to the Board of Education.[33] It is not clear what school would have been built on it, although a reference in 1879, by Dr. Roy from the American Missionary Association (AMA) while on a field trip to the area, seems to indicate there was a public school operating in the area.[34] His final transaction took place in 1887 when he took a mortgage with a Jenny Lassiter. By 1893, the land was involved in a dispute between his nieces, Adelaide Dunson Kearns and Ellen Dunson Smitherman, and their husbands.[35] Colier,

---

[31] Emsley and Susan Lassiter, et al, to Calier Phillips, 1851, recorded 1855, Deed Book 29:495. FHLM #0470233.

[32] Colier Lassiter to Samuel Hill (Tr), 1855, Deed Book 30:15. FHL #0470234.

[33] Colier and Katie Lassiter to Board of Education, 1874, Randolph County Deed Book 38:288. FHL #0470237.

[34] Roy, 1879, p. 33(11):335.

[35] Anderson Smitherman et al, v Solomon Kearns, et Ux. Final Decree, 1893, Randolph County Deed Book 248: 156. FHL #0470851.

himself, was dead by this time. His heirs were allotted 150 acres in the final decree.[36]

Additional land records which have been preserved by Colier's descendants include: an 1808 deed from Elijah Bingham to William Arnold for one hundred acres; a land grant (#2406) to Christopher Bundy in 1801,with another copy of the same grant dated 1818 also for one hundred acres "on the waters of the Uharie;" and finally there is a plat and description for eighteen acres of land, location not mentioned, but identified as "Calier Lassiter's Clearing," containing an upper piece of 9 acres and 4 rods, and a lower piece of 9 acres and 59 rods.[37]

Colier's name also appeared in a number of other records. In the spring of 1857, he was charged in Superior Court with unlawfully carrying firearms.[38] In 1867 his name (recorded as "Calvin") appeared in the records of the Bureau of Refugees, Freedmen and Abandoned Lands ("Freedmen's Bureau") as a delegate to the Constitutional Congress for North Carolina.[39] Colier died sometime between 1887 and 1893. He was

---

[36]*See:* Williams, 2011.

[37]Harold Lassiter Papers.

[38] State v Colier P. Lassiter, Spring Term 1857, Minutes of the Superior Court. FHL #0470215.

[39] Delegate to the Constitutional Congress, North Carolina, Lassiter Mills District, Calvin Lassiter. Bureau of Refugees, Freedmen, and Abandoned Lands. NARA #M843, Roll 32:107.

reportedly buried at Uwharrie Friends Cemetery, Asheboro, but looking at the information on that cemetery presented here (*See* "Part I: Uwharrie Cemetery"), it is perhaps more likely that he was buried at Strieby. Since there is no marker in either cemetery which was common at the time in this heavily Quaker community, there is nothing to corroborate this information either way. His wife, Katherine (Polk) Lassiter ("Granny Kate") died 19 December 1906 and was buried in Strieby Cemetery. Granny Kate was a founding member of Strieby Church.[40]

[40] *See also:* Williams, 2011.

Figure 17: Granny Kate Lassiter Tombstone. Photo by Margo Lee Williams, 1982.

Uwharrie Friends Meeting House, 1793-1856. Friends who were meeting in the Uwharrie area before 1780 built this house in 1793 and met in it until 1856 when the meeting was laid down. The building stood for several years.

Figure 18: Uwharrie Friends Meeting House.
Courtesy of the Randolph Room, Randolph County Library.

Uwharrie Friends and Rocky Branch

The Rev. Islay Walden's church and school were not the first to serve the people of Hill Town and Lassiter Mill. Uwharrie Friends Meeting was established in 1793. Uwharrie Friends were apparently strongly antislavery. On at least one occasion the Meeting, on behalf of the North Carolina Yearly Meeting, was deeded a family of slaves, from Abraham Simmons (Symmons), which was a first step in helping them achieve freedom. That family eventually found freedom when they went to Carthage, Indiana around 1830, as part of the Quaker migration to the Midwest. There they were known as Lassiters and the

Figure 19: Henry Newby House, Carthage, Indiana. Photo by Nancy Barry Kline, 2013.

community believed them to be cousins of Emsley Lassiter, Miles' oldest son, who had also migrated to the Carthage area along with Uwharrie Meeting member, Henry Newby and his family.[41]

---

[41] Williams, 2013

Figure 20: Uwharrie Friends Meeting and Cemetery (1793-1864) marker. Photo by Margo Lee Williams, 2011

Uwharrie Cemetery

The Meeting House was used until 1856 and the Meeting itself was discontinued in 1864. The building was "roofed" (torn down) in 1867, and the land, excluding the cemetery, was sold in 1877. The history of the cemetery is unclear. In keeping with the "plain" life, "[i]t was often customary for Friends to leave their graves unidentified by anything more than a stone slate because to do more would be a "worldly excess."[42] In 1994, 250 gravesites were identified inside the cemetery boundaries, however, "[t]he East side of graveyard was used by the colored people," wrote Lillian H(ill) Thornburg in 1941 to a Mrs. Worth.[43] The last burial of a person of color was reportedly John Sanders, according to Morrison (2009), but a date was not given in the article and no death date has been identified in any current databases, nor was he found in the census after 1880.[44] This was presumably the John F. Sanders found as a boy living in Union Township, in the Hill Town area, the son of Samuel and Mary Sanders, and next door to his brother Henry, who had married Wiley Lassiter's daughter, Juliann.[45] This is where Miles was most likely buried in 1850, although he may have been buried inside the cemetery proper because he was in fact a member of the Meeting.[46]

---

[42] Morrison, 2009, p. 3

[43] Letter of Lillian Hill Thornburg to Mrs. Worth, 1941, p. 2

[44] Morrison, 2009, p. 3.

[45] 1880; Census Place: Union, Randolph, North Carolina; Roll: 978; Family History Film: 1254978; Page: 196C; Enumeration District: 224; Image: 0683. *Ancestry.com*. John F. Sanders, lines 37 & 38.

[46] *See* Williams, 2011.

Rocky Branch Church and School

After Uwharrie Friends Meeting was laid down, the African American community in the Lassiter Mill area as well as those at Hill Town, were given permission to use the Meeting House for worship. Lillian Thornburg wrote: "Uwharrie Friends Church was built in 1797. It was a spacious meeting house. When no longer used as a meeting of Friends the colored people held revivals in it."[47] Thornburg, who was born in 1872 and died in 1949,[48] recalled a time when her parents took her to one of these revivals, "Well I remember when about seven years old my parents took me with them to one of the revivals, and my terror when the halleluiahs rolled."[49] Since the Meeting House was "roofed" in 1867 and the land sold in 1877, when Thornburg would have been only five years old, it is not likely that the revival she attended was at the old Meeting House.

---

[47] Lillian Hill Thornburg Letter, 1941, p. 1.

[48] North Carolina Death Certificates 1909-1976 [Database on-line]. *Ancestry.com*. Lillian Thornburg, 8 Dec 1949.

[49] Lillian Hill Thornburg Letter, 1941, p. 1.

When the Meeting House was being used by the people of Hill Town (and Lassiter Mill as well as others in New Hope Township), it was known as the Rocky Branch Church and School House, and some say it was the first school building for African Americans in Randolph County. The teachers were reportedly Quakers and the school was attended by both white and black children. Thornburg references the use of the Meeting House as a school: "The old meeting house was used as a school house for some time. What was called then 'subscription schools' were taught in it."[50]

From Rocky Branch to Hill Town

Exactly who was leading the spiritual community at Rocky Branch is not clear. However, this was during the time that the Rev. Daniel Worth, a Guilford County native, former Quaker turned Wesleyan, rabid abolitionist preacher, and agent for the American Missionary Association was active in Randolph County. Worth's antislavery preaching caught the attention of the authorities after John Brown's failed revolt in Harper's

---

[50] Lillian Hill Thornburg Letter, 1941, pp. 2-3.

Ferry, West Virginia. In 1859, he was arrested in Guilford County and subsequently convicted for inciting possible slave revolts by distributing a pamphlet called, *The Impending Crisis of the South,* written by Hinton Rowan Helper. After learning, while out on bail, that the State Supreme Court had upheld his lower court conviction, he fled North Carolina and went to New York.[51] The impact and memory of Worth's preaching, and antislavery witness, were reportedly remembered by the community for many years. In fact, Worth's historical preaching was mentioned in 1879, by the Rev. Joseph Roy, a field superintendent for the American Missionary Association when reporting on the Rev. Islay Walden's return to Randolph County and Hill Town to plant a Congregational church there:

> In the back country of Randolph County, N.C., twenty-five miles away from the railroad, I looked up Rev. Islay Walden, a former slave in that region... This is in the neighborhood of one of the churches of our antebellum missionary, Rev. Daniel Worth, whom all our colored friends and some of the whites remembered affectionately. His church, a

---

[51] Garner, 2009.

former Wesleyan, has been taken up by the M.E. Church, so that they are well cared for.[52]

Figure 21: Old Barn on Lassiter Family Farm. Photo by Margo Lee Williams, 1982.

[52] Roy, 1879, pp. 33(11):334-335. The Methodist church to which he refers is probably the current Salem United Methodist Church.

PART TWO:

THE AMERICAN MISSIONARY ASSOCIATION and EDUCATION

Figure 22: The American Missionary Magazine

Figure 23: The Rev. Dr. Joseph E. Roy, Field Secretary of the American Missionary Association.

The American Missionary Association

The American Missionary Association (AMA) was formed in Albany, New York on 3 September 1846, at a meeting of antislavery organizations.[53] Its mission, as described in the first issue of the *American Missionary* was to preach the gospel to the poor, to help "feeble" churches, to be missionaries to free people of color, and to preach "deliverance" to slaves.[54] The AMA was officially non-sectarian, but most of its officers and members were from the Congregational church communities. According to Clara DeBoer (2015),

> Although the AMA was not begun primarily for black persons, more of them served on its board and were commissioned by it than is true of any other predominantly white benevolent organization. More than five hundred black persons, officers, teachers, and missionaries, can be identified (not always easy in view of the color-blind nature of the AMA) among the AMA workers during the period covered by the [Amistad] archives. This remarkable record was achieved because of the uncompromising belief in freedom and equality on the part of the founders of the AMA.[55]

Even before the end of the Civil War, AMA missionaries came to North Carolina eager to spread the

---

[53] Hollyday, 2005.
[54] Hollyday, 2005, p. 18.
[55] DeBoer, 2015.

gospel, fight against slavery, and feed the hunger for education. "The American Missionary Association was the most significant educational society for blacks during the Civil War and Reconstruction," according to Maxine Jones (1985).[56] The Association itself wrote:

> Let it be remembered, 1) that the American Missionary Association was the first to enter the work of educating and uplifting the Freedmen of the South, and the first to introduce industrial training into the schools; 2) that it has done the largest work in that field, having spent more money and educated more pupils than any other society.[57]

Clara DeBoer (2015) quoted the US Board of Education's comments in 1916, when it said that, "'No denominational schools surpass those of this group in educational standards or administrative efficiency.'"[58]

AMA Common Schools

AMA Common Schools or ungraded, one (and sometimes two) teacher, elementary schools were often in isolated, rural communities where no public schools were located. They were frequently associated with churches.

---

[56] Jones, 1985, p. 103.
[57] American Missionary Association, 1895, p. 49(5):153.
[58] DeBoer, 2015.

By 1891, the AMA had fifty-one (51) schools across the South. Some of these schools had been established by graduates of their own AMA normal schools or colleges. Despite these schools and their commitment to not forget "the ignorant and weak," the AMA relinquished their schools to the public school system whenever possible, believing that their commitment to education was best served by their secondary and normal schools, and their colleges.[59]

The AMA believed that young black women were important as educational, social, and religious community leaders. Most of the AMA's black teachers were women. Their commitment to women was seen in their commitment to female boarding schools where young black women were prepared to take their place as leaders in their families, communities, churches and as teachers. As a result, even some of the poorest rural AMA schools had well trained teachers, unlike common schools for black children run by local boards of education.[60]

---

[59] Richardson and Jones 2009, p. 1.
[60] Richardson and Jones 2009.

In addition to young black teachers, there were also white rural teachers. By contrast, these women were usually older, and their devotion to their black students often resulted in their ostracism by the white community. On the other hand, the white teachers were not readily trusted by black communities because of the experiences of oppression, fear and predation at the hands of white men. The psychological need to resist any and all white authority, a carryover from slavery and a reaction to Jim Crow, often made it difficult for white teachers to gain trust and respect. However, if the community was convinced the white teacher was sincere the community would be supportive.

Regardless of color, teachers were then as now, overworked and underpaid. Because these teachers were viewed as "missionaries," in addition to teaching academic subjects, they also organized Sunday Schools and visited students' families, providing a variety of assistance, including farming advice, medical assistance, teaching basic hygiene, maintaining the school buildings, and planting gardens. "They did all this for twenty dollars a day, and room and board."[61] However, rural isolation and poor salaries had a detrimental effect on teacher retention with better-educated teachers seeking and finding better opportunities in the more affluent urban communities of Atlanta, New Orleans, or Memphis, where they had attended college. In addition, those who came south from northern cities often had no experience either with rural life or poverty. Unprepared for these difficulties, attrition was high. Even those who had been born in rural communities were frequently reluctant to return once they had been exposed to the greater experiences and financial opportunities of urban life.[62]

School attendance was adversely affected by the need by parents for the extra hands of their children, both at planting time and harvest.

> In December 1936, Myrtle W. Wright, Cotton Valley [Alabama] principal wrote that some students could not attend classes until the corn and peas were picked, cane stripped and syrup made, sweet potatoes dug and buried, and peanuts packed and stacked. Some would still be enrolling after

---

[61] Richardson and Jones 2009, p. 8.

[62] Richardson and Jones, 2009.

> Christmas. ... [and in] 1946, teacher Lorene Hastings said that by March most of her second grade 'will drop out to plow'.[63]

Despite these limitations, hundreds of poor, rural, black children finished their local common school and went on to secondary schools, normal schools, college, and beyond. Those who were unable to go on nevertheless acquired basic educational skills in the three "R's:" Reading, 'Riting, and 'Rithmetic.

By 1905, the number of AMA common schools had declined to 16, going back up to 23 in 1907. By 1920, the AMA had only four common schools left. The last school, Cotton Valley (Alabama), closed in 1961. The AMA had always insisted that elementary education was the responsibility of the state, and they discontinued schools as public education became available. However, they would not abandon a school if no other alternative was possible. A report in 1895 in the *American Missionary* explained their viewpoint.

> ... [W]e are obliged by peculiar demands, and for reasons which we cannot overcome, to maintain certain common and elementary schools. Such

---

[63] Richardson and Jones, 2009, p. 11.

> schools are now coming to be chiefly cared for - after a fashion - by the respective States. ... Where we are planting churches, and in some places where multitudes of children would be left without any instruction we have planted our common schools with two or three Christian teachers to keep each other company and to unite their faith and work.[64]

This was the case with Cotton Valley, in Alabama. The Board of Education refused to provide a school, or pay its teachers, so the AMA continued the Cotton Valley School. They eventually struck an agreement with the county Board of Education, who then agreed to pay the teachers. After the school burned in 1961, however, the AMA transferred the property to the county, thus closing the last AMA common school and transferring local elementary education completely to the county.[65]

Some ungraded schools were discontinued as common schools because they were "upgraded" (turned into graded schools). Such was the case with Strieby School. Thus, Strieby School under the auspices of the AMA, bridged the scattered educational efforts of sympathetic Friends (Quakers) among Free People of

---

[64] American Missionary Association, 1895, pp. 49(5):352-353.
[65] Richardson and Jones, 2009.

Color before Emancipation, and its absorption by the public school system in the 1920s.

Figure 24: The Rev. (Alfred) Islay Walden.

A Thirst for Education

The American Missionary Association (AMA) believed education was not all that was needed to help the Freedmen make a smooth transition into mainstream life. They believed that Christian education was equally as important. They recognized that survival in a slave culture meant the use of questionable ethical and moral behaviors, such as lying and deceit. While useful coping mechanisms in slavery, they were decidedly maladaptive behaviors in freedom. Thus, the AMA paired churches with their schools.[66]

The gospel message of justice delivered by the American Missionary Association and its educational efforts in Southwestern Randolph County were not new when the Rev. (Alfred) Islay Walden returned to preach and teach in 1879. What made his witness different was that he was a former slave, not a white man. He was from Southwestern Randolph County, he was returning to his people. This time the establishment of a church and school for the people of Hill Town and neighboring Lassiter Mill was permanently sustained by the self-determination of its people. Uwharrie Friends Meeting, Rocky Branch Church, the Rev. Daniel Worth had all been stepping stones along the way.

The Rev. (Alfred) Islay Walden

The Rev. (Alfred) Islay Walden was born a slave circa 1843 in Randolph County, North Carolina. Though his first name was "Alfred," he dropped that name after a

---

[66] DeBoer, 2015.

tragic lynching involving a man named "Alfred."[67] According to his obituary in the *Congregational Yearbook,* of the Congregational Church, published in 1885, he was the son of Ruth and Branson (Garner) Walden.[68] In addition, a previously unidentified marriage between Alfred I. Walden and Amelia Frances "Fannie" Harris, in Wake County, 17 October 1867, listed Branson Walden and Ruth Walden as his parents, which would be consistent with the Congregational Yearbook assertion.[69]Although family members claim his father was a Free Man of Color, William D. Walden Jr.,[70] an article written about his ordination at the New Brunswick Theological Seminary (NBTS) in New Jersey, appearing in the New York *Evening Post,* on 2 July 1879, stated that his father escaped from slavery on "forged papers," and fled to Indiana.[71]

---

[67] Walden 1873.

[68] National Council, 1885, p. 7:37.

[69] North Carolina, Marriage Records, 1741-2011 [Database on-line]. *Ancestry.com*. Alfred I. Walden [Abstract erroneously labels the capital cursive "I" as a "J"] and Amelia Frances Harris, 17 Oct 1867, Wake County. No other mention of Amelia has been identified to date.

[70] Garner, 2009, p. 52.

[71] *Evening Post,* 1879, n. p.

As a young man Islay reportedly worked as a laborer, hotel servant, and at the gold mines of Randolph County. His unusual math abilities and quick mind were recognized early in his life by his master, who was the first to call him a "poet," after hearing his first rhyme recited upon the death of an ox.[72]

Gone North

Shortly after Lee surrendered Walden learned of his freedom from his master.[73] By the winter of 1867-68, though nearly-blind from birth, Walden walked to Washington, D.C., determined to get both eye-glasses and an education. It was during this trip that he married Amelia Frances Harris, but there is no information about what became of her.

In Washington, DC, Walden supported himself by selling poems and political ballads on the streets, doing manual labor, and organizing Sabbath schools for black children. His work with the Sunday school was significant enough that an article appeared in the *Washington Bee*

---

[72] Walden, 1873 & 1877.
[73] Walden, 1873 & 1877.

newspaper in 1898, over 20 years after his death. In a column entitled, Flotsam and Jetsam, his work was described:

> Islay Walden, an odd genius, poet and preacher, during his collegiate days at Howard University, some twenty odd years ago, conducted a very well attended non-denominational Sunday school here. The teachers, young men and women, were drawn from the departments and the University. The singing of the school was a most attractive feature. ... Walden after graduation, entered the service of the American Missionary Association, and a humble grave in a remote corner of North Carolina marks the scene of labors that duplicated his academic missionary services.[74]

Among those singing with this group included future renowned journalist, Bruce Grit (John Edward Bruce), whose bass voice "could always be heard distinctly above all others, those days when the skill of his right hand had not been so universally acknowledged."[75] This undoubtedly was a reference to his future journalistic skills. According to the biographical sketches in his poetry volumes, a professor from Rutgers College who

---

[74] Chase, 17 September 1898, p. 4.
[75] Chase, 17 September 1898, p. 4.

befriended him was able to encourage the Second Reformed Church to grant him a scholarship to study at Howard University.[76] The Howard University Normal School Directory of 1871 shows Islay Walden enrolled.[77]

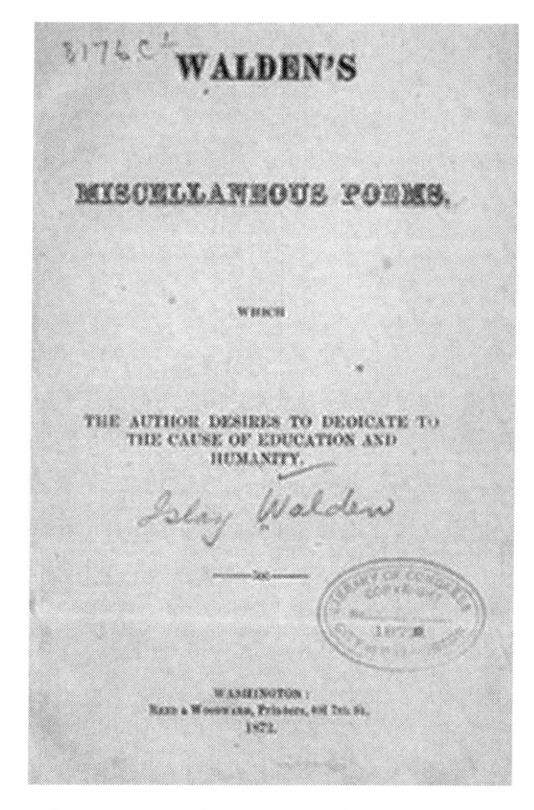

WALDEN'S

MISCELLANEOUS POEMS,

WHICH

THE AUTHOR DESIRES TO DEDICATE TO
THE CAUSE OF EDUCATION AND
HUMANITY.

Islay Walden

WASHINGTON:
[illegible]
1872.

Figure 25: Walden's *Miscellaneous Poems.*

[76] Walden, 1873 & 1877.

[77] U.S., School Catalogs, 1765-1935. *Ancestry.com*. Islay Walden, 1871.

Walden's Poetry

To support himself while a student at Howard, Walden published his *Miscellaneous Poems: Which the author desires to dedicate to the cause of education and humanity.* An introductory recommendation therein by J. L. H. Winfield, of the War Department, encouraged people to purchase the volume. Among his comments he stated, "... whatever may be the faults of metre, critics will not lose sight of the eloquence, originality and real beauty of thought that are found in his work."[78] There was also an introductory biographical essay written by C. C. Harper ("C.C.H."), founder of the American Colonization Society. He commented that he found it remarkable that only a little over a year before, Walden did not even know anything about books.[79] Announcement of the publication of this volume of poetry appeared in several publications around the country, between 18 July and 8 August 1873, including: the *Patriot* (Harrisburg, Pennsylvania),[80] the *Goodhue*

---

[78] Walden, 1873, p. 4.
[79] Walden 1873.
[80] American Antiquarian Society and Newsbank. (2004). Personal: Islay Walden, in *Patriot, IV* (1873, 18 July):1.

County Republican (Redwing, Minnesota),[81] the *Rockford Journal* (Rockford, Illinois),[82] and the *Brooklyn Daily Eagle* (Brooklyn, New York). It was noted in the *Brooklyn Daily Eagle* that,

> Islay Walden, a student of Howard University, Washington, and now visiting this city, has published a volume of poems, religious, secular and miscellaneous. The author is heartily commended by Professor A. Barber and other people of the Federal Capital.[83]

Most of the poems in this volume reflect on his personal experiences and emotions. Joan Sherman, Professor Emerita of English Literature at Rutgers University included Walden and his poems in all three of her books on 19th century African American poetry. In her 1992 *Anthology* she wrote,

> His frankness, affectionate regard for people, naïve waggish humor, and natural joy in

---

[81] American Antiquarian Society and Newsbank. (2014). Personal and Literary: Islay Walden, in *Goodhue County Republican*, (1873, 24 July), p. 2.

[82] American Antiquarian Society and Newsbank. (2004). Personal and Literary: Islay Walden, in *Rockford Journal* (1873, 26 July), p. 6.

[83] *The Brooklyn Daily Eagle*, 8 August 1873, p. 4. Professor A. Barber was ProfessorAmzi Barber, Principal of the Normal Department at Howard University.

> living give special charm to verses on love and such homespun occasions as eating at school, ice skating, and needing a winter overcoat.[84]

In 1877, while studying at NBTS, he published *Walden's Sacred Poems with a Sketch of His Life.* These poems were more spiritual and reflected on various biblical passages, especially the psalms. This volume of poetry also attracted attention with notices of its publication in *The North State,* published in Greensboro, North Carolina and *The Torchlight*, published in Oxford, Granville County, North Carolina.[85] Both notices appeared in August 1878.

Sherman (1992) was not a fan of this volume, reportedly calling it "uninspired and repetitious."[86] Ben Friedlander (2009) noted that after acquiring an education, he no longer expressed his poetry in a "folk" manner. Friedlander explained that unlike Langston Hughes, Walden "didn't live at a time when he might have been both sophisticated and folk."[87] On the other hand, Dickson

---

[84] Sherman, 1992, p. 221.
[85] *The North State*, 1 August 1878, p. 2; Davis, 6 August 1878, p. 2.
[86] Friedlander, 8 October 2009.
[87] Friedlander, 8 October 2009.

Bruce (1992) wrote in his book, *Black American Writing from the Nadir: The Evolution of a Literary Tradition 1877-1915,* that:

> At the center of Walden's poetry was a deep devotionalism. The poems focused on an emotional relationship between the believer and God and on the hope for a heavenly union.[88]

Echoing this sentiment. Simmons-Henry, Henry, and Speas (1990) in *The Heritage of Blacks in North Carolina* noted that "the Christianity that Walden preached, he exemplified in his life."[89]

Both of Walden's collections have been reprinted in recent years and made available to the public once again. His poems are considered to be important examples of 19th century African American poetry and are included in several anthologies as well as poetry websites including, *Over the River and through the Wood: An Anthology of Nineteenth-Century American Children's Poetry* and *The Poetry Foundation.*[90]

---

[88] Bruce, 1992, pp. 22-24.
[89] Simmons-Henry, *et al.*, 1990, I:70.
[90] Kilcup and Sorby, 2013.

Blyden Jackson in "Black Victorian Writers of North Carolina" (1984) said that Walden was "the first Black North Carolina writer who could be called Victorian."[91] Dicksen Bruce (2001) expanded on this in the *Concise Oxford Companion to African American Literature*, saying that Walden and other Reconstruction era/Victorian era African American writers "created paeans to nature, love, and a sentimental piety. They broke with other Victorians only in persistently linking their writing to protesting prejudice and discrimination."[92] On the other hand, Gene Jarrett (2006) wrote in his introduction to *African American Literature beyond Race: An Alternative Reader* that if one agreed with the critique that there were poets who emphasized form over content, a neoclassical hallmark, then Walden would be considered a "neoclassical" poet.[93] Jarrett quotes Joan Sherman, saying that writers such as Walden "'show a decided bias for neoclassical decorum, heightened poetic diction, and technical virtuosity.'"[94] Later in *Deans and Truants: Race and Realism in African*

---

[91] Jackson, 1984, p. 55.
[92] Bruce, 2001, p. 464.
[93] Jarrett, 2006, p. 12.
[94] Jarrett, 2006, p. 12.

American Literature, Jarrett (2013) notes that Walden and his African American contemporaries "produced enough poems to suggest that their literary tradition was not an anomaly, but a racial fixture."[95] In addition, *The Cambridge Companion to Nineteenth-Century American Poetry* noted that Walden was one of the 19th Century African American poets who also wrote about American Indians.[96]

Perhaps the most important indication that Walden's poetry was not an insignificant contribution to nineteenth century poetry can be seen in an article that appeared in the *Pittsburgh Courier,* then a relatively new publication, but one that went on to be considered a giant among African American newspapers. On 2 September 1911, they ran an article written by N. Barnett Dodson about the founding of a new historical research society dedicated to preserving African American history by A. A. Schomberg and John E. Bruce, aka Bruce Grit, the same Bruce Grit who sang for Walden's Sunday School at Howard University.

---

[95] Jarrett 2013, p. 43.
[96] Larsen, 2011, p. 52n.

The new organizatiion was called the Negro Society for Historical Research and was established for "the purpose of gathering information from books and through correspondence of historical value to the Negro race."[97] The article stated that the Society had already acquired 150 titles: "A few of the more important ones are here given: ...'Poems of Islay Walden,' blind poet of North Carolina, 1875..."[98] This article was also published in the *Lexington Standard*, Lexington, Kentucky, on 21 October 1911.[99] This collection and other titles and photographs would eventually become part of the Schomburg Center for Research in Black Culture, in New York City.

There is some information that Walden wrote another volume of poems around 1875, called *The Ritual of the Golden Circle.*[100] The exact nature of the poems is not known. Alas, there are no copies known to have survived.

---

[97] Dodson, 2 September 1911, p. 4.
[98] Dodson, 2 September 1911, p. 4.
[99] Dodson, 21 October 1911, p. 1.
[100] National Council, 1885, p. 7:37.

Seminary Years

While Walden's poems provide a glimpse into 19th century African American thought, it was his work in ministry and education that ultimately had the greatest impact. Walden earned his teaching certificate from Howard's Normal program in June 1876.[101] The *National Republican* reported on the ceremonies and noted that he presented, "A Glance at the Sentence," for his graduation recitation.[102] However, the *Evening Star* reported that his recitation was entitled "A Glance at *Science* (emphasis mine)," which seems more plausible.[103] After graduation, he returned to New Jersey in hopes of attending seminary.

According to an article in the New York paper, *Evening Post*, Walden first applied to Princeton College, but was turned down. He was accepted at the New Brunswick Theological Seminary (NBTS) with the help of Professor George W. Atherton of Rutgers College. His ability to attend the seminary was made possible by

---

[101] Howard University, 1896, p. 44.

[102] *The National Republican*, 15 June 1876, p. 4.

[103] American Antiquarian Society and Newsbank, (2004), Local News: Howard University—Normal Class, in *Evening Star* (1876, 16 June), p. 5.

scholarship money bequeathed by a member of a Reformed Church in Yonkers, New York, for the education of a "colored man."[104]

Walden and another young man, John H. Bergen, were the first two African Americans to study at NBTS.[105] It is interesting to note that both young men had vision problems which led them to petition the school in 1877 in order to be excused from the Greek language requirement.[106] It was granted them and they were able to continue their studies.

During Walden's years there, despite his own struggles with poverty and near-blindness, Walden established a mission school for needy African Americans.[107] The school (called the "Students' Mission Sabbath-school") and its activities turned up in a series of articles and advertisements in New Brunswick's *The Daily Times* from December 1878 to June 1879.

On 4 December 1878, *The Daily Times* noted that the school had celebrated its first anniversary the previous

---

[104] *Evening Post,* 2 July 1879, n. p.
[105] Bruggink and Baker, 2004, p. 103.
[106] Minutes of General Synod, 1877, pp. 607 & 689.
[107] Walden 1877; NBTS, e-story.

Sunday at the YMCA. Not only parents and family were in attendance, but also members of the First and Second Reformed Churches. The program was described as including prayer, scripture readings, and musical offerings. Monies were also raised in support of the mission for which they said Walden had "worked laboriously."[108]

On 21 December, a small article advertised the upcoming "Panorama and Concert" to be presented on New Year's evening in Saenger Hall at the Seminary. This time the proceeds would go to "the clothing and shoeing of the poor colored children under the care of the mission."[109] Another ad for this event appeared on 28 December.[110] The 4 January edition reported on the concert in an article called "Shoes for the Poor."[111] The event was hailed as a financial success, based in large part on the sale of tickets, notwithstanding the theft of $4.00, for which Walden offered a reward for the arrest of the perpetrator. Also noted in the article were "the young ladies who

---

[108] *The Daily Times*, 4 December 1878, p. 3.
[109] *The Daily Times*, 21 December 1878, p. 3.
[110] *The Daily Times*, 28 December 1878, p. 3.
[111] *The Daily Times*, 3 January, 1879, p. 3; & 4 January 1879, p. 3.

labored to make this and other entertainments of the mission successful," including an "E. Farmer," and "P. Farmer," no doubt the Eleanora Farmer who would become his second wife and her sister, Phoebie Farmer, who would marry Lassiter descendant Harris Dunson and move to the Lassiter Mill community.[112]

Walden's efforts and sacrifices on behalf of the mission school were referenced eloquently in a letter Walden wrote to Professor David Demarest at NBTS. The letter, as transcribed, is not dated, but probably was written about 1878, possibly around the time of the anniversary in December.[113] Walden explained in the letter that he still owed money for room rent and for reading and copying of class notes. He went on to explain that although he felt that, in general, he had the same advantages as others at the seminary, who accepted preaching engagements to

---

[112] *The Daily Times*, 3 January, 1879, p. 3; & 4 January 1879, p. 3. *See also*: 1880 US Federal Census; Census Place: New Brunswick, Middlesex, New Jersey; Roll: 789; Family History Film: 1254789; Page: 79B; Enumeration District: 122; Image: 0586. John V. Farmer, head; Elinore W. Farmer, daughter; Phoebie A. Farmer, daughter. *See also*: North Carolina, Marriage Records, 1741-2011 [Database on-line]. *Ancestry.com*. Harris Dunson & Phoebe Farmer, 3 Apr 1890.

[113] Letter to Prof. David Demarest from Islay Walden, n.d.

earn money, he was unable to do so because of his eyesight as well as the lack of "colored" churches at which he could hope to preach. Instead, he explained, over the "last 11 months" he had created a "students' mission" with,

> 60 odd scholars most of which were gathered from the streets, some of which were so poor and destitute that we were not only compelled to fix them up but in many cases I had to buy soap that the peculiar scavengers might be removed.[114]

Walden's program, he explained, was not confined to just academic subjects. One issue he addressed directly was that of temperance. He noted that two thirds of the students in his mission were the children of drunkards. Realizing that preaching to these drunken parents was not likely to make an impact; he organized temperance societies with the children and had the children go out into the community preaching the virtues of sobriety. He claimed to have had at least some success with this, saying that "Some parents have entirely reformed."[115]

---

[114] Letter to Prof. David Demarest from Islay Walden, n.d.
[115] Letter to Prof. David Demarest from Islay Walden, n.d.

While music and a sewing circle are understandable school programs, Walden embarked on another program not typically found in a school:

> There is another evil we are trying to remedy, when there is a sickness or death among this people they are nearly all compelled to solicit aid. Now this is the remedy[:] to organize a benevolent society making it beneficial at once instead of delaying six or eight months as most societies do. We are to have no initiation fee but twenty five cents month tuition in case of sickness. Each member is taxed 5 cents a week and 50 cents at the death of a member. ... This is simple and can be done if there are two in the society but the more the merrier.[116]

This was confirmed in *The Daily Times,* which reported that according to Walden:

> There has been much suffering and sickness among the colored people and as far as possible relief has been given. The Superintendent solicits aid from any who feel disposed to assist in this benevolent work.[117]

Walden was also candid about the "prejudice against the mission" he experienced.

---

[116] Letter to Prof. David Demarest from Islay Walden, n.d.

[117] *The Daily Times*, 29 March 1879, p. 3.

> ...But the worst struggle has been to overcome the overwhelming prejudice against the mission but this has been done to a great extent by solid steady march, turning neither to the right or left and whatever men have thought of this mission, those that have had courage enough to visit it have gone away commending the work, giving up and *[sic]* unreasonable and senseless prejudice based upon this fact that it has been reported that five or six of these scholars have left other schools. ... But our school like all others has some Teachers and scholars who at some time did belong to other schools. Our most trouble came from the hand of a missionary which resulted in a newspaper fight, for he with no knowledge of this school went around telling the benevolent people that this school was a nuisance and an expense that ought not to be and as he was not a competent judge, I did what any other man would in the defense of an institute which he represents.[118]

Walden went on to suggest that this mission school should come under the care of the Reformed Church in America's (with which the seminary was associated) board of domestic missions. He felt that then the students and staff could take ownership of the mission and be able to say that they, like those at other institutions, such as Princeton and Yale, had shown compassion for the African

---

[118] Letter to Prof. David Demarest from Islay Walden, n.d.

American community in New Brunswick. He said he felt a particular sense of duty because some of the students were now even attending Friday night "prayer meetings."[119]

Having completed those explanations, Walden came back to his original point. He couldn't possibly pay for his room, gas, or reading assistance. He needed help. He indicated that unless these bills were paid he would not be able to be recommended for "classis" (i.e., graduation) at the end of the academic year. Besides, he went on, his mission "Sunday School" had outgrown the space at the seminary that they were currently using and he would have to seek another location, requiring more monetary outlays no doubt.[120] His plea was undoubtedly successful because he would, in fact, graduate and be ordained in the summer of 1879.

Ordination

Walden and John H. Bergen graduated in June 1879, the first two African Americans to graduate from the

---

[119] Letter to Prof. David Demarest from Islay Walden, n.d.
[120] Letter to Prof. David Demarest from Islay Walden, n.d.

NBTS. An article appeared in *The Daily Times* on 16 May 1879, saluting their accomplishment:

> Fourteen young men will graduate from the Theological Seminary this Spring, and go forth to their ministerial fields. Of the fourteen, two are colored students, J. H. Bergen, being a native of this city, and the other, Islay Walden, being an ex-slave and hailing from Randolph County, North Carolina. Mr. Bergen will probably remain north, but Mr. Walden expects to go to his native place and labor there.[121]

Walden's intended return to North Carolina was not new, it had already been mentioned in *The Daily Times* on 24 March 1879, in a brief notice about a successful annual "entertainment" that was intended to raise money but was not so financially successful because of inclement weather. The notice ended seemingly tersely, saying, "The Superintendent of the Mission, Mr. Islay Walden, expects to leave for the south when his term at the seminary closes."[122]

On Saturday, 28 June 1879, an article in *The Daily Times* was dedicated to the ordination of Rev. E. S. Booth,

---

[121] *The Daily Times*, 16 May 1879, p. 3.
[122] *The Daily Times*, 24 March 1879, p. 3.

who had graduated at the same time as Walden. The same article noted that Walden would also soon be ordained:

> Mr. Islay Walden, the young colored gentleman who graduated at the same time as Mr. Booth, will be ordained in the Second Reformed Church of this city on Tuesday next at two o'clock p. m. He has been appointed by the American Missionary Board to go forth and labor as a teacher and missionary among his colored brethren.[123]

One more notice was published on 30 June 1879, which noted that Walden would be ordained the next day and that he had preached on Sunday evening at the Mt. Zion A(frican) M(ethodist) E(piscopal) Church.[124]

Walden was ordained on 1 July 1879, the first African American to be ordained by the Reformed Church in New Jersey. The ordination was attended by numerous church dignitaries and professors, including the Rev. Dr. W. H. Campbell, President of Rutgers College and the Rev. Dr. Strieby, Secretary of the "American Board of Missions" (American Missionary Association). Dubbed "An Interesting Ordination," the *Evening Post*, a prominent New York newspaper published a lengthy article the next

---

[123] *The Daily Times*, 28 June 1879, p.3.
[124] *The Daily Times*, 30 June 1879, p.3.

day on Walden's ordination.[125] The article explained that Bergen had not yet found a post with the Reformed Church and therefore, though licensed to preach, was not yet ordained. It went on to say that because the Reformed Church did not have any missions in the South, Walden signed with the American Missionary Association (AMA), missionary arm of the Congregational Church.[126]

[125] *Evening Post,* 2 July 1879, n. p.
[126] *Evening Post,* 2 July1879, n. p.

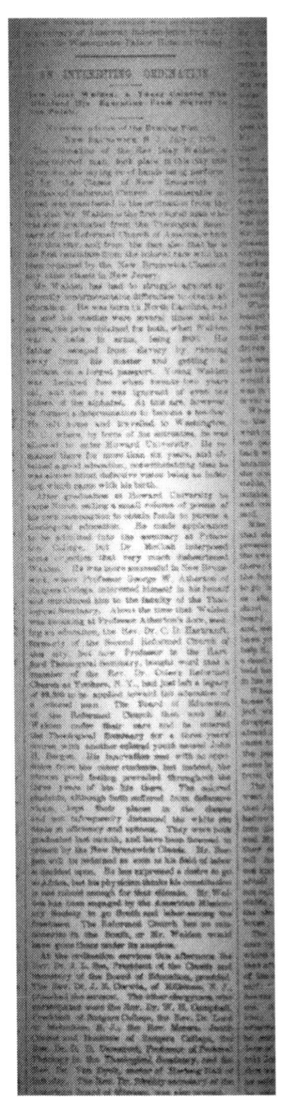

Figure 26: "An Extraordinary Ordination," in *Evening Post*, 2 July 1879.

Returning South

Walden began his journey south shortly after ordination in early July 1879. He wrote about his trip in a letter to the editor of the *New Brunswick Times (The Daily Times)*, saying that he was writing them as promised.[127] His report appeared not only in the *Times*, on 23 July, but also in the *Goldsboro Messenger* (NC), on 28 August, 1879. From his report, it appears that he went from New Jersey to Norfolk and Portsmouth, Virginia, by boat, arriving on 11 July. He reported that the men he met on the docks were almost all men of color. He said that those he met were hard working and that they reported reasonably good relations with their white counterparts.[128]

Walden went on to say that he continued his journey south, going to Mount Olive, North Carolina, today the home of the University of Mount Olive, a small Christian university. It would seem that this leg of his journey was by railroad, since, as he noted in his article, there were four railroad lines that passed through nearby Goldsboro, Wayne County, North Carolina, including the

---

[127] Walden, 28 Aug 1879, p. 2.
[128] Walden, 28 Aug 1879, p. 2.

Norfolk and Western Railroad. He observed that, "At all the stations along the railroads white and colored men seemed to be laboring together as brothers, each trying to earn something to support himself and family."[129] He described Mount Olive as a place where much progress had been made. "Many a young man owns his horse and buggy, and nearly all the families own their homes and farms."[130]

After leaving Mount Olive, he stopped in nearby Dudley, where he said he "found the moral standard of this people far superior to any place I was ever at."[131] Dudley had an AMA affiliated school and an educational standard "beyond that of New Brunswick."[132] He described the living standard to be quite substantial:

> Here I find men owning their own saw and shingle mills, all worshipping under their own 'vine and fig tree.' Colored men own about this place from one to five or six hundred acres of land. [133]

---

[129] Walden, 28 Aug 1879, p. 2.
[130] Walden, 28 Aug 1879, p. 2.
[131] Walden, 28 Aug 1879, p. 2.
[132] Walden, 28 Aug 1879, p. 2.
[133] Walden, 28 Aug 1879, p. 2.

Regarding prejudice, Walden noted that there was substantial prejudice by the "lower class of the whites toward the colored people," but that "those who were wealthy before the war are kindly disposed to them."[134] Walden returned to Goldsboro on 19 July. He noted that when he had left North Carolina he did not think it would be a good place to be, but on returning he found it to be a "fine missionary field."[135] He described it as a city of about 4000 people, half of whom were people of color. He noted that not only did it have four rail lines, but two more were planned. He said it was the "great cotton market of Eastern North Carolina."[136] He also described it as the "centre of the colored population" and so much so that the state legislature had established an asylum for people of color there.[137] He said there were three churches for people of color, one Baptist and two Methodist. He noted that there were 800 children in schools, although only 300 could be accommodated in the common schools, with the remainder being taught in Sunday Schools. Because there

---

[134] Walden, 28 Aug 1879, p. 2.
[135] Walden, 28 Aug 1879, p. 2.
[136] Walden, 28 Aug 1879, p. 2.
[137] Walden, 28 Aug 1879, p. 2.

was so much education being pursued in Goldsboro he said he was "at home" there and was being implored to stay and establish a high school.[138] He said the Presbyterian minister sent letters to newspapers introducing Walden and his work. He then got letters from all the elders and sent them to Dr. Strieby of the AMA saying they would be pleased if Walden were to be assigned to a mission there. Walden seemed especially impressed because the minister had previously been a large slaveholder, but was now "highly honored by the colored people and beloved by all who know him."[139] He went on to say that the Baptist minister also endorsed the letter inviting him to call on him whenever necessary. The Methodist minister told him that it was "a field very much in need of cultivation," while the Episcopalian minister was said to call it "an excellent field."[140] Walden concludes his report by saying that, "… other citizens of high standing will write to Dr. Strieby giving their

---

[138] Walden, 28 Aug 1879, p. 2.
[139] Walden, 28 Aug 1879, p. 2.
[140] Walden, 28 Aug 1879, p. 2.

testimony of the importance of the field."[141] It would appear from this letter that Walden anticipated staying in Goldsboro and was even excited to do so. In fact, this may be the lucrative offer that he ultimately turned down to return to Randolph County, not an offer in New Jersey. Thus, for reasons not completely evident, in the end, Walden did not stay in Goldsboro. By the 1880 census, he had returned to Randolph County and was living with his sister and her family in Hill Town.[142]

---

[141] Walden, 28 Aug 1879, p. 2.

[142] 1880 US Federal Census; Census Place: Union, Randolph, North Carolina; Roll: 978; Family History Film: 1254978; Page: 196C; Enumeration District: 224; Image: 0683. Emsley Hill, head; Islay Walden, boarder.

Figure 27: Old Strieby Church, originally The First Congregational Church of Randolph County. Photo courtesy of Patrice Lassiter Bryant.

Return to Hill Town

Under the auspices of the AMA, Walden returned to the Lassiter's Mill postal area of southwestern Randolph County, North Carolina. There he established a Congregational church and "common school," as AMA one or two teacher schools were called, in an area in the Uwharrie Mountains called "Hill Town." It is likely that he ultimately decided to take this post because it was in the same community where his sister, Sarah (Callicutt/Walden) Hill, wife of Emsley Hill, lived.

The church reportedly was called first, "Promised Land Church." According to Aveus "Ave" Lassiter Edmondson, in an article that appeared in *Asheboro Magazine* in 2011, Priscilla Hill, (affectionately known as "Granny Prissy") Emsley Hill's mother, helped build the brush arbor that was used as this early meeting place. Walden's job as AMA missionary, however, was to plant a permanent Congregational church for the community. This church was called the *First Congregational Church of Randolph County*. DeBoer (2015) noted that "If a church in the South is named First Congregational and was founded during Reconstruction, it is generally a predominantly black church started by the AMA."[143]

Walden's church would eventually be named Strieby Congregational Church and School, after the Rev.

---

[143] DeBoer, 2015.

Dr. Strieby, the same prominent Congregational minister and Corresponding Secretary of the AMA that attended his ordination. Kate Lassiter Jones believed that it was Rev. Strieby who helped Walden found the church, but it was apparently the Rev. Joseph Roy, the Field Superintendent, who assisted. In Roy's 1879 Field Report he stated, "The Field Superintendent assisted him in organizing a Congregational Church of thirty members."[144] Roy stated that a man in Hill Town offered "three acres of land and timber in the tree for all the lumber needed for a church school-house, and that man was an ex-slave."[145] It is not clear to whom he was referring since the Hill and Lassiter families were free families dating back before 1850.

In 1880, Walden, as agent for the AMA purchased a six acre plot of land from a neighboring white family, Addison and Cornelia Lassiter, on which the church was built:[146]

> Men and women gathered from every direction to plan for the building. A two-wheeled ox cart hauled six huge rocks for the foundation. Logs, lumber and

---

[144] Roy, 1879, pp. 33(11): 334-335.
[145] Roy, 1879, pp. 33(11):334-335.
[146] Addison and Cornelia Lassiter to H. W. Hubbard, 22 May 1880.

service were given. The weather boarding for the 60′x30′ building was finished by hand, mostly by our late Uncle Julius Hill.[147]

---

[147] Jones, 1972, p. 2.

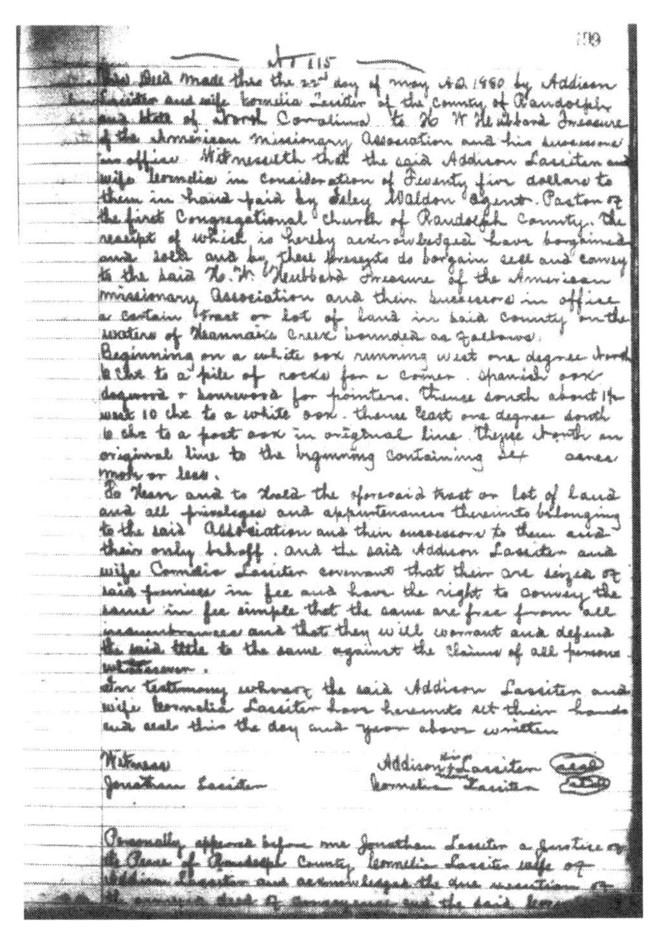

119

No 115

This Deed made this the 22nd day of May AD 1880 by Addison Lassiter and wife Cornelia Lassiter of the County of Randolph and State of North Carolina to H W Hubbard Treasurer of the American Missionary Association and his successors in office. Witnesseth that the said Addison Lassiter and wife Cornelia in consideration of Twenty five dollars to them in hand paid by Isley Waldon Agent. Pastor of the first Congregational Church of Randolph County. the receipt of which is hereby acknowledged have bargained and sold and by these presents do bargain sell and convey to the said H. W. Hubbard Treasurer of the American Missionary Association and their successors in office a certain tract or lot of land in said County on the waters of [illegible] Creek bounded as follows.

Beginning on a white oak running west one degree North [illegible] chs to a pile of rocks for a corner. Spanish oak dogwood & sourwood for pointers. Thence south about [illegible] west 10 chs to a white oak. thence East one degree South [illegible] chs to a post oak in original line. Thence North on original line to the beginning containing six acres more or less.

To have and to hold the aforesaid tract or lot of land and all privileges and appurtenances thereunto belonging to the said Association and their successors to them and their only behoff. and the said Addison Lassiter and wife Cornelia Lassiter covenant that they are seized of said premises in fee and have the right to convey the same in fee simple that the same are free from all incumbrances and that they will warrant and defend the said title to the same against the claims of all persons whatsoever.

In testimony whereof the said Addison Lassiter and wife Cornelia Lassiter have hereunto set their hands and seals this the day and year above written

Witness
Jonathan Lassiter

Addison (his mark) Lassiter (seal)
Cornelia Lassiter (seal)

Personally appeared before me Jonathan Lassiter a Justice of the Peace of Randolph County Cornelia Lassiter wife of Addison Lassiter and acknowledged the due execution of the annexed deed of conveyance and the said [illegible]

Figure 28 Addison & Cornelia Lassiter to H W Hubbard, Treasurer, American Missionary Association, paid by Islay Walden, Agent & Pastor, First Congregational Church of Randolph County.

Figure 29: Strieby Church, School, and Cemetery Site Map—Tax Parcel 29596.

Roy noted that he met with three committees, one from Hill Town, one from what would become Salem Church, in Concord Township about eight miles away, and one from Troy, in neighboring Montgomery County, where the AMA was in the process of establishing Peabody Academy. At this point they did not have an ordained preacher for each location so it was decided there would be a circuit:

> So we organized a circuit for Brother Walden, one Sabbath at Troy and the other at Salem Church and Hill Town, with one sermon at each place. The Quakers promise a school at Salem. A public school will serve Hill Town for the present, and a competent teacher must be secured for the Academy.[148]

The Church members at Hill Town quickly became involved in the wider life of the Congregational Church and the American Missionary Association. A report of the 1880 Conference held at Dudley, N.C., noted that representatives traveled 130 miles to attend. In describing the progress of the church at Hill Town, it said, "A gracious revival and a meeting-house under way are the

---

[148] Roy, 1879, p. 33(11):335.

fruits of the first six months of the life of this church."[149] This may have been the revival to which Thornburg referred, as she would have been about seven by this time.[150]

The following year, in 1881, the report again mentioned Rev. Walden and others from the congregation:

> Rev. Islay Walden and his delegate, Deacon Potter, together with three others, came fifty miles in a one-horse wagon to attend the Conference. One of the party, Mrs. Hill, now a widow, has had twelve children, forty grand-children and twelve great-grand-children. She had never seen the (train) cars nor heard a railroad whistle till she came to the Conference. ...The sermon Friday night was by Rev. Islay Walden; text, the first Psalm.[151]

Most certainly the "Mrs. Hill," referenced here was Granny Prissy. "Deacon Potter" could have been Thomas Potter, her son-in-law, married to her daughter Mary Jane Hill, or Thomas' brother, Ira Potter, married to daughter Charity Hill.

---

[149] American Missionary Association, 1880, p. 34(3):72.
[150] Lillian Hill Thornburg Letter 1941, p. 1.
[151] American Missionary Association, 1881, p. 35(7):211.

Figure 30: Strieby Church Cemetery.
Photo by Margo Lee Williams, 1982.

Walden also married in 1881 to a woman he had met while in New Jersey, Eleanora Wilhelmina Farmer.[152] Despite her urban northern roots, she became a vital part of Walden's work in Hill Town, becoming a teacher and principal of the school at Hill Town.[153]

[152] New Jersey Marriages: Alfred I. Walden and Elenor W. Farmer, 18 May 1881.
[153] American Missionary Association, 1884, p. 38(3):45.

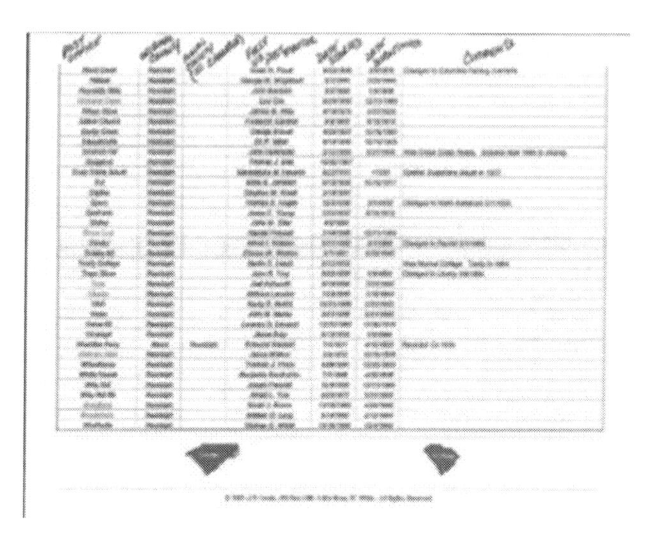

Figure 31: US Postmasters-Strieby

In 1883, Walden successfully petitioned the government for a postal office thus eliminating the long ride to the Lassiter's Mill post office and thereby making "Strieby" the official name of the community. Walden became the first Postmaster. In February 1884, *The American Missionary* reported this achievement:

> Rev. Islay Walden's school and church whose post-office was formerly that of Lassiter's Mill, have now secured a new post route and their own post-office, called by the government Strieby, and served by the pastor as postmaster.[154]

---

[154] American Missionary Association, 1884, p. 38(3):45.

Alas, even as the achievement of the post office was being reported, Walden's ministry and career were being cut short by his untimely death from Acute Bronchitis (more likely pneumonia) on 2 February 1884, at age 35-40. *The American Missionary* eulogized him,

> ... He rallied the people, developed a village with school-house and church, secured a post-office and became postmaster. Here he labored four years, blessed with revivals, and was honored by the people, black and white. His wife an educated and judicious missionary teacher was of great assistance to him in all his work ...[155]

He was buried in Strieby Church Cemetery.[156]

[155] American Missionary Association, 1884, p. 38(4):98.

[156] National Council, 1885, p. 7:37.

Figure 32: The Rev. Islay Walden cemetery marker, Strieby Church Cemetery. Photo by Margo Lee Williams, 2014.

Figure 33: Bench from Old Strieby Church.
Photo by Margo Lee Williams, 2014.

A Widow Carries On

Despite Walden's death, his desire for a legacy of education and spirituality lived on at Strieby. His widow, Eleanora Farmer Walden, continued as the principal teacher as well as postmistress. "Mrs. Elenora Walden continues the school work of her husband, greatly confided in by the people."[157] The ministerial work was assumed by the Rev. Zachariah Simmons who was the pastor at Salem Congregational Church.

In 1888, Henry Ruffin Walden, reportedly a cousin of Islay Walden's, married Eleanora Walden, Islay's widow.[158] Henry was apparently about to enter his last year as a student at Hampton Normal School (Hampton, VA). He graduated in 1889, returning to Strieby to become a teacher there. An entry for his name in a Hampton Institute publication stated: "Teaching with his wife (whom he married before entering the Senior class) the American Missionary School at Strieby, NC."[159] This seems to indicate that Strieby had become a two teacher school, since Eleanora was still a teacher there.

In 1891, Henry wrote an extensive article for *The American Missionary* magazine about the teaching and missionary work at Strieby. In it he wrote about the need for a separate schoolhouse that was built:

---

[157] American Missionary Association, 1884, p. 38(6):164-165.
[158] North Carolina, Marriage Index, 1741-2004 [Database on-line].*Ancestry.com*. H R Walden and Eleanor W Walden, 13 Dec 1888.
[159] Hampton Institute, 1893, p. 290.

> ... I took my axe one day and had some of the rest follow me into the woods, and there we cut the foundation of a school building ...We must have a school building because it is needed. The school has a good reputation far and wide, among both white and colored.[160]

He also wrote about the great progress in education commenting that already there had been "a young girl, who went out last winter as teacher in another community, carrying the good seed of the word from this church and school."[161] There is no way to know her level of expertise. One could assume it was rather rudimentary by urban standards, but it was undoubtedly a source of pride for the Strieby community and Walden went on to say it was greatly appreciated by the receiving community: "She planted the truth there and the people were well-pleased with her good work."[162]Alas, he does not give us the name of this young missionary woman.

---

[160] Walden, 1891, p. 45(5):167.
[161] Walden, 1891, p. 45(5):166-167
[162] Walden, 1891, p. 45(5):167.

Sadly, Eleanora Walden died in early 1892. Her obituary appeared in the March 1892 issue of *The American Missionary*. Therein it stated, at the time of her death, she held the position of Principal of Garfield Academy, at Strieby, was postmistress, and was working very hard in a series of meetings which were being held and in which several of her pupils had found the Saviour.[163] Eleanora was also buried in Strieby Cemetery next to Islay.

Figure 34: Eleanora W. Walden Gravestone.
Photo by Margo Lee Williams, 2014.

Eleanora's husband, Henry Ruffin Walden, who had gone on to become the teacher at the AMA's school at Salem Church in Concord Township, about eight miles

---

[163] American Missionary Association, 1892, p. 46(3):91.

away, returned to Strieby to take over her duties as teacher and postmaster.[164] The following year he wrote one more report about the work at Strieby, which seemed to indicate a certain frustration with older generations, but he was not specific. He commented that progress depended on the work with the young and though while slow, he felt they were improving, but other than commenting on their prayer life, he was, yet again, not specific. His advice for others was to concentrate on the young; the older generations were largely a lost cause.[165]

In 1898, Henry Walden married Theodosia Hargrave, also a teacher.[166] By 1910, he and his new family had moved to Richmond County, where his wife had taken a teaching position.[167] At some point Henry, like his cousin Islay, became a minister serving Congregational

---

[164] American Missionary Association, 1892, p. 46(3): 41 & 91.
[165] Walden, 1893.
[166] North Carolina, Marriage Records, 1741-2011 [Database on-line]. *Ancestry.com*. Henry R Walden and Theodocia E Hargrave, 13 Sep 1898.
[167] 1910 US Census. *Ancestry.com*. Henry R Waldener [*sic*], farmer; Theodosia Waldener [*sic*], teacher.

churches in Charlotte[168] and High Point,[169] where he died in 1951, at age 84.[170]

Figure 35: The Rev. Henry Ruffin Walden. Photo courtesy of Tina Walden Spruill.

[168] U.S. City Directories, 1821-1989, Charlotte, 1917 [Database on-line]. *Ancestry.com*. Henry R Walden, pastor, Emanuel Congregational Church.
[169] U.S. City Directories, 1821-1989, High Point, 1935 [Database on-line]. *Ancestry.com*. Rev Henry R Walden, pastor, Pilgrim Congregational Church.
[170] North Carolina Death Certificates [Database on-line]. *Ancestry.com*. Henry Ruffin Walden, 20 Jan 1951.

Figure 36: Site of Strieby Church School-left side of church. Photo by Margo Lee Williams, 2014.

The Common School Era Ends

As public education became more available, some AMA "common schools" closed or were "upgraded." Strieby reportedly upgraded.

> In 1905, the community led by Talledegan Reverend O.W. Hawkins, pastor and principal, erected a larger building with the intent to transform its institution from common school into a graded and normal school. Local blacks donated four thousand feet of lumber, nails, and other material, and were

> doing the construction themselves. The AMA promised only forty dollars for school furniture.[171]

Alas, this new two room school would not achieve its intended goal:

> Just when plans were being completed to advance the church school to Garfield Academy, the gold mines became exhausted and the distillery closed down. The wave of families moving in ceased. Daily laborers turned to their land for making a living. Soon the children became of age to seek further education and employment elsewhere. Eventually, family heads sold their land and moved away, or deceased.[172]

By the 1920s, like other AMA common schools across the South, Strieby became part of the North Carolina public school system. This was consistent with the AMA's belief that basic elementary education was the state's responsibility and that the AMA's mission was to extend education beyond the elementary level to high school, "normal" school, and college. Indeed the number of prominent AMA-affiliated Historically Black Colleges is impressive, including Berea College, Talladega College,

---

[171] Richardson and Jones, 2009, p. 14.
[172] Jones, 1972, p. 2.

Tougaloo College, Hampton University, Straight (now Dillard) University, Atlanta University (now Clark Atlanta University), and Fisk University, among the better known colleges.[173] Nevertheless, the AMA also acknowledged that the common schools had "assisted its churches," and had "stimulated interest in public education."[174]

---

[173] DeBoer, 2015.
[174] Richardson and Jones, 2009, p. 14.

PART THREE:

EDUCATION IN NORTH CAROLINA AND AT STRIEBY IN THE TWENTIETH CENTURY

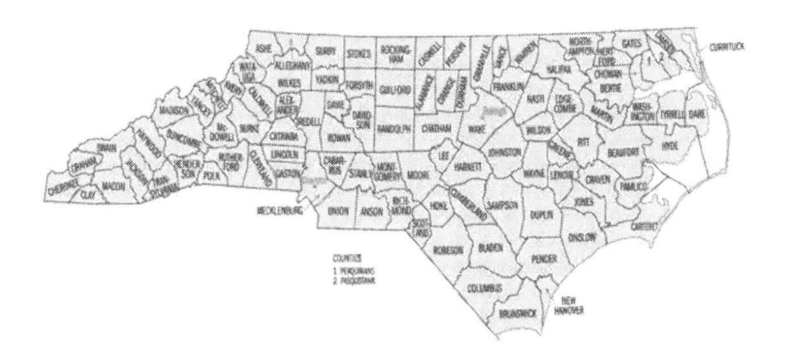

Figure 37: North Carolina County Map.
Photo courtesy of US Census Quickfacts - North Carolina.

Figure 38: Professor Jacobs' school, Lake Waccamaw, Columbus County. Photo Courtesy of the Library of Congress.

Public Education in North Carolina

Although the North Carolina constitution of 1776 included education at public expense, the first law enacted was in 1839. The law established school districts for white children only. No provision was made for free black children and it was forbidden to teach slaves to read or write, or to give or sell them books.[175] According to Eric Foner (2015), at the end of the Civil War, in 1865, Jonathan

[175] North Carolina Advisory Committee, 1959-62, p. 99.

Worth, by then Governor of North Carolina, though previously supporting public education, convinced the state legislature to eliminate the public school system for fear of having to finance schools for "negroes." In their place, they authorized tax-supported private academies.[176] A few years later, in 1871, in *Lane v Stanly*, the North Carolina Supreme Court ruled that the Constitution established the public school system and the General Assembly, counties, and boards of education must provide for it through public taxes. It said the system should be general and uniform, providing for every child.[177] However, almost 30 years later, in 1900, the beginning of the twentieth century and 35 years after the end of the Civil War, public school education and education resources were still not available to every child, black or white, in North Carolina.

---

[176] Foner, 2015, [Kindle Version] Image 2089.
[177] North Carolina Advisory Committee, 1959-62, p. 100.

Buildings, Teachers, and Other Resources

In 1900, the 5028 white school districts had school buildings valued at $231 each. Many were in poor condition. Nevertheless, they were in better condition than the 2236 colored school districts whose school buildings were valued at only $136 each. Surprisingly, these districts were the lucky ones. There were another 830 school districts that had no school building. Differences did not end there.

The quality of the teachers varied as well. Few teachers had more than an elementary school education, especially teachers in schools for children of color. By 1919, 16 percent of white teachers and 43 percent of black teachers had not finished high school. The graduation rate for black teachers could hardly be surprising since there was not a single "standard" high school for black students, and all schools for black children, books and other equipment were "crude," often used and outdated.[178] Interestingly, teacher salaries in 1884 for white and black teachers were relatively close, with black teachers

---

[178] North Carolina Advisory Committee 1959-62, pp. 100-101.

receiving 94 percent of white teacher salaries. This would be the closest they would be until after 1940. By contrast, in the early 1900s, the salary disparity would be 2:1.[179] These conditions were very likely the inspiration for *Hooker v. Greenville*. Decided in 1902, *Hooker v. Greenville* provided that a white child and a "colored" child should have the same amount of money per capita, and that "... both races shall have equal opportunities for an education so far as the public money is concerned."[180] Unfortunately three years later the court, with four new judges, reversed itself.

That disparity in educational spending was noted by the North Carolina Advisory Committee in its 1959-60 report.[181] In 1944-45, library expenditures per book for white students was $0.73, but only $0.35 for black students. The gap was even wider in 1957-58, when expenditures were $1.84 for white students but only $1.28 for black students, even though this was 3-4 years after *Brown v Board of Education*. It can be further inferred from the

---

[179] North Carolina Advisory Committee 1959-62, p. 101.
[180] North Carolina Advisory Committee 1959-62, p. 100.
[181] North Carolina Advisory Committee 1959-62, p. 105.

disparity in circulation of library books. In 1944-45, 17 books on average, per white student, were in circulation, while only 6 books on average, per black student, were in circulation. Again, the gap had widened even more by 1957-58. It would appear that white students were encouraged to believe, and did believe, that reading was important and would open doors to a world that a black child would never have access to, no matter how much they read.

School Attendance

It is interesting to note that prior to the late 1950s, the dropout rate was *lower* for African American students than white students.[182] That trend would be reversed after 1959. One could speculate about why that would be the case. This writer believes that the socioeconomic-cultural importance of education for those, who for the most part, were one generation from slavery, was far greater than for white counterparts, whose very white group membership gave them status and opportunity denied their African American neighbors.

---

[182] North Carolina Advisory Committee, 1959-62, p. 104.

While the pre-1960 dropout rate may have been lower, absenteeism among African American students was always slightly higher.[183] Again, this writer speculates that economic demands dictated these differences. North Carolina was, and is still, largely a rural, farm state. Pre-1960, African American farmers, whether independent, tenant farmers, or hired farm laborers, needed the extra hands of their children. The need for all family members, including children, to provide labor that could enhance the economic success of the family unit was far greater for statistically poorer African American farm families than for white families.

One, Two, and Three Teacher Schools

One, two, and three teacher schools, such as Strieby School, could not be accredited by the State:

> No doubt some of the teachers in these schools are capable and there may be special geographical and economic factors affecting the location and enrollment of these schools, nevertheless it can be said that such schools do not offer the students the

---

[183] North Carolina Advisory Committee, 1959-62, p. 104.

> same educational opportunity as other schools in the State with larger faculties and facilities.[184]

This was one of the reasons schools began to consolidate in the mid-1920s and continued to do so in the following decades. One might have hoped that this would have impacted students of color as much as their white counterparts. Apparently, it did not.

Public schools circa 1960 were 70 percent white and 30 percent nonwhite. If race was not a factor, the percent of white students in small, one, two, or three teacher schools would have reflected the same numbers. They did not. Of the 111 such elementary schools, 32 were composed of all white students, 79 of all nonwhite students (74 Negro [*sic*], 5 Indian or other). Of the 29 such high schools, 11 were composed of all white students, 18 of all nonwhite students (11 Negro [*sic*], 7 Indian or other).[185] Perhaps, more tragic were the circumstances in *Clay*, *Graham* and *Mitchell* counties, where there were *no* elementary schools to which any black child was assigned, and the counties of Alleghany, *Clay*, *Graham*, Madison,

---

[184] North Carolina Advisory Committee 1959-62, p. 111.
[185] North Carolina Advisory Committee 1959-62, p. 112.

Mitchell, Swain, and Transylvania where there were *no* high schools to which black students were assigned. In fact, there were no school facilities even nearby for these students.[186] It was precisely these impoverished conditions that had led the AMA to continue to maintain some of its Common and Elementary schools.

> ... The instruction in these rural public schools is necessarily inadequate as in many cases the children have no appropriate school facilities or appointments and have eight or nine months to forget what they tried to learn in three or four. But these poor people that are out of the way, who are by far the great majority, through sheer eagerness to know, do learn something and often are stimulated to find their way out of the places of darkness to our larger schools.[187]

Accreditation

In 1959-60 when the North Carolina Advisory Committee made its report. Six years after *Brown v Board of Education,* there was great variation across the state in terms of accredited and state approved high schools. Not a single high school for nonwhite students was able to meet the same standards as those of white students. However,

---

[186] North Carolina Advisory Committee 1959-62, p. 112.
[187] American Missionary Association, 1895, pp. 49(6):352-353.

schools could be *accredited* by the State Department of Public Education. In 1959-60, of the 240 schools for nonwhite students, 223 were accredited by the State, representing, 93 percent of nonwhite high schools, with an enrollment of 68,255. By contrast, 621 of the 634 white high schools were accredited by the State, representing 98 percent and 192,923 white students. In addition, 109 white schools, or 17 percent, were accredited by the Southern Association, but only 47 nonwhite schools, or 19 percent, met the criteria to be approved. This represented 68,280 white students or 35 percent, but only 21,563 nonwhite students, or 32 percent of the 11 states accredited by the Southern Association, but that is somewhat misleading. Schools for nonwhite students could be considered "approved" by the Association if they met the Southern Association of Colleges and Secondary Schools' requirements. North Carolina ranked 11th, or last, for the percent of white students in an accredited school, yet it ranked 7th for the percent of nonwhite students in approved schools.[188] Unfortunately, Randolph County did

---

[188] North Carolina Advisory Committee 1959-62, p. 106.

not have any nonwhite students enrolled in schools approved or accredited by the Southern Association, but Randolph High School, in Liberty, was accredited by the State Department of Public Education.[189] Regardless, public elementary schools such as Strieby had a significant educational impact on their communities.

---

[189] Historic Landmark Preservation Commission, 2012.

Figure 39: Abigail (Henley) Ratliff's "Marbury" Water Dipper from Strieby School. Photo by Eric Ratliff, Sr.

Education at Strieby.

When Strieby School began circa 1880, schools provided only three months of classroom teaching. This did not change until the 1920s when it was increased to four months. In 1927, the classroom time increased to six months, and then in 1929, to eight months. The eight-month term remained until after the 1930s when nine-months became the norm.[190]

[190] Auman & Auman, 1976, p. 19.

**Figure 40: Barzilla "Zill" Harrison Hill.
Photo courtesy of Richard Jackson.**

Circa 1920, schools in Randolph County were divided into township areas. New School Committeemen were elected for the new districts. Many schools were consolidated into one new school, thereby reducing the total number of schools. Strieby District was represented on the Committee by Zill (Barzilla) Lassiter (who lived in the Lassiter Mill area of New Hope Township), grandson of Miles and Healy Lassiter and B.H. Hill (Brazilla Harrison Hill of Strieby proper), grandson of Ned and Priscilla Hill.[191]

---

[191] Auman & Auman, 1976, p. 1.

Figure 41: Sarah Juanita (Smitherman) Lassiter, 1902-1975.

In the late 1920s leaders of the school districts believed that consolidation would improve the quality of education. Petitions from various areas were received by the School Board. Delegates from the three schools of color in Southwestern Randolph County (*Red House*, *Salem*, and *Strieby*), asked the School Board to consolidate these three schools. Teachers at Strieby during this time were: Amanda Capel (1921-23); Vella A. Lassiter (1923-24); Annie

Mae Hill (1925); Clara Cranford (1926-27); and Eunice K. Brown (1929-30).[192]

Thus, Strieby School continued well into the 20th century, producing teachers, doctors, nurses, ministers, and others for the African American community of Southwestern Randolph County and beyond. Local graduates and family members who came back to Strieby to teach there, included:

- Novella "Vella" Anna Lassiter (1923-24): Vella was the daughter of Winston Lassiter and his wife Ora Kearns, and great grandchild of Miles Lassiter. Vella is buried at Strieby.
- Clara Cranford (1926-1927): Clara was the daughter of Hal B. Cranford and Belle Cassady, and great granddaughter of Ned and Priscilla Hill. Clara is not buried at Strieby.
- Annie Mae (Cave) Hill (1925): Annie Mae was the wife of Ernest Marvin Hill Sr., who was the son of Julius Hill and his wife Elizabeth Davis, and grandson of Ned and Priscilla Hill. Annie Mae is not buried at Strieby.

---

[192] Auman & Auman, 1976, pp. 19-20.

- Sarah (Smitherman) Lassiter (1940, with the combined "common school"): Sarah was the daughter of Mary (Hill) Smitherman and Charlie Smitherman, wife of Ulysses "Grant" Lassiter, and great granddaughter of Ned and Priscilla Hill. Sarah is buried in Strieby Cemetery.

Of the other two teachers mentioned above, Amanda Capel was a professional teacher from neighboring Montgomery County, and Eunice Brown was the wife of the pastor. Neither is buried at Strieby.

Figure 42: Aveus Lassiter Edmondson 101st birthday, 4 July 2014. Photo by Margo Lee Williams.

A Student Reminisced: Aveus Lassiter Edmondson

Aveus Lassiter Edmondson ("Ave"), who was 101 years old at this writing, remembered her days at Strieby School fondly. She said that she, her siblings, and others from the Lassiter Mill community would walk through the woods usually in order to get to school. When asked if she wasn't afraid of snakes, she said, "No, the boys were with us." However, she noted that several local white people commented that it was a shame that "those young'uns

Figure 43: Oberia (Hill) Hill (R), and Daughter, Bettie Marie Hill (L). Photo courtesy of the Late Bettie-Marie Hill.

can't ride the bus."

When asked about the school building, she remarked that it stood next to the church on the left when facing it (the cemetery is to the rear and right). She said it had 4 or 5 rooms where different age groups studied, but all were led by one teacher who rotated through the class rooms. When asked if any of the rooms served as a library, she said that there was no library, nor books for circulation. Among her classmates, she said, were cousins, Oberia Hill and Maxine Hill who lived at Strieby.

Ave remembered several of the teachers named above. She remembered Amanda Capel, whom she didn't think was very knowledgeable. She remembered Annie Mae Hill but didn't know if she was related to the Hills of Strieby (she was, by marriage). She said that Clara Cranford actually lived in Asheboro and commuted to the school, a trip of about 10-12 miles. She especially remembered Eunice Brown because she was the wife of the minister at Strieby. She was not sure whether Sarah Smitherman taught actually at Strieby or only at the combined Common School that included Salem and Red House. This is not surprising since Sarah was not teaching until about 1940, when Ave had already left the community to pursue her studies in nursing, after finishing Peabody Institute, in Troy, Montgomery County.

When asked if the gold mines, store, or Post Office that used to be at Strieby at one time were still functioning when she was a young girl, she said that did not remember any of them being there. However, she did remember the

Marbury Dipper that had been in the possession of her cousin, Abigail Henley Ratliff. She remembered that it was used to get water from the well bucket. She did not know to whom it belonged.

Figure 44: Clarence Edmondson & Aveus Lassiter.
Photo courtesy of Patrice Lassiter Bryant

After leaving Randolph County, as stated, Ave went on to become a nurse, living and working in Queens, New York, with her husband, Clarence Edmondson. There they attended Lemuel Haynes Congregational Church, in

Jamaica, Queens. Ave and Clarence were very active church members there, including taking several missionary trips abroad.

In the 1970s Ave and Clarence returned to live at the home-place on Lassiter Mill Road and resumed their membership at Strieby. Ave continued to work as a nurse at Mountain View Nursing Home in nearby Denton, in neighboring Davidson County. In September 1985, Ave was ordained a Deacon at Strieby. She was also one of the Trustees until her death.

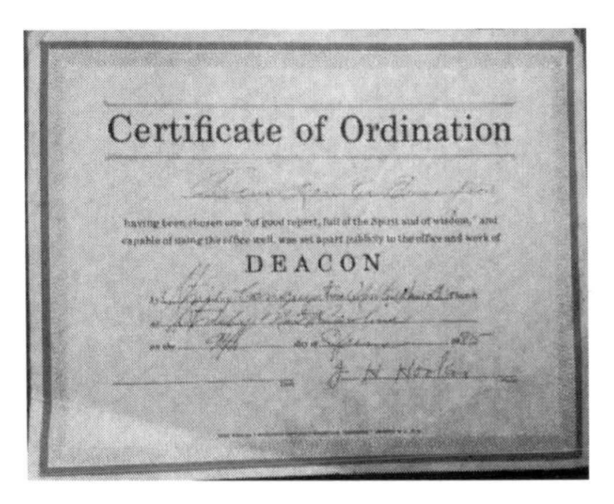

Certificate of Ordination

DEACON

Figure 45: Certificate of Ordination-Aveus Lassiter Edmondson. Photo courtesy Patrice Lassiter Bryant.

Ave's beloved husband, Clarence, died in 1982 and was buried at Strieby.[193] After 101 years of life, Ave died on 19 October 2014, in Greensboro, North Carolina where she had gone to live and be cared for by her niece, Patrice Lassiter Bryant. She was laid to rest in Strieby's cemetery, beside Clarence, the following Saturday, 25 October 2014, at a service presided over by her nephew, the Rev. Winston Lassiter, his wife, the Rev. Tanya Lassiter, and her godson and cousin, the Rev. Eric Ratliff Sr., in the presence of her many family members and friends. It was the end of an era.[194]

---

[193]*See* Strieby Cemetery Listing below.

[194] From an interview with the Author, 6 July 2014

Figure 46: Strieby Church Sign at Strieby Church Road and High Pine Church Road. Photo by Margo Lee Williams, 2014.

Impact of Strieby Church and School

The impact of Strieby Church and School on the community of "Hill Town" cannot be overlooked. According to the 1870 census, there were only 4 independent households of families of color in Union Township, containing 21 individuals. In 1880, when the Rev. Islay Walden first started the church and school, Hill Town, in Union Township, had grown to 10 families containing 60 people. According to the report written by Henry Walden in 1891, this was a poor, backward, uneducated, and morally bankrupt community.

> The place that is now called "Strieby," was once a desolate place called "Hilltown" with a few cabins in it. The people did not respect one another nor themselves. ... One person here - the mother of six - had never heard a sermon until she heard Rev. Islay Walden preach in the beginning of this work. Others heard such preaching as was going about in that day and time. ... In place of the old houses are new ones. Instead of one room the houses have two or three now. Instead of one bed there are beds in different rooms. Impurity has come under condemnation.[195]

This view of Strieby as a poor and backward community no doubt is true, but Walden's description also hints of Victorian hyperbole, moral judgment, and denominational arrogance. In addition, Walden was not from Strieby/Hill Town, or even from neighboring New Hope Township. He had grown up in a completely different county. He never knew Hill Town. It had already become Strieby by the time he and his mother, Julia (Ritter) Walden, arrived. This author has found no other deprecating description, either written by the Rev. Islay Walden or any other contemporary individual. It is very

[195] Walden, 1891, p. 45:166.

likely that there were one room cabins. This would not be peculiar for a rural community of that time. The implications that Henry Walden draws from this seem to be colored by Victorian expectations. Nevertheless, the missionary work of his predecessors and his own efforts undoubtedly had a strong impact on the community, religiously, morally, and educationally:

> This Congregational work has raised the standard of the community beyond what could have been expected. In domestic affairs about the home, in Christian living, in speech, in education and in manners the progress has been great.[196]

According to the 1880 census, already 13 children were attending school in Hill Town. By the 1900 census, the community included 21 families, containing 101 people, with 33 children in school. (*See:* 1900 Census below)

[196] Walden, 1891, p. 45:166.

1900 US Census Randolph County - Families of Color								
Strieby - Union Township								
Dwelling#	Name	Color	# in Home	Occup	Read	Write	In School	Comments
69	A(sp?) Holmes	B	9	Farmer	4	0	5	
80	Anthony Davis	B	8	Farmer	3	3	1	
82	Henry Walden	B	4	Farmer	3	3	1	Julia (Ritter) Walden - Mother-Midwife
83	Edward Stratton	B	4	Minister	2	2	0	From: South Carolina
84	Charles Gray	B	1	Day Labor	0	0	0	
90	Josiah McCloud	B	9	Farmer	8	7	4	
91	John McRay	B	4	Farmer	2	1	1	
92	Stephen Lassiter	B	1	Day Labor	0	0	0	
93	James Lilly	B	10	Farmer	6	6	7	
103	Richard Wallace	B	7	Day Labor	6	5	4	
104	Sherman Hill	B	4	Farmer	1	1	0	Son of Ned Hill
105	Calvin Hill	B	5	Farmer	3	3	0	Son of Ned Hill
106	Brazilla Hill	B	4	Farmer	4	4	2	
107	Israel Coble	B	6	Farmer	2	2	0	
108	Alexander Hill	B	3	Farmer	1	1	0	Priscilla Hill - Mother/Widow of Ned Hill
109	William Fisher	B	5	Farmer	4	4	2	
110	Dockery Potter	B	3	Farmer	2	2	0	Grandson of Ned Hill
111	Julius Hill	B	6	Farmer	2	1	2	Son of Ned Hill
112	Charity Potter	B	3	Day Labor	3	0	1	Daughter of Ned Hill
113	Mary Smitherman	B	5	Day Labor	2	2	3	Daughter of Ned Hill
	Total		**101**		**58**	**47**	**33**	**57.4% Overall Literacy**
Elsewhere in Union Township								
162	Noah Cagle	B	2	Farmer	0	0	0	2 white boarders not counted
164	John Bean	B	1		0	0	0	Son of Rachel Bean - "W"
169	Charles Smith	B	1	Servant	0	0	1	Home of Nathan Luck
	Total		**4**		**0**	**0**	**1**	**0% Overall Literacy**

Figure 47: 1900 US Census, Randolph County-Union

1900 US Census Randolph County - Families of Color								
Lassiter Mill - New Hope Township								
Dwelling#	Name	Color	in Home	Occup	Read	Write	In school	Comments
14	Clark Hill	B	5	Farmer	4	2	2	Brother-in-law of Winston Lassiter
15	Winson Lassiter	B	8	Farmer	2	2	0	Brother-in-law of Clark Hill
16	Amos Lassiter	B	8	Farmer	5	5	3	Brother of Wins[t]on Lassiter
17	Postell Henley	B	3	Farmer	3	2	0	Brother-in-law of Amos and Winston Lassiter
18	George Phillips	B	4	Farmer	2	2	0	Brother of Amos Lassiter's wife- Harriett
20	Alex Adderton	B	7	Farmer	5	5	3	Brother-in-law of Amos and Winston Lassiter
21	James Redwine	B	2	Farmer	0	0	0	Son-in-law of Ned Hill
22	Myranda Scarlett	B	3	Day Labor	1	0	0	
26	Alex Burk	B	4	Day Labor	0	0	0	
29	Rachel Hearn	B	1	Servant	0	0	0	In Home of Miles Hopkins
	Total		**45**		**22**	**18**	**8**	**48.9% Overall Literacy**

Scattered in New Hope Township								
Dwelling #	Name	Color	# in home	Occup	Read	Write	n Schoo	Comments
43	Adam Reeves	B	4	Day Lab	0	0	1	
69	Solomon Kearns	B	7	Farmer	5	4	1	Wife Adelade-fist cousin of Winston and Amos Lassiter
73	George Sanders	B	8	Day Lab	5	2	5	
74	Robert Walker	B	7	Day Lab	0	0	0	
79	John R Haywooc	B	1	Day Lab	0	0	0	In home of James Luther
92	Lee Wootian	B	1	Servant	0	0	0	In home of Joseph Stafford
110	William Taylor	B	7	Farmer	4	1	3	
148	Tommie Hearn	B	1	House Servant	0	0	0	In home of Nelson Hopkins
159	Garfield Kearns	B	1	Farm La	1	1	0	In home of Queen Walker
160	Emma Kearns	B	4	Day Lab	3	3	0	
197	William Stokes	B	7	Farmer	3	3	3	
205	Charlie Cross	B	8	Farmer	5	5	4	
207	Franklin Taylor	B	3	Day Lab	0	0	0	
216	Robert Kearn	B	4	Day Lab	0	0	0	
217	Isabel Dorsett	B	1	Day Lab	0	0	0	
222	Sarah Dorsett	B	3	Day Lab	0	0	0	
224	Rainer Dorsett	B	1	Day Lab	0	0	0	
225	David Barber	B	1	Day Lab	1	1	0	
234	Harris Harrison	B	2	Day Lab	1	1	0	Winburn Hill - lodger
	Total		**67**		**28**	**21**	**17**	**41.8% Overall Literacy**

Figure 48: 1900 US Census Randolph County-New Hope Township

By comparing the names of the young boys listed on the 1900 census from Strieby and Lassiter Mill who would then be of age to be drafted in World War I and who would, if able, sign their draft registrations, another measure of community literacy can be established.[197]

Name	**Signed**	**Comments**
Calvin J Coble		Nothing found
Rodna (Rodney) Coble		Died: 26 Jun 1917[198]
Albert Hill	Yes	
Arthur Haze Hill	Yes	
Carl Edward Hill	Yes	
Gurnie Calvin Hill	Yes	Nothing found
Ulysses Grant Hill	No	
Cornie [sp?] Holmes		Nothing found
George Lilly	Yes	
Isley A Lilly	Yes	
Walter Lilly		Nothing found
Jeremiah W McCloud	Yes	
Charlie Potter	Yes	

[197] U.S., World War I Draft Registration Cards, 1917-1918 [Database on-line]. *Ancestry.com.*
[198] North Carolina, Deaths, 1906-1930 [Database on-line]. *Ancestry.com.* Rodney Coble, 26 Jun 1917.

Ayer [sp?] Sanders		Nothing found
Birtis Smitherman	Yes	
Harrison Smitherman	Yes	
Winston Smitherman	Yes	
Samuel Stratton		Nothing found; son of minister from SC
Henry C D D Wallace		Nothing found
Irving Wallace	Yes	Deaf & Dumb
William H Wallace		Nothing found

If the Lassiter Mill names are added:

Greeley Davis[199]		Died: 24 Jul 1918
Franklin Harrison		Nothing found
Lonnie Harrison	Yes	
George Henley	No	
James Hill		Nothing found
Colon Charles	Yes	

[199] North Carolina, Death Certificates, 1909-1975 [Database on-line]. *Ancestry.com*. Graley [*sic*] Davis, 24 Jul 1918.

Lassiter		
Harris Lassiter	Yes	
Willie James Lassiter	Yes	
Willie Loflin	Yes	
Hubert/Herbert Phillips	Yes	
Linzie Scarlett		Nothing found
Samuel Scarlett		Nothing found

Of those Draft records identified, all but two people signed their own draft cards. One person, Ulysses Grant Hill, said in the 1900 census that he could read and write. Unfortunately, there is no way to sort out the discrepancy. The other person, George Henley said in 1900 that he could read, but not write. Even so, young men educated at Strieby, identified in the draft, confirm a significant level of literacy. Within Strieby itself, the literacy level of 57.4% appears to be slightly higher than the national average for African Americans which was about 50% in 1900.[200] On the other hand, the Lassiter Mill community was just under the national average with a level of 48.9%.

---

[200] Margo, 1990, p. 8.

Also striking is the identification of one young man, Irving Wallace, in draft records as "deaf and dumb," even though he was so identified, he signed his own draft card. When double checking the 1900 census, it was noticed that it said nothing about him being "deaf and dumb."[201] It did say that he could read and write, seemingly confirmed by his signature on the draft card.[202] However, it also said that he did not speak English. What this seems to confirm is that he did not speak in an easily comprehended manner, which the draft characterized as "dumb." More importantly, it says that someone in Strieby, most likely his teacher, took extra care to help him learn to read and write even though he could not hear. That teacher, given his age, (born about 1881) would have been first, Eleanora Walden, and after her death, Henry Walden. This would indicate that this was a community that cared about its members and, it would seem, had great aspirations for its children.

---

[201] 1900 US Federal Census; Census Place: Union, Randolph, North Carolina; Roll: 1213; Page: 6A; Enumeration District: 0099; FHL microfilm: 1241213. *Ancestry.com*. Richard Wallace, head; Irvin J Wallace, age 20.

[202] U.S., World War I Draft Registration Cards, 1917-1918 [Database on-line]. *Ancestry.com*. Irving Wallace, b. 5 Jul 1881.

By the 1910 census, Strieby had seen some out-migration, but it still had 17 families with 77 members, 22 children in school, and an overall literacy of 58.4%. The Lassiter Mill area had 11 families with 58 individuals and 18 children in school. Their overall literacy was slightly lower at 51.7%. Scattered around the rest of New Hope Township were 17 other families of color, totaling 85 individuals with 14 children in school, for an overall literacy of 27.1%. What is striking about these numbers is that the further one gets from Strieby Church and School, the more significant the drop in literacy. Additional research would be needed to determine how close these families were to the other two schools in Southwest Randolph, Salem and Red House. In any event it is obvious that Strieby School had a significantly positive impact on the Strieby and Lassiter Mill communities.

1910 US Census Randolph County - Union Township								
			#in					
Dwelling#	Name	Color	home	Occup	Read	Write	#in schl	Comments
6	John McRay	B	7	Farmer	3	3	2	
9	Thomas Chandler	Mu	8	Farmer	2	1	4	Jina Coble servant
22	Israel Coble	B	9	Farmer	4	4	1	
23	Jane Edie	Mu	2	Farmer	1	1	0	
24	Ulysses Hill	Mu	7	Farmer	3	3	3	
25	Elizabeth Hill	Mu	2	Farmer	1	1	0	
26	Stephen Hill	Mu	2	Farmer	0	0	0	Priscilla Hill: Mother
27	William Fisher	B	4	Farmer	4	4	1	
28	Brazilla Hill	B	3	Farmer	3	3	0	
29	James Shamburger	B	5	Farmer	4	4	3	
30	Thomas Loflin	B	4	Farmer	2	2	0	
31	Hines King	B	2	Minister	2	2	0	From: Connecticut
32	Dockery Potter	B	5	Farmer	4	3	1	Mo:Charity Hill Pottr
33	Julius Hill	B	6	Farmer	4	3	3	
34	Angeline Davis	B	3	Farmer	1	1	0	
35	Mary Smitherman	B	6	Farmer	5	5	4	
43	Richard Wallace	B	2	Farmer	2	1	0	
		Total	77		45	41	22	
						Overall Literacy		58.40%

1910 US Census Randolph County - New Hope Township								
	Lassiter Mill area							
			#in				#in	
Dwelling#	Name	Color	home	Occup	Read	Write	School	Comments
3	Dell Davis	B	1	Servant	1	1	0	
7	George Harrison	B	9	Farmer	0	0	4	
9	Zill (Amos) Lassiter	B	7	Farmer	6	6	2	Fa: Colier Lassiter
10	Postell Henley	B	3	Farmer	3	3	0	w: Martitia Lassiter
11	Winston Lassiter	B	11	Farmer	8	8	5	Fa: Colier Lassiter
12	James Redwine	B	3	Farmer	1	1	0	w: "Thanie" Hill
13	Alex Adderton	B	8	Farmer	5	5	2	w: Rhodemia Lassitr
14	Mattie Cagle	B	8	Self-Empl	1	1	2	
17	Alphons Holmes	B	5	Laborer	3	3	3	
20	Joseph Powell	Mu	2	Farm Lab	2	2	0	
22	Will Matthews	Mu	1	Laborer	0	0	0	
		Total	58		30	30	18	
						Overall Literacy		51.70%
Elsewhere in New Hope Township								
65	Cicero Harris	B	2	Farm Lab	2	0	0	
71	Elisha Ingram	B	7	Farm Lab	0	0	0	
77	Greeley Davis	B	6	Farmer	2	2	1	
102	Willie Kearns	B	5	Laborer	0	0	0	
128	William Stokes	B	6	Farmer	1	1	0	
129	Calwell Miller	B	4	Farmer	1	1	0	
130	Andrew Kearns	B	5	Laborer	1	1	0	
131	Adam Hearns	B	5	Laborer	1	0	0	
133	Robert Walker	B	9	Farmer	2	2	4	
142	Birchie Cross	B	4	Farm Lab	2	2	0	
147	James D Birkhead	B	4	Farm Lab	2	2	1	
148	Myrna Redwine	B	4	Laborer	1	1	1	
154	Adam Reeves	B	5	Farm Lab	0	0	1	
166	Henry Harris	B	8	Farm Lab	1	0	4	
169	Charlie Cross	B	5	Farmer	5	5	2	
175	Eunice Kearns	B	3	None	0	0	0	
218	James Short	B	3	Farm Lab	2	2	0	
		Total	85		23	19	14	
					Overall Literacy			27.10%

Figure 49: 1910 US Census, Randolph County Union and New Hope Townships.

In 1920, just before the consolidation of the Strieby, Salem, and Red House schools (all schools for children of color), there were 14 families, with 68 individuals. The closing of the gold mines and resulting loss of extra income, along with the growth of factories elsewhere encouraged out migration. Nevertheless, all 15 children at Strieby, who were school-age, were in school, and the entire adult population of 52 could read, with only 1 of those marked as unable to also write. It should be noted that these numbers do not take into account the families that lived in the nearby Lassiter Mill area of neighboring New Hope Township, who were also educated at Strieby. This was not the picture nationwide.

Dwelling #	Name	in home	Occup	Read	Write	in school	Comments
	1920 US Census Randolph County -Strieby						
154	Bertis Smitherman	6	Farmer	6	6	0	Mary Hill Smitherman-mo
155	James Davis	3	Farmer	3	3	0	
156	Winburn Hill	2	Farmer	2	2	0	Thanie Redwine - mo
157	Sylvester Simmons	4	Farmer	2	2	0	2 children not in school
158	William Fisher	2	Farmer	2	2	0	
159	Arthur Hill	6	Farmer	3	3	1	3 children not in school
160	Julius Hill	8	Farmer	5	5	2	2 children not in school
161	Stephen Hill	1	Farmer	1	1	0	
162	Brazille Hill	2	Farmer	2	2	0	
163	Dockery Potter	5	Farmer	4	4	2	1 child not in shool
164	Allie Davis	8	Farmer	5	5	2	2 children not in school
165	Israel Coble	11	Farmer	9	8	4	4 dhildren not in school
166	Ulysses Hill	9	Farmer	7	7	4	2 children not in school
167	Charity Potter	1	Servant	1	1	0	
	14 Families	**68**		**52**	**51**	**15**	**16 children not in school were underage**
				100% literacy of all who were of age			
				76.5% literacy of the total population			
			New Hope Township -- Lassiter Mill				
156	Jesero Stokes	2	Farm Lal	1	1	0	No children
158	John C Bright	4	Farmer	2	2	0	2 children too young
174	Thomas Loflin	8	Farm Lal	6	6	4	2 children too young
180	George Harrison	7	Farmer	7	7	5	All children in school
181	Diffie Reeves	6	Farmer	2	2	0	4 children too young
186	Alice Moose/Mose	1	Servant	1	1	0	No children
196	Zill Lassiter	5	Farmer	5	5	1	4 adults
197	George Henley	3	Farmer	2	2	0	1 child 2 young 4 school
198	Winston Lassiter	13	Farmer	11	11	5	6 ad'lts; 2 child'n 2 young
	9 Families	**49**		**37**	**37**	**15**	**11 children 2 young 4 school**
				97% Literacy of all who were of age			
				75.5% Literacy of total population			

Figure 50: 1920 US Census, Randolph County - Strieby and Lassiter Mill

**Figure 51: Mary Harrison,
Daughter of George Harrison,
Lassiter's Mill.
Photo by Margo Lee Williams, 1982.**

Nationwide, in 1900 literacy across the country for communities of color was around 50%.[203] Strieby's literacy was slightly higher at 58%, while Lassiter Mill'swas slightly lower at 47%. Similarly, in 1910, Strieby's literacy was 58.4%, while Lassiter Mill's had increased to 51.7%. However, in 1920, Strieby's overall literacy was 76% with 100% for those old enough to read and that of Lassiter Mill, similarly, at 75.5% overall and 97% for all old enough to read, as measured by the

---

[203] Margo, 1990.

census. Nationwide literacy for African Americans old enough to read was slightly lower than 75%.[204] Strieby may have been a small community, but it had a strong commitment to education.

In 1940, exact school grade levels finished, for those still living in the Strieby area of Union Township are listed in the census. The census does not call the area Strieby, but these individuals have already been identified in previous census records, or are identified here as their children.[205] Some of the youngest individuals, under age 20, have most likely been educated in the combined school (Strieby, Salem, and Red House) then located in Cedar Grove Township. Again, unlike the rest of the country, Strieby was displaying a 95% literacy rate, male and female. Nationwide the African American literacy was only around 83-90%.[206]

Name	Age	Grade finished
James A Davis	58	6
Lovie (Potter) Davis	52	6
(Moses) Henderson Davis	71	3
Bertis Smitherman	56	6

---

[204] Margo, 1990.

[205] 1940 US Federal Census; Census Place: Union, Randolph, North Carolina; Roll: T627_2962; Pages: 1B & 2A; Enumeration District: 76-15.

[206] Margo, 1990.

Harris(on) Smitherman	50	6
Sallie Smitherman	38	7
Wins(t)on Smitherman	40	6
Sarah (Juanita) Smitherman	23	C(ollege) 1
Charlie Hill	22	7
Clifton Hill	25	7
Lizzie (Eadie) Potter	62	5
(Fred) Joseph Potter	16	8
Arthur (Haze) Hill	52	7
Lizzie (Lassiter) Hill	53	6
E. L. Hill	17	7
A. L. Hill	17	7
Marie Hill	12	6
John C. Hill	25	7
Howard Hill	22	7
Milton Hill	18	6
(Syl)Vester Simmons[207]	57	--

[207] Abstract reads "Victor" Simmons, but the original more closely resembles "Vester," agreeing with the 1920 census listing "Sylvester Simmons."

Figure 52: (L-R) Zane "Zev" Perkins, Bettie-Marie Hill, (grandchildren) and Arthur Hill. Photo courtesy of Richard Jackson.

It should be noted that two of the three people listed above that did not complete at least sixth grade were Henderson Davis, who was much older, and Lizzie Eadie Potter, who was not from Strieby. The third, Sylvester Simmons, is not listed as having any education, but the 1920 census above said that he could read and write, a discrepancy with no means of resolution. Of the twenty individuals listed here, eight finished sixth grade, eight finished seventh grade, and one finished eighth grade. One, Sarah Juanita Smitherman, had finished one year of college and was now a teacher in the Common School, most likely the combined school located in Cedar Grove Township. These numbers are similar to those among African Americans nationwide. If the three anomalies are excluded (Henderson Davis, Lizzie Eadie Potter, and Sarah Juanita Smitherman) the average number of years of schooling for the Strieby community in 1940 were 6.8 years. However, what Sarah Juanita Smitherman's one year of college completed hints at, are those young people who have already left Strieby to acquire secondary schooling and a college education. If we control for adults over the age of 20, we get a mean of 6.5 years. It is noteworthy that this small, remote, primarily farming and milling community of mixed race African Americans had successfully taken advantage of the elementary school education provided by Strieby.

Looking at the Lassiter Mill community in 1940, whose children were also educated at Strieby, there were the following individuals:[208]

---

[208] 1940 US Federal Census; Census Place: New Hope, Randolph, North Carolina; Roll: T627_2962; Enumeration District: 76-23. *Ancestry.com.*

Name	Age	Grade completed
Harriet Lassiter	78	8
Ruth Lassiter	16	H(igh School) 3
Fay Lassiter	13	8
Avon Lassiter	6	0
Ora Lassiter	65	8
Willie J Lassiter	40	7
Leonard Lassiter	24	H4
Harold Lassiter	22	C(ollege) 1
Walter Henley	14	5
Abbey Henley	10	0
Bud McDonald	30	0
Lillian McDonald	28	6
Carel J Bright	54	7
Mable C (Lassiter) Bright	47	7
Ora C Bright	17	H2
Lassiter J Bright	9	3
Alex Cross	53	0
Picilla [sic] Cross	62	4
Willie A Cross	14	5
Lem Millen	35	3
Elevena Millen	19	5
Martha R Millen	10	2
Nella M Millen	3	0
John E Millen	1	0
Tom Laughlin	61	2
Zina (Hill) Laughlin	54	H2
Lester M Laughlin	24	H2
Hill L Laughlin	20	7
Frank F Laughlin	17	6
Dellar (Potter) McRae	60	3
Elzevan McRae	26	4
Raymond E McRae	21	5

Jerrell [sic] McRae	14	5
Harris Lassiter	48	7
Cora C Lassiter	37	7
Fay H Lassiter	13	7
Max H Lassiter	10	3
Albert [*sic*-Elbert] J Lassiter	3	0

Figure 53: (L-R), A Lassiter cousin (Avon Lassiter?, 1933-1950), Elbert Lassiter Sr (1937-1971) & Max Harris Lassiter. Photo courtesy of Elbert Lassiter Jr.

Figure 54: Abbey (Henley) Ratliff (1930-2009). Photo courtesy of Eric Ratliff Sr.

First, it is evident that three children, and possibly a fourth (Lassiter J Bright) were too young for school. For these purposes, four will be set aside. The next thing of note is that, unlike the admittedly smaller community at Strieby, Lassiter Mill has four people who completed some high school. They also had one person who was in college. It is also true, however, that there is a greater spread of grades completed of more people. The spread here goes from second grade to first year of college. This creates a mean number of years attended of 5.8. Thus despite the inclusion of several individuals who had gone beyond their Common School years, the mean years attended was clearly affected by the additional number of individuals who had only completed two or three years, and a couple of adults who had not attended at all. It should be noted that two adults who had no schooling were not from traditional Strieby or Lassiter Mill families. Of the 7 adults over the age of 20 who had completed less than 6 years of school, four of them were not from Lassiter Mill or Strieby originally. The last three did grow up in Strieby and were Hill descendants. They do seem anomalous, but without information about their personal circumstances no reliable conclusions can be drawn. Therefore, if one controls for those 14 individuals known to have grown up in either Strieby or Lassiter Mill, a mean of 7.6 years of school attended is observed. For those 14 adults, the overall literacy is 100%.

Figure 55: Ruth (Lassiter) Laughlin (1922-2000). Photo by Margo Lee Williams, 1982.

The statistical comparisons presented here do have some limitations. First and foremost because Strieby was, even at its largest, always a small community, as was the Lassiter Mill community of color. However, even though now shrunken from its heyday in the 1890s and early 1900s, the small 1870 community of *Hill Town,* containing only a couple of African American families, primarily the family of Ned and Priscilla (Mahockly) Hill, did grow to be a thriving community. It became a center for local African Americans with church, school, and Post Office called *Strieby.*

Figure 56: Original Strieby Church Bell.
Photo by Margo Lee Williams, 2014.

Strieby Church was, and is, a perfect example of what the American Missionary Association hoped to accomplish and, in fact, did accomplish in the rural South:

> Our churches are generally small and poor, but they have stood steadfastly for human rights, for Christian equality and freedom of church membership, and for moral and religious education. While their work has been slow, their influence has been deep and pervasive, as has been that of our schools, small and great.[209]

---

[209] American Missionary Association, 1895, pp. 49(5):160-161.

Figure 57: Strieby Church Cornerstone. Photo by Margo Lee Williams, 2014.

Figure 58: Novella Anna Lassiter, "Vella," 1894-1994. Photo courtesy of Patrice Lassiter Bryant.

A Civil Rights Story: Vella Lassiter

Vella Lassiter was one example of both the legacy of educational excellence encouraged by schools in the American Missionary Association tradition, as well as their stance against injustice. Born Novella Anna Lassiter, "Vella" was the second of thirteen children (twelve of whom survived) of Winston and Ora (Kearns) Lassiter, of the Lassiter Mill community in Randolph County, North Carolina.

Bennett College
Greensboro, North Carolina.
To whom it may concern, Greeting:
Vella Anna Lassiter
Normal
Bennett College
DIPLOMA

Figure 59: Vella Lassiter's Bennett College Diploma.

Vella attended Strieby Church School. From there she went on to Peabody Academy in Troy, in neighboring Montgomery County, and then to Bennett College, in Greensboro. Vella graduated in 1913 from the Normal program and eventually earned her Master's degree from Miner Teachers College, in Washington, DC. (Miner became part of DC Teachers College which became the foundation for the Department of Education at the University of the District of Columbia.) Vella went on to become a teacher, first back at Strieby, then the combined school at Red House School in the nearby Mechanic area, and eventually at a school in Reidsville, in Rockingham County, North Carolina, where she taught for 40 years. However, being close to her family, she often came home on weekends to visit.

So it was in 1937. Vella was returning to Reidsville on Easter Monday afternoon. She was on the first of her two bus trips. The first bus would take her from Asheboro to Greensboro, about 35 miles away in Guilford County. From there she would take a bus to Reidsville. She had bought her ticket and was seated on the bus - next to a white person; the bus was crowded; there were no more seats. The bus driver apparently objected to Vella sitting next to a white person. Vella was asked to give up her seat, get off the bus, and wait for the next one. Anyone who knew Vella knew she was a force of nature. Vella said *"No."* The bus driver attempted to force her off the bus. Vella resisted. Eventually two policemen were needed to drag her to the door and throw her onto the sidewalk. She would later tell people there was no way she would make it easy for them to throw her off that bus. After all, she had bought a ticket and she was just as good as any white person.[210]

Vella called one of her brothers to come and take her to Reidsville, but she also called a lawyer, her cousin, prominent High Point, North Carolina, African American attorney, T. F Sanders (grandson of Wiley Phillips Lassiter and great grandson of Miles Lassiter). With his assistance (and that of prominent civil rights attorney, F.W. Williams, of Winston Salem) Vella sued the *Greensboro-Fayetteville Bus Line*, on the grounds that they had sold her the ticket for that specific bus trip and consequently were required to transport her. To everyone's surprise they won the case in a jury trial in November of that year. She was awarded $300 in damages. The bus company appealed to the North Carolina State Supreme Court. Two years later in 1939, the decision was upheld by Judge Allen H. Gwyn.[211] Vella had won. In reporting the victory on 18 August 1939, *The Carolina Times* newspaper, published in Raleigh, wrote that:

---

[210] Jones, 1993, pp. 343-344.
[211] *The Carolina Times,* 1939, p. 6.

> Possibly the most significant victory regarding the rights of Negroes was won in Randolph County last month when attorney P.[*sic*] W. Williams, prominent Winston-Salem lawyer emerged victorious in a suit against the Greensboro-Fayetteville Bus Line.[212]

Her success was particularly significant because there was only one other lawsuit like it that had gone to the North Carolina State Supreme Court and won before hers, that was a 1914 housing segregation lawsuit in Winston-Salem.[213]

Figure 60: Strieby Church Sign
In Memory of Novella "Vella" Lassiter.
Photo by Margo Lee Williams, 2014.

---

[212] *The Carolina Times,* 1939, p. 3.
[213] Gershenhorn, 2010, p. 85; Williams, 2013.

PART FOUR:

THE FAMILIES OF STRIEBY

Figure 61: Hill, Lassiter, and Associated Families, 1987.
Photo by Clyde Foust.

Figure 62: Lassiter, Hill, and associated Families, 1996. Photo courtesy of Margo Lee Williams.

The Hill and Lassiter Families

As noted above, the two principal families who were among the founders of Strieby were the Hill and Lassiter families. Many of the other families whose names were noted in various census years had family members who intermarried with these two families. Therefore, only the four generation genealogies of the two main families, Hill and Lassiter, are presented here. It is the author's belief that there is enough information in these genealogies to be able to expand into other families, as necessary, by any given descendant or researcher.[214]

Figure 63: Priscilla (Mahockly) Hill.
Photo courtesy of Ruth Howard.

Descendants of EDWARD and PRISCILLA HILL

[214] Please note: References found here will not be duplicated in the Sources section. They are presented here as completely as possible to provide the researcher enough information to pursue additional resource information.

Generation 1

1. **EDWARD "NED"**[1] **HILL** was born about 1805 in Randolph County, North Carolina.[215] He died between 1870-1880 in Hill Town, Union, Randolph, North Carolina.[216] He married **PRISCILLA MAHOCKLY** (called "**HARRIS**" on the death certificate of her daughter, **CHARITY HILL POTTER**,[217] but "**MAHACKLEY**" on the death certificate of her daughter **BETHANIA "THANIE" REDWINE**[218]before 1834 in Randolph County, North Carolina. She was born about May 1800 in North Carolina.[219] She died in 1911 in

---

[215] 1870 US Federal Census; Census Place: Union, Randolph, North Carolina; NARA Roll: M593-1156; Page: 506B; Image: 466; Family History Library Film: 552655. *Ancestry.com*. Ned Hill, head. *Note:* the 1850 and 1860 censuses say he was born in 1820 and 1810 respectively, but the 1805 date is more consistent with the ages of his children.
[216] 1880 US Federal Census; Census Place: Union, Randolph, North Carolina; NARA Roll: 978; Family History Film: 1254978; Page: 195B; Enumeration District: 224; Image: 068. *Ancestry.com*. Priscella Hill, head – "Widowed."
[217] North Carolina, Deaths, 1906-1930 [Database on-line]. *Ancestry.com*. Charity Potter; Priscilla Harris, mother.
[218] North Carolina, Deaths, 1906-1930 [Database on-line]. *Ancestry.com*. Thanie Redwine; Priscilla Mahackley, mother.
[219] 1850 US Federal Census; Census Place: Southern Division, Randolph, North Carolina; NARA Roll: M432_641; Page: 133B; Image: 273. *Ancestry.com*. Edward Hill, head; Priscilla Hill, age 50. There is no corroborative information for the birth date on her tombstone of 1792. *See:* Priscilla Hill, 1792-1911, at: *Find-a-Grave*.

Strieby, Union, Randolph, North Carolina and is **buried in Strieby Church Cemetery.**[220]

a. EDWARD "NED" HILL and PRISCILLA MAHOCKLY had the following children:

   i. **NATHAN[2] (CASE) HILL** was born about 1830 in Randolph County, North Carolina.[221] He married **SARAH POLK,** (probably) the daughter of **MARY POLK** and granddaughter of **CHARITY (POLK?) LASSITER** on 15 Sep 1853 in Randolph County, North Carolina.[222] She was born in 1833 either in Davidson County or Randolph County, North Carolina.[223]

   ii. **CHARITY HILL** was born in May 1834 in Strieby, Union, Randolph, North Carolina. She died 31 Mar 1921 in Strieby,

---

[220] Priscilla Hill, 1792-1911. Strieby Congregational United Church of Christ. *Find-a-Grave*.

[221] 1860 US Federal Census; Census Place: Western Division, Randolph, North Carolina; NARA Roll: M653-910; Page: 213; Image: 431; Family History Library Film: 803910. *Ancestry.com.* Nathan Hill, head.

[222] North Carolina, Marriage Bonds, 1741-1868 [Database on-line]. *Ancestry.com*. Nathan Case and Sarey Poke, 15 Sep 1853, Calier Lassiter, Bondsman. See also: *U.S., Social Security Applications and Claims Index, 1936-2007* [Database on-line]. *Ancestry.com*. Cora Rush; Father: Nathan Hill; Mother: Sarah Poak [*sic*].

[223] 1850 US Federal Census; Census Place: Southern Division, Randolph, North Carolina; NARA Roll: M432-641; Page: 136A; Image: 278. *Ancestry.com*. Jack Lassiter, head; Charity Lassiter, age 55; Sarah Lassiter, age 17.

Union, Randolph, North Carolina.[224] She married **IRA POTTER**, son of **JESSE POTTER** and **LUVENIA "LOVEY" HENLEY** on 10 October 1855 in Asheboro, Randolph, North Carolina.[225] He was born between 1827 and 1831 in Randolph County, North Carolina.[226] **CHARITY (HILL) POTTER** was **buried in Strieby Church Cemetery**.

iii. **CALVIN HILL** was born in April 1838 in Strieby, Union, Randolph, North Carolina.[227] He married **ELIZABETH CHANDLER** about 1856-1857, in Randolph County, North Carolina,[228] She was born between 1835 and 1841.[229] Calvin apparently died before 1910 when

---

[224] North Carolina, Death Certificates, 1909-1975 [Database on-line]. *Ancestry.com*. Charity Patter [sic-original says "Potter"], 31 Mar 1921.
[225] North Carolina, Marriage Records, 1741-2011 [Database on-line]. *Ancestry.com*. Charity Hill and Ira Potter, 10 October 1855.
[226] 1850 US Federal Census; Census Place: Southern Division, Randolph, North Carolina; NARA Roll: M432-641; Page: 103A; Image: 211. *Ancestry.com*. Ire [*sic*] Potter, age 19.
[227] 1850 US Federal Census; Census Place: Southern Division, Randolph, North Carolina; NARA Roll: M432_641; Page: 133B; Image: 273. *Ancestry.com*. Edward Hill, head; Calvin Hill, age 12.
[228] North Carolina, Deaths, 1906-1930 [Database on-line]. *Ancestry.com*. Ulysses Grant Hill; Calvin Hill, father, Elizabeth Chandler, mother.
[229] 1900 US Federal Census; Census Place: Union, Randolph, North Carolina; NARA Roll: 1213; Page: 6B; Enumeration District: 0099; FHL microfilm: 1241213. *Ancestry.com*. Calvin Hill, head; Elizabeth Hill, Jun 1841.

Elizabeth says she is a widow.[230] Elizabeth herself is not found after 1910.

iv. **BETHANA HILL** was born in 1842 in Strieby, Union, Randolph, North Carolina.[231] She died 29 Oct 1922 in Strieby, Union, Randolph, North Carolina.[232] She married (1) **BENJAMIN LUTHER** on 03 December 1867 in Asheboro, Randolph, North Carolina.[233] He was born in 1830 in Randolph County, North Carolina. She married (2) **JAMES REDWINE** about 1886 in Asheboro, Randolph, North Carolina.[234] He was born in 1834 in Davidson County, North Carolina.[235] **BETHANA "THANIE" HILL REDWINE** was **buried in Strieby**

---

[230] 1910 US Federal Census; Census Place: Union, Randolph, North Carolina; NARA Roll: T624-1128; Page: 2A; Enumeration District: 0100; FHL microfilm: 1375141. *Ancestry.com*. Elizabeth Hill, head, widowed.

[231] 1850 US Federal Census; Census Place: Southern Division, Randolph, North Carolina; NARA Roll: M432_641; Page: 133B; Image: 273. *Ancestry.com*. Edward Hill, head; Thany Hill, age 8.

[232] North Carolina, Death Certificates, 1909-1975 [Database on-line]. *Ancestry.com*. Thanie Redwine, 29 Oct 1922.

[233] North Carolina, Marriage Records, 1741-2011 [Database on-line]. *Ancestry.com*. Bethania Hill and Benjamin Luther, 3 Dec 1867.

[234] 1900 US Federal Census; Census Place: New Hope, Randolph, North Carolina; NARA Roll: 1213; Page: 2A; Enumeration District: 0090; FHL microfilm: 1241213. *Ancestry.com*. James Redwine, married 14 years.

[235] 1900 US Federal Census; Census Place: New Hope, Randolph, North Carolina; NARA Roll: 1213; Page: 2A; Enumeration District: 0090; FHL microfilm: 1241213. *Ancestry.com*. James Redwine, born Jun 1834.

Church Cemetery.

v. **EMSLEY HILL** was born in September 1841 in Hill Town, Union, Randolph, North Carolina.[236] He died on 08 July 1913 in Cincinnati, Hamilton, Ohio.[237] He married **SARAH WALDEN CALLICUTT**, daughter of **WILLIAM D WALDEN** Jr and **RUTH GARNER** on 23 February 1871 in Asheboro, Randolph, North Carolina.[238] She was born in September 1843 in Randolph, North Carolina. She reportedly died in West Virginia in 1920, where her daughter was living,[239] but no document for has been identified to date by this researcher.

vi. **MARY JANE HILL** was born in 1845 in Hill Town, Union, Randolph, North

---

[236] 1850 US Federal Census; Census Place: Southern Division, Randolph, North Carolina; NARA Roll: M432_641; Page: 133B; Image: 273. *Ancestry.com*. Edward Hill, head; Emsley Hill, age 9.

[237] Ohio, Deaths, 1908-1932, 1938-2007 [Database on-line]. *Ancestry.com*. Emsley Hill, 8 Jul 1913.

[238] North Carolina, Marriage Records, 1741-2011 [Database on-line]. *Ancestry.com*. Emsley Hill and Sarah Callicutt, 23 Feb 1871.

[239] 1920 US Federal Census; Census Place: Blue Sulphur, Greenbrier, West Virginia; NARA Roll: T625-1953; Page: 4A; Enumeration District: 45; Image: 625. *Ancestry.com*. Robert Wilson, head; Sarah Hill, mother-in-law. *See also*: West Virginia, Deaths Index, 1853-1973 [Database on-line]. *Ancestry.com*. Lucretia Clark, born: Cincinnati, Ohio; died: 22 Oct 1967, Hinton, West Virginia; father: Emsley Hill; mother: Sarah Hill.

Carolina.[240]She died 28 Nov 1923 in Strieby, Union, Randolph, North Carolina.[241]She married (1) **THOMAS POTTER**, son of **JESSE POTTER** and **LUVENIA "LOVEY"HENLEY** on 03 December 1867 in Asheboro, Randolph, North Carolina.[242] He was born about 1823-1827 in Randolph County, North Carolina.[243]He may have died between 1884 and 1888 when Mary Jane married (2) **JOSEPH EADIE**, possibly the son of **JAMES EADIE** and **PATSY LOMACK**, on 26 Dec 1888 in Randolph County, North Carolina.[244] He was born in 1844 in North Carolina and died between 1900 and 1910 when Mary Jane ("Jane") reported being widowed.[245] **MARY**

---

[240] 1850 US Federal Census; Census Place: Southern Division, Randolph, North Carolina; NARA Roll: M432_641; Page: 133B; Image: 273. *Ancestry.com*. Edward Hill, head; Mary Hill, age 5.

[241] North Carolina, Death Certificates, 1909-1975 [Database on-line]. *Ancestry.com*. Jane Eady, 28 Nov 1923.

[242] North Carolina, Marriage Records, 1741-2011 [Database on-line]. *Ancestry.com*. Mary Jane Hill and Thomas J Potter, 28 Dec 1867.

[243] 1850 US Federal Census; Census Place: Southern Division, Randolph, North Carolina; NARA Roll: M432_641; Page: 3A; Image: 211. *Ancestry.com*. Thomas Potter, age 23 [sic].

[244] North Carolina, Marriage Records, 1741-2011 [Database on-line]. *Ancestry.com*. Mary J. Potter and Joseph Eadie, 26 Dec 1888.

[245] 1910 US Federal Census; Census Place: Union, Randolph, North Carolina; NARA Roll: T624_1128; Page: 2A; Enumeration District: 0100; FHL microfilm: 1375141. *Ancestry.com*. Jane Edie, age 60, widowed.

JANE "JANE" HILL EADY was **buried in Strieby Church Cemetery**.

vii. **SARAH "SALLY" HILL** was born in 1846 in Hill Town, Union, Randolph, North Carolina. She married (1) **EDMUND/EDWARD CRANFORD** on 15 August 1870 in Asheboro, Randolph, North Carolina. [246]When and where Sally died is not known but was most likely sometime before 1896 when **EDMUND** married **MINNIE HEARN.**[247]

viii. **STEVEN MARMADUKE HILL** was born in 1850 in Strieby, Union, Randolph, North Carolina. [248] He died 17 November 1922 and is **buried in Strieby Church Cemetery.**

---

[246] North Carolina, Marriage Collection, 1741-2004 [Database on-line]. *Ancestry.com*. Sarah Hill and Edward Cranford, 15 Aug 1870.
[247] North Carolina, Marriage Collection, 1741-2004 [Database on-line]. *Ancestry.com*. Edmon [*sic*] Cranford and Minnie Hearn, 29 Jan 1896.
[248] 1870 US Federal Census; Census Place: Union, Randolph, North Carolina; NARA Roll: M593_1156; Page: 506B; Image: 466; Family History Library Film: 552655. *Ancestry.com*. Ned Hill, head; Marmaduke Hill, age 20.

Figure 64: Julius "Uncle Juke" Hill.
Photo courtesy of London Hill.

b. **JULIUS HILL** was born in Mar 1854 in Hill Town, Union, Randolph, North Carolina.[249] He died after 1930 and before 1940 in Strieby, Union, Randolph, North Carolina, when he is last found in the census.[250] He married (1) **MARTHA ANN DUNSON**, daughter of **CALVIN DUNSON** and **NANCY PHILLIPS LASSITER** about 24 Jan 1883 in Wadesboro, Anson County, North Carolina.[251] She was born in 1863 in Lassiter Mill, New Hope, Randolph, North Carolina.[252] She died between 1885-1886 in Lassiter Mill, New Hope, Randolph, North Carolina.[253] He married **(2) ELIZABETH J. DAVIS**, daughter of **ANTHONY DAVIS** and **ANN CRUMP/HEARN** on 09 Sep 1886 in

---

[249] 1880 US Federal Census; Census Place: Union, Randolph, North Carolina; NARA Roll: 978; FHL #1254978; Page: 195B; Enumeration District: 224; Image: 0682. *Ancestry.com*. Priscella Hill, head; Julias Hill, age 26. *See also*, 1900 US Federal Census; Census Place: Union, Randolph, North Carolina; NARA Roll: 1213; Page: 6B; Enumeration District: 0099; FHL #1241213. *Ancestry.com*. Julius Hill, head, born Mar 1855.
[250] 1930 US Federal Census; Census Place: Union, Randolph, North Carolina; NARA Roll: 1715; Page: 6A; Enumeration District: 0034; Image: 427.0; FHL #2341449.*Ancestry.com*. Julius Hill, head.
[251] North Carolina, Marriage Records, 1741-2011 [Database on-line]. *Ancestry.com*. Julius Hill and Martha Dunson, 24 Jan 1883.
[252] 1870 US Federal Census; Census Place: New Hope, Randolph, North Carolina; Roll: M593_1156; Page: 400B; Image: 250; FHL #552655. *Ancestry.com*. Calvin Dunson, head; M Ann Dunson, age 7.
[253] Vidales. (2011). Randolph County Estates, Dunbar-Duty: William Dunston. *The Genealogical Journal by the Randolph County Genealogical Society*, Volume XXXV, No. 2: 45-46.

Randolph County, North Carolina.[254] She was born in Jan 1860 in Randolph County, North Carolina. She died on 06 Mar 1940 in Strieby, Union, Randolph, North Carolina and is buried in **Strieby Congregational Church Cemetery**.[255]Around 1920, he "married" (3) ANNIE in Randolph County, North Carolina. There is no official record of this marriage. She was born in 1901 in North Carolina.[256]

i. **JOHN HILL** was born in 1856 in Strieby, Union, Randolph, North Carolina.[257]

ii. **JESSE HILL** was born in 1858 in Strieby, Union, Randolph, North Carolina.[258]

iii. **ALEXANDER HILL** was born in Apr 1859 in Strieby, Union, Randolph, North

---

[254] North Carolina, Marriage Index, 1741-2004 [Database on-line].*Ancestry.com*. Elizabeth J Davis and Julius Hill, 09 Sep 1886.

[255] North Carolina, Death Certificates, 1909-1976 [Database on-line].*Ancestry.com*. Elizabeth J Hill, 06 Mar 1940, widowed, husband's name: Julius Hill.

[256] 1930 US Federal Census; Census Place: Union, Randolph, North Carolina; NARA Roll: 1715; Page: 6A; Enumeration District: 0034; Image: 427.0; FHL #2341449. *Ancestry.com*. Julius Hill, head; Annie Hill, wife, age 29, first marriage age 19.

[257] 1870 US Federal Census; Census Place: Union, Randolph, North Carolina; NARA Roll: M593-1156; Page: 506B; Image: 466; FHL #552655. *Ancestry.com*. Ned Hill, head; John Hill, age 15.

[258] 1860 US Federal Census; Census Place: Western Division, Randolph, North Carolina; NARA Roll: M653-910; Page: 212; Image: 428; FHL #803910. *Ancestry.com*. Ed Hill, head; Jesse Hill, age 2.

Carolina.[259]

Generation 2

2. **NATHAN[2] (CASE) HILL** (EDWARD "NED"[1]) was born in 1830 in Randolph County, North Carolina. He married **SARAH POLK,** the (probable) daughter of **MARY POLK** and granddaughter of **CHARITY (POLK) LASSITER,** on 15 Sep 1853 in Randolph County, North Carolina. She was born in 1833, most likely Davidson County or Randolph County, North Carolina.[*See Entry Above*]
    a. NATHAN HILL and SARAH POLK had the following children:
        i. **CLARKSON[3] HILL** was born about March 1853 in Union, Randolph County, North Carolina.[260] He married **(1) ELLEN DAVIS** on 30 December 1882 in Randolph County, North Carolina.[261] She was born in Randolph County, North Carolina. She may have died before 1894 in Randolph County, North Carolina, when he married **(2) JANNETTA**

---

[259] 1870 US Federal Census; Census Place: Union, Randolph, North Carolina; NARA Roll: M593-1156; Page: 506B; Image: 466; FHL #552655. *Ancestry.com*. Ned Hill, head; Alexander Hill, age 10.
[260] 1860 US Federal Census; Census Place: Western Division, Randolph, North Carolina; Roll: M653-910; Page: 213; Image: 431; FHL #803910. *Ancestry.com*. Nathan Hill, head; Clarkson Hill, age 7.
[261] North Carolina, Marriage Records, 1741-2011 [Database on-line].*Ancestry.com*. Clarkson Hill and Ellen Davis, 30 Dec 1882.

"NETTIE" KEARNS, daughter of **CLARKSON KEARNS and RANAH** on 16 November 1894 in Randolph County, North Carolina.[262] She was born in Feb 1865 in New Hope, Randolph, North Carolina.[263] She died on 08 Apr 1912 in Randolph County, North Carolina.[264]

ii. **WILIE HILL** was born in 1858 in Union, Randolph County, North Carolina.[265] He died on 12 February 1926 in Albemarle, Stanly, North Carolina.[266]He married **IDA STEELE** (called **IDA LITTLE** in the marriage records), daughter of **LOUISA STEELE**, on 2 Oct 1882.[267] She was born Dec 1862 and died 27 Mar 1925 in Albemarle, Stanly, North Carolina.[268]

---

[262] North Carolina, Marriage Records, 1741-2011 [Database on-line]. *Ancestry.com*. Clarkson Hill and Nettie Kearns, 16 November 1894.

[263] 1870 US Federal Census; Census Place: Concord, Randolph, North Carolina; NARA Roll: M593_1156; Page: 337A; Image: 123; Family History Library Film: 552655. *Ancestry.com*. Clark Kearns, head, Jannetta Kearns, age 6.

[264] North Carolina, Death Indexes, 1908-2004 [Database on-line]. *Ancestry.com*. Nettie Hill, 08 Apr 1912.

[265] 1860; Census Place: Western Division, Randolph, North Carolina; NARA Roll: M653_910; Page: 213; Image: 431; Family History Library Film: 803910. *Ancestry.com*. Nathan Hill, head; Wilie Hill, age 2.

[266] North Carolina, Death Certificates, 1909-1976 [Database on-line]. *Ancestry.com*. Wiley Hill, 12 Feb 1926.

[267] North Carolina, Marriage Records, 1741-2011 [Database on-line]. *Ancestry.com*. Wiley Hill and Ida Little, 4 Oct 1882.

[268] U.S. Find A Grave Index, 1600s-Current [Database on-line]. *Ancestry.com*. Edna [sic] Hill, 27 Mar 1925.

iii. **MARY HILL** was born in 1855 in Union, Randolph County, North Carolina.[269]

iv. **LEANDER HILL** was born in 1860 in Union, Randolph County, North Carolina.[270]

---

[269] 1860 US Federal Census; Census Place: Western Division, Randolph, North Carolina; NARA Roll: M653_910; Page: 213; Image: 431; FHL #803910. *Ancestry.com*. Nathan Hill, head; Mary Hill, age 5.

[270] 1860 US Federal Census; Census Place: Western Division, Randolph, North Carolina; NARA Roll: M653_910; Page: 213; Image: 431; Family History Library Film: 803910. *Ancestry.com*. Nathan Hill, head; No Name Hill, age 1/12. *See also*, 1870 US Federal Census; Census Place: New Hope, Randolph, North Carolina; NARA Roll: M593_1156; Page: 409A; Image: 267; FHL #552655. *Ancestry.com*. Nathan Hill, head; Lander Hill, age 8; *and* 1880; Census Place: Union, Randolph, North Carolina; NARA Roll: 978; Family History Film: 1254978; Page: 195B; Enumeration District: 224; Image: 0682. *Ancestry.com*. Nathan Hill, head; Leander Hill, age 21.

Figure 65: Left, Milton Hill. Right, Sarah Ann (Leak) Hill. Photos courtesy of Sharon Shanks.

v. **MILTON L HILL**[271] was born in December 1865 in Union, Randolph County, North Carolina.[272] He died in Jefferson County, Arkansas.[273] He

---

[271] Photos in this family line were shared from: Sharon Shanks Family Tree. *Ancestry.com*. Retrieved from: http://person.ancestry.com/tree/27703817/person/12260183901/facts

[272] 1870 US Federal Census; Census Place: New Hope, Randolph, North Carolina; NARA Roll: M593-1156; Page: 409A; Image: 267; Family History Library Film: 552655. *Ancestry.com*. Nathan Hill, head; Milton Hill, age 6.

[273] U.S., Social Security Applications and Claims Index, 1936-2007 [Database on-line]. *Ancestry.com*. Milton Hill. Although family members have posted a death date in 27 Nov 1949, Chicago, Cook, Illinois (See: *Sharon Shanks Family Tree* on *Ancestry.com*). There does not seem to be a discernible entry for Milton Hill in the SSDI, despite this application and claim. The family has

married **SARAH ANN LEAK** on 26 May 1888 in Jefferson County, Arkansas.[274] She was born about 1867 in Richmond County, North Carolina.[275] She died 20 Jun 1936 in Jefferson County, Arkansas.[276]

vi. **DEMPSEY HILL** was born in 1866 in Union, Randolph County, North Carolina.[277]

vii. **CORAH HILL** was born in 1867 in Union, Randolph County, North Carolina.[278]She married (1) **CALVIN "CAP" WALL** on 1 Jan 1885, in Richmond County, North Carolina.[279] She married (2) **CALVIN RUSH** on 2 Aug 1905, in Stanly County, North

---

not cited a specific source for his date of death (i.e. bible records, death certificate).

[274] Arkansas, County Marriages Index, 1837-1957 [database on-line].*Ancestry.com*. Milton Hill and Sarah Ann Leak, 26 May 1888.

[275] 1870 US Federal Census; Census Place: Steeles, Richmond, North Carolina; NARA Roll: M593-1156; Page: 595A; Image: 644; Family History Library Film: 552655. *Ancestry.com*. Sarah A. Leak, age, 3.

[276] Arkansas Death Index, 1914-1950 [Database on-line].*Ancestry.com*. Sarah Tea [sic] Hill, 20 Jun 1936.

[277] 1870 US Federal Census; Census Place: New Hope, Randolph, North Carolina; NARA Roll: M593-1156; Page: 409A; Image: 267; FHL #552655. *Ancestry.com*. Nathan Hill, head; Dempsey Hill, age 4.

[278] 1870 US Federal Census; Census Place: New Hope, Randolph, North Carolina; NARA Roll: M593-1156; Page: 409A; Image: 267; FHL #552655. *Ancestry.com*. Nathan Hill, head; Cora Hill, age 2.

[279] North Carolina, Marriage Records, 1741-2011 [Database on-line]. *Ancestry.com*. Calvin Wall and Cora Hill, 1 Jan 1885.

Carolina.[280]Calvin Rush died 20 April 1929, in Stanly County, North Carolina.[281]

viii. **CHRISTINA HILL** was born in July 1870 in New Hope, Randolph, North Carolina.[282]

---

[280] North Carolina, Marriage Records, 1741-2011 [Database on-line]. *Ancestry.com*. Cal Rush and Cora Wall, 2 Aug 1905. Some have suggested that Cora married Fletcher Rush. However, the Cora who married Fletcher Rush was Cora Julia Tomlinson. Both Cora and Fletcher were born about 1880. It was Cora Julia Tomlinson Rush who died 10 Jun 1955, not Cora Hill Rush. *See*: North Carolina, Death Certificates, 1909-1976 [Database on-line]. *Ancestry.com*. Cora Julia Rush 10 Jun 1955; Father: Frank Tomlinson. Fletcher Rush was the son of Calvin Rush by his first wife, Dora (Turner) Rush, *See*: North Carolina, Marriage Records, 1741-2011 [Database on-line]. *Ancestry.com*. Fletcher Rush and Cora Tomlinson; Father: Calvin Rush; Mother: Dora Rush.

[281] North Carolina, Death Certificates, 1909-1976 [Database on-line].*Ancestry.com*. Calvin Rush, 20 Apr 1929.

[282] 1870 US Federal Census; Census Place: New Hope, Randolph, North Carolina; NARA Roll: M593-1156; Page: 409A; Image: 267; FHL #552655. *Ancestry.com*. Nathan Hill, head; Christina Hill, age 2/12 year.

Figure 66: Left-Thomas Julius Hill. Right-Julia Ella (Woods) Hill. Photos courtesy Sharon Shanks.

ix. **THOMAS JULIUS HILL**[283] was born on 15 March 1871 in Union, Randolph County, North Carolina. He died on 01 July 1975 in St Louis, Missouri.[284] He married **JULIA ELLA WOODS** on 10 February 1894 in Jefferson County, Arkansas.[285] She was born in August 1878

[283] Photos in this family line were shared from: Sharon Shanks Family Tree. *Ancestry.com*. Retrieved from: http://person.ancestry.com/tree/27703817/person/12260183907/facts

[284] U.S. Social Security Death Index, 1935-Current [Database on-line]. *Ancestry.com*. Thomas Hill, Jul 1975.

[285] Certification of Marriage License, Book I: 172, Jefferson County, Arkansas (2 May 1938). Thos Hill and Ella Woods, 7 Feb 1894. Digital copy. Retrieved from Sharon Shanks Family Tree at Ancestry.com. (http://trees.ancestry.com/tree/27703817/family).

in Arkansas.[286] She died in September 1961 in Kirkwood, St Louis, Missouri.[287]

x. **EARNEST HILL** was born in 1875 in Union, Randolph County, North Carolina.[288]

3. **CHARITY[2] HILL** (EDWARD "NED"[1]) was born in May 1834 in Hill Town, Union, Randolph, North Carolina. She died 31 Mar 1921 in Strieby, Union, Randolph, North Carolina. She married **IRA POTTER**, son of **JESSE POTTER** and **LUVENIA "LOVEY" HENLEY** on 10 Oct1855 in Asheboro, Randolph, North Carolina. He was born in 1827 in Randolph County, North Carolina. She's **buried in Strieby Church Cemetery**. *[See Entry Above]*

    a. IRA POTTER and CHARITY HILL had the following children:[289]

        i. **JAMES[3] POTTER** was born in 1850 in

---

[286] 1880 US Federal Census; Census Place: Moro, Bradley, Arkansas; NARA Roll: 39; FHL #1254039; Page: 26B; Enumeration District: 016; Image: 0382. *Ancestry.com*. Norred Wood, head; Julier Wood, age 2.

[287] U.S., Find A Grave Index, 1700s-Current [Database on-line]. *Ancestry.com*. Mrs. Ella Hill, 1878-1961.

[288] 1880 US Federal Census; Census Place: Union, Randolph, North Carolina; NARA Roll: 978; FHL #1254978; Page: 196C; Enumeration District: 224; Image: 0683. *Ancestry.com*. Nathan Hill, head; Earnest Hill, age 5.

[289] In the 1900 census, Charity said she had borne 11 children, 8 of whom were still alive. *See*: 1900 US Federal Census; Census Place: Union, Randolph, North Carolina; NARA Roll: 1213; Page: 6B; Enumeration District: 0099; FHL #1241213. *Ancestry.com*. Charity Hill, head (widowed).

Randolph County, North Carolina.[290]

ii. **ELIAS POTTER** was born in 1852 in Randolph County, North Carolina.[291]

iii. **MARY ELIZA POTTER** was born in 1856 in Randolph County, North Carolina.[292] She had an undetermined relationship with a **LEWIS WOOTEN.**[293]

iv. **CHRISTOPHER POTTER** was born in 1859 in Randolph County, North Carolina.[294] He married **IDA HEPLER**, on 4 Oct 1900, in Forsyth County, North Carolina. She was the daughter of **ALEX HEPLER** and his wife **CORA BUTNER**.[295]

v. **ISABEL POTTER** was born in 1863 in Cedar Grove, Randolph, North

---

[290] 1860 US Federal Census; Census Place: Western Division, Randolph, North Carolina; NARA Roll: M653_910; Page: 221; Image: 447; FHL #803910. *Ancestry.com.* Ira Potter, head; James Potter, age 10.

[291] 1860 US Federal Census; Census Place: Western Division, Randolph, North Carolina; NARA Roll: M653_910; Page: 221; Image: 447; FHL #803910. *Ancestry.com.* Ira Potter, head; Elias Potter, age 8.

[292] 1860 US Federal Census; Census Place: Western Division, Randolph, North Carolina; NARA Roll: M653_910; Page: 221; Image: 447; FHL #803910. *Ancestry.com.* Ira Potter, head; Eliza Potter, age 4.

[293] North Carolina, Death Certificates, 1909-1975 [Database on-line]. *Ancestry.com.* Charlie M. Potter, 30 Jul 1968, Mother: Mary Potter; Father: Lowes [*sic*] Wooten.

[294] 1860 US Federal Census; Census Place: Western Division, Randolph, North Carolina; NARA Roll: M653-910; Page: 221; Image: 447; FHL #803910. *Ancestry.com.* Ira Potter, head; Chris Potter, age 1.

[295] North Carolina, Marriage Records, 1741-2011 [Database on-line]. *Ancestry.com.* Christopher Potter and Ida Hepler, 4 Oct 1900.

Carolina.[296]

vi. **JESSE POTTER** was born in 1866 in Cedar Grove, Randolph, North Carolina.[297]

vii. **EMSLEY P. POTTER** was born in 1868 in Cedar Grove, Randolph, North Carolina.[298] He married **ANNIE M. BARRETT**, daughter of **SHEPARD BARRETT and MARY BARRETT**, on 16 September 1896, in Carthage, Moore, North Carolina.[299]

viii. **CALVIN DUCKERY POTTER** was born in 1870 in Cedar Grove, Randolph, North Carolina.[300] He died 27 Jan 1940 in Strieby, Union, Randolph, North Carolina.[301] He married **ELIZABETH**

---

[296] 1870 US Federal Census; Census Place: Asheboro, Randolph, North Carolina; NARA Roll: M593-1156; Page: 284B; Image: 18; FHL #552655. *Ancestry.com*. Ira Potter, head; Isabel Potter, age 7.

[297] 1870 US Federal Census; Census Place: Asheboro, Randolph, North Carolina; NARA Roll: M593-1156; Page: 284B; Image: 18; FHL #552655. *Ancestry.com*. Ira Potter, head; Jesse Potter, age 4.

[298] 1870 US Federal Census; Census Place: Asheboro, Randolph, North Carolina; NARA Roll: M593-1156; Page: 284B; Image: 18; FHL #552655. *Ancestry.com*. Ira Potter, head; Emsley Potter, age 2.

[299] North Carolina, Marriage Records, 1741-2011 [Database on-line]. *Ancestry.com*. E. P. Potter and Annie M. Barrett, 10 Sep 1892 (original is difficult to read but appears to say 16 Sep 1892).

[300] 1870 US Federal Census; Census Place: Asheboro, Randolph, North Carolina; NARA Roll: M593-1156; Page: 284B; Image: 18; FHL #552655. *Ancestry.com*. Ira Potter, head; Potter, male, age 10 months.

[301] North Carolina, Death Certificates, 1909-1975 [Database on-line]. *Ancestry.com*. Calvin D. Potter, 27 Jan 1940.

EADY, daughter of **JOSEPH EADIE and JANE KEARNS** on 12 October 1895 in Asheboro, Randolph, North Carolina. She was born in 1874 in Cedar Grove, Randolph, North Carolina. [302] He is **buried in Strieby Church Cemetery**.

ix. **ADA POTTER** was born in 1872 in Cedar Grove, Randolph, North Carolina.[303]

x. **ALEXANDER POTTER** was born in 1877 in Cedar Grove, Randolph, North Carolina.[304]

4. **CALVIN[2] HILL** (EDWARD "NED"*[1]*) was born in April 1838 in Hill Town, Union, Randolph, North Carolina. He married **ELIZABETH CHANDLER** about 1860 in Randolph County, North Carolina. She was born in June 1841. Calvin apparently died before 1910 when Elizabeth says she is a widow. Elizabeth herself is not found after 1910. [*See Entry Above*]

    a. CALVIN HILL and ELIZABETH CHANDLER had the following children:

---

[302] 1880 US Federal Census; Census Place: Cedar Grove, Randolph, North Carolina; NARA Roll: 978; FHL #1254978; Page: 158B; Enumeration District: 220; Image: 0611. *Ancestry.com*. Joseph Eady head; Elizabeth Eady, age 6.

[303] 1880 US Federal Census; Census Place: Cedar Grove, Randolph, North Carolina; NARA Roll: 978; Family History Film: 1254978; Page: 153C; Enumeration District: 220; Image: 0598. *Ancestry.com*. Ira Potter, head; Adah Potter, age 8.

[304] 1880 US Federal Census; Census Place: Cedar Grove, Randolph, North Carolina; NARA Roll: 978; FHL #1254978; Page: 153C; Enumeration District: 220; Image: 0598. *Ancestry.com*. Ira Potter, head; Alexander Potter, age 3.

i. **MARY LOUISA[3] HILL** was born in 1860 in Hill Town, Union, Randolph, North Carolina.[305]

ii. **JOHN PRESLEY HILL** was born in 1861 in Hill Town, Union, Randolph, North Carolina.[306]

Figure 67: Izetta Rewine. Photo courtesy Ruth M. Howard.

iii. **DAVID SHERMAN HILL** was born in

---

[305] 1870 US Federal Census; Census Place: Union, Randolph, North Carolina; NARA Roll: M593-1156; Page: 506B; Image: 466; FHL #552655. *Ancestry.com*. Calvin Hill, head; Mary Hill, age 10. *See also*: 1880 US Federal Census; Census Place: Union, Randolph, North Carolina; NARA Roll: 978; FHL #1254978; Page: 195B; Enumeration District: 224; Image: 0682. *Ancestry.com*. Calvin Hill, head; Louisa Hill, age 20.

[306] 1870 US Federal Census; Census Place: Union, Randolph, North Carolina; NARA Roll: M593-1156; Page: 506B; Image: 466; FHL #552655. *Ancestry.com*. Calvin Hill, head; John Hill, age 8. 1880 US Federal Census; Census Place: Union, Randolph, North Carolina; NARA Roll: 978; FHL #1254978; Page: 195B; Enumeration District: 224; Image: 0682. *Ancestry.com*. Calvin Hill, head; Priscilla [*sic*] Hill, age 19.

1863 in Hill Town, Union, Randolph, North Carolina.[307] He married **IZETTA REDWINE**, daughter of **JAMES REDWINE** and **DIAN JANE STAFFORD**, on 17 April 1898 in Asheboro, Randolph, North Carolina.[308] She was born in November 1877 in Davidson County, North Carolina.[309] David died between 1900 and 1903 when **IZETTA** married his brother, **ULYSSES GRANT HILL** *(see below)*. She was last identified definitively, in 1940, in New York, New York, living with her sons, **SHERMAN, EDWARD AND JAMES HILL**.[310]

iv. **SARAH J. HILL** was born in 1866 in Hill

---

[307] 1870 US Federal Census; Census Place: Union, Randolph, North Carolina; NARA Roll: M593-1156; Page: 506B; Image: 466; FHL #552655. *Ancestry.com*. Calvin Hill, head; David Hill, age 6. *See also*: 1880 US Federal Census; Census Place: Union, Randolph, North Carolina; NARA Roll: 978; FHL #1254978; Page: 195B; Enumeration District: 224; Image: 0682. *Ancestry.com*. Calvin Hill, head; Sherman Hill, age 16.

[308] North Carolina, Marriage Records, 1741-2011 [Database on-line]. *Ancestry.com*. Sherman Hill and Zettie Redwine, 17 Apr 1898.

[309] 1880 US Federal Census; Census Place: Alleghany, Davidson, North Carolina; NARA Roll: 961; Family History Film: 1254961; Page: 307C; Enumeration District: 049; Image: 0630. *Ancestry.com*. James Redwine, head; Icetta Redwine, age 1.

[310] 1940 US Federal Census; Census Place: New York, New York, New York; NARA Roll: T627-2668; Page: 14A; Enumeration District: 31-1837. *Ancestry.com*. Therman [*sic* – original reads Sherman] Hill, head; Izetta Hill, mother.

Town, Union, Randolph, North Carolina.[311]

Figure 68: Barzilla Hill & Elizabeth (Hearn) Hill. Photo courtesy of Richard Jackson.

v. **BARZILLA "ZILL" HARRISON HILL** was born on 18 July 1866 in Hill Town, Union, Randolph, North Carolina.[312]He

311 1880 US Federal Census; Census Place: Union, Randolph, North Carolina; NARA Roll: 978; FHL #1254978; Page: 195B; Enumeration District: 224; Image: 0682. *Ancestry.com*. Calvin Hill, head; Sarah J. Hill, age 14.

312 1870 US Federal Census; Census Place: Union, Randolph, North Carolina; NARA Roll: M593-1156; Page: 506B; Image: 466; FHL #552655. *Ancestry.com*. Calvin Hill, head; David Hill, age 6. *Seealso*: 1880 US Federal

died 2 Dec 1933.[313] He married **ELIZABETH HEARN**, the daughter of **ROLLIN HEARN** and **REBECCA DAVIS** on 01 Jan 1885 in Asheboro, Randolph, North Carolina.[314] She was born in Feb 1865 in Randolph County, North Carolina and died 4 May 1936.[315] They are **both buried in Strieby Cemetery**.

vi. **ULYSSES GRANT HILL** was born on 30 Jun 1873 in Hill Town, Union, Randolph, North Carolina.[316] He died on 20 Aug 1925 in Strieby, Randolph, North Carolina.[317] He married **IZETTA REDWINE**, then widow of his brother, **DAVID SHERMAN HILL** (*See above*), on 08 Nov 1903 in Randolph County,

---

Census; Census Place: Union, Randolph, North Carolina; NARA Roll: 978; FHL #1254978; Page: 195B; Enumeration District: 224; Image: 0682. *Ancestry.com*. Calvin Hill, head; Sherman Hill, age 16.

[313] North Carolina, Death Certificates, 1909-1975 [Database on-line]. *Ancestry.com*. Zell Hell [*sic*], 2 Dec 1933.

[314] North Carolina, Marriage Collection, 1741-2004 [Database on-line]. *Ancestry.com*. Brazilla Hill and Lizzie Hearn, 1 Jan 1885.

[315] U.S., Find A Grave Index, 1700s-Current [Database on-line]. *Ancestry.com*. Lizzie Bell Hill, 4 May 1936.

[316] 1880 US Federal Census; Census Place: Union, Randolph, North Carolina; NARA Roll: 978; Family History Film: 1254978; Page: 195B; Enumeration District: 224; Image: 0682. *Ancestry.com*. Calvin Hill, head; Ulijaus [*sic* – original reads "Ulissus"], age 7.

[317] North Carolina, Deaths, 1906-1930 [Database on-line]. *Ancestry.com*. Ulysses Grant Hill, 20 Aug 1925.

North Carolina. Izetta was last identified in New York City living with her sons Sherman, Edward, and James Hill.[318] **ULYSSES HILL** was **buried in Strieby Church Cemetery.**

5. **BETHANA[2] HILL** (EDWARD "NED"*1*) was born in 1842 in Hill Town, Union, Randolph, North Carolina. She died 29 Oct 1922 in Strieby, Union, Randolph, North Carolina. She married (1) **BENJAMIN LUTHER** on 03 December 1867 in Asheboro, Randolph, North Carolina. He was born in 1830 in Randolph County, North Carolina. She married (2) **JAMES REDWINE** in 1886 in Asheboro, Randolph, North Carolina. He was born in Randolph County, North Carolina. She is **buried in Strieby Church Cemetery**. [*See Entry Above*]
    a. BETHANA HILL had the following child with a **JOHN BELLI (BELLU?)**[319]
        i. **ELIZABETH[3] HILL** was born in 1861 in Hill Town, Union, Randolph, North Carolina. She died 2 Oct 1933 in High Point, Guilford, North Carolina.[320] She married **WILLIAM FISHER** around

---

[318] 1940 US Federal Census; Census Place: New York, New York, New York; NARA Roll: T627-2668; Page: 14A; Enumeration District: 31-1837. *Ancestry.com*. Therman [*sic* – original reads Sherman] Hill, head; Izetta Hill, mother.

[319] North Carolina, Death Certificates, 1909-1975 [Database on-line]. *Ancestry.com*. Elizabeth Fisher, 2 Oct 1933.

[320] North Carolina, Death Certificates, 1909-1975 [Database on-line]. *Ancestry.com*. Elizabeth Fisher, 2 Oct 1933.

1885 in Randolph County.[321] He was born in 1840 in North Carolina. He died sometime between 1920 and 1930 when Elizabeth is listed as a widow.[322]

b. BETHANA HILL had the following child with **JESSE POTTER (Jr.)** son of **JESSE POTTER** and **LOVENIA "LOVEY" HENLEY**:[323]

   i. **THOMAS WINBORN HILL** was born in 1863 in Hill Town, Union, Randolph, North Carolina. He died 9 Sep 1929 in Strieby, Union, Randolph, North Carolina.[324] He never married. He is **buried in Strieby Church Cemetery**.

c. BETHANA HILL and **BENJAMIN LUTHER** had the following children:

   i. **EMMA LUTHER** was born in May 1870 in Hill Town, Union, Randolph, North Carolina. She died 16 Apr 1952 in High Point, Guilford, North Carolina.[325] She

---

[321] 1900 US Federal Census; Census Place: Union, Randolph, North Carolina; NARA Roll: 1213; Page: 6B; Enumeration District: 0099; FHL #1241213. *Ancestry.com*. William Fisher, head; Elizabeth Fisher, wife; years married: 15.

[322] 1930 US Federal Census; Census Place: High Point, Guilford, North Carolina; NARA Roll: 1696; Page: 35A; Enumeration District: 0060; Image: 71.0; FHL #2341430. *Ancestry.com*. Elizabeth Fisher, widowed.

[323] North Carolina, Death Certificates, 1909-1975 [Database on-line]. *Ancestry.com*. Winburn [Abstract reads, "Minburn"] Hill, 2 Sep 1929.

[324] North Carolina, Death Certificates, 1909-1975 [Database on-line]. *Ancestry.com*. Winburn [Abstract reads, "Minburn"] Hill, 2 Sep 1929.

[325] North Carolina, Death Certificates, 1909-1975 [Database on-line]. *Ancestry.com*. Emma Luther, 16 Apr 1952.

never married despite reporting being a widow on the 1940 census.[326]She was **buried in Strieby Church Cemetery.**

ii. **CORRINA LUTHER** was born in 1875 in Hill Town, Union, Randolph, North Carolina.[327]

iii. **FANNY LUTHER** was born in 1876 in Hill Town, Union, Randolph, North Carolina.[328]

iv. **HATTIE B. LUTHER** was born in 1879 in Hill Town, Union, Randolph, North Carolina.[329]

6. **EMSLEY[2] HILL** (EDWARD "NED"[1]) was born in September 1844 in Hill Town, Union, Randolph, North Carolina. He died on 08 July 1913 in Hamilton, Ohio. He married **SARAH WALDEN CALLICUTT**, daughter of **WILLIAM D WALDEN Jr** and **RUTH GARNER** on 23 February 1871 in Asheboro, Randolph,

---

326 1940 US Federal Census; Census Place: High Point, Guilford, North Carolina; NARA Roll: T627-2921; Page: 5B; Enumeration District: 41-92. *Ancestry.com*. Emma Luther, widowed.

327 1880 US Federal Census; Census Place: Union, Randolph, North Carolina; NARA Roll: 978; Family History Film: 1254978; Page: 195B; Enumeration District: 224; Image: 0682. *Ancestry.com*. Corrina [Abstract reads, "Cossener"] Luther, age, 5.

328 1880 US Federal Census; Census Place: Union, Randolph, North Carolina; NARA Roll: 978; FHL #1254978; Page: 195B; Enumeration District: 224; Image: 0682. *Ancestry.com*. Benjamin Luther, head; Fannie Luther, age 4.

329 1880 US Federal Census; Census Place: Union, Randolph, North Carolina; NARA Roll: 978; Family History Film: 1254978; Page: 195B; Enumeration District: 224; Image: 0682. *Ancestry.com*. Benjamin Luther, head; Hattie B. Luther, age 1.

North Carolina. She was born in September 1843 in Randolph County, North Carolina. She reportedly died in West Virginia in 1920, where her daughter was living. [*See Entry Above*]

a. EMSLEY HILL and SARAH WALDEN CALLICUTT had the following children:

   i. **MARY A.**[3] **HILL** was born in 1870 in Hill Town, Union, Randolph, North Carolina.[330]

Figure 69: William Julius Hill. Photo courtesy of the late Evie Ruth (Hill) Grady.

   ii. **WILLIAM JULIUS HIL**L was born on 17 December 1871 in Hill Town, Union,

[330] 1880 US Federal Census; Census Place: Union, Randolph, North Carolina; NARA Roll: 978; Family History Film: 1254978; Page: 196C; Enumeration District: 224; Image: 0683. *Ancestry.com*. Emsley Hill, head; Mary A. Hill, age 10.

Randolph, North Carolina.[331] He died on 28 May 1925 in Mt. Washington, Hamilton, Ohio. He married **FLORA ELIZABETH SETTLES** on 02 November 1898 in Ohio.[332] She was born on 22 Sep 1877 in Brah Hill, Clermont, Ohio.[333] She died on 01 Mar 1949 in Cleveland, Cuyahoga, Ohio, USA.[334]

iii. **CLAUDIA G. HILL** was born in 1873 in Hill Town, Union, Randolph, North Carolina.[335]

iv. **ISLAY THOMAS HILL** was born on 06 October 1876 in Hill Town, Union, Randolph, North Carolina.[336]He married **MARY CARROLL** about 1896.[337] He died 4 Aug 1970, in Dayton, Montgomery,

---

[331] 1880 US Federal Census; Census Place: Union, Randolph, North Carolina; NARA Roll: 978; FHL #1254978; Page: 196C; Enumeration District: 224; Image: 0683. *Ancestry.com*. Emsley Hill, head; William J. Hill, age 8.

[332] Garner, 2009, p. 52.

[333] Ohio, Births and Christenings Index, 1800-1962 [Database online]. *Ancestry.com*. Flora E. Settle, 22 Sep 1877.

[334] Ohio, Deaths, 1908-1932, 1938-2007 [Database on-line]. *Ancestry.com*. Flora Hill, 1 Mar 1949.

[335] 1880 US Federal Census; Census Place: Union, Randolph, North Carolina; NARA Roll: 978; FHL #1254978; Page: 196C; Enumeration District: 224; Image: 0683. *Ancestry.com*. Emsley Hill, head; Claudis [sic] G. Hill, age 7.

[336] 1880 US Federal Census; Census Place: Union, Randolph, North Carolina; NARA Roll: 978; FHL #1254978; Page: 196C; Enumeration District: 224; Image: 0683. *Ancestry.com*. Emsley Hill, head; Islay T. Hill, age 3.

[337] 1900 US Federal Census; Census Place: Dayton Ward 7, Montgomery, Ohio; NARA Roll: 1307; Page: 10A; Enumeration District: 0063; FHL #1241307. *Ancestry.com*. Iolay [*sic* – original reads Islay] Hill, head.

Ohio.[338]

v. **ROBERT HILL** was born about 1877 in Hill Town, Randolph, North Carolina.[339]

vi. **ESTELLA J HILL** was born in Oct 1879 in Hill Town, Union, Randolph, North Carolina.[340] She reportedly died 15 Oct 1934.[341]

vii. **LUCRETIA HILL** was born on 22 Feb 1881 in Hill Town, Union, Randolph, North Carolina.[342] She died 22 Oct 1967 in Hinton, Summers, West Virginia.[343] She married first, **ROBERT L WILSON**.[344] He died between 1930 and 1940 when

---

338 Ohio, Deaths, 1908-1932, 1938-2007 [Database on-line]. *Ancestry.com.* Thomas I. Hill, 4 Aug 1970.

339 Brigitte Hopkins Hill Family Tree. *Ancestry Family Trees.* (*Ancestry.com*). Robert Hill, born 1877.

340 1880 US Federal Census; Census Place: Union, Randolph, North Carolina; NARA Roll: 978; FHL #1254978; Page: 196C; Enumeration District: 224; Image: 0683. *Ancestry.com.* Emsley Hill, head; Estella J. Hill, age 1.

341 Breazeale Family Tree. *Ancestry Family Trees.* (*Ancestry.com*). Estella J. Hill, 15 Oct 1934.

342 1900 US Federal Census; Census Place: Milford, Clermont, Ohio; Roll: 1247; Page: 7B; Enumeration District: 0036; FHL #1241247. *Ancestry.com.* Emsly Hill, head; Nucretia *[sic]* Hill age 16.

343 West Virginia, Deaths Index, 1853-1973 [Database on-line]. *Ancestry.com.* Lucretia Clark, 22 Oct 1967.

344 1920 US Federal Census; Census Place: Blue Sulphur, Greenbrier, West Virginia; NARA Roll: T625-1953; Page: 4A; Enumeration District: 45; Image: 625. *Ancestry.com.* Robert L. Wilson, head; Lucretia Wilson, wife.

Lucretia was listed as a widow.[345]She married a man whose last name was "**CLARK,**" sometime before she died, but no other information is known about him at this time.[346]

viii. **ELINORA HILL** was born on 30 Jan 1882 in Hill Town, Randolph, North Carolina.[347] She died 6 Oct 1894, in Milford, Clermont, Ohio.[348]

---

[345] 1940 US Federal Census; Census Place: Alderson, Greenbrier, West Virginia; NARA Roll: T627_4404; Page: 10A; Enumeration District: 13-3. *Ancestry.com.* Lucretia B. Wilson, widowed.

[346] West Virginia, Deaths Index, 1853-1973 [Database on-line]. *Ancestry.com.* Lucretia Clark, 22 Oct 1967.

[347] Brigitte Hopkins Hill Family Tree. *Ancestry Family Trees. Ancestry.com.* Elinora Hill, 30 Jan 1882.

[348] Brigitte Hopkins Hill Family Tree. *Ancestry Family Trees.* (*Ancestry.com*). Elinora Hill, 6 Oct 1894.

Figure 70: C.J. Nettie Hill Tombstone, Strieby Church Cemetery. Photo by Margo Lee Williams, 2014

ix. **C. J. NETTIE HILL** was born 15 Jul 1885 and died 20 Dec 1888.[349] She is **buried in Strieby Church Cemetery.**

x. **ANNA HILL** was born Jul 1899, in Milford, Clermont, Ohio.[350]

7. **MARY JANE[2] HILL** (EDWARD "NED"[1]) was born in 1845 in Hill Town, Union, Randolph, North Carolina. She died 28 Nov 1923 in Strieby, Union, Randolph,

---

349 C. J. Nettie Hill Tombstone, Strieby Church Cemetery. C, J, Nettie daughter of Emsley S. Hill. Born 15 July 1885; Died 20 Dec 1888.

350 1900 US Federal Census; Census Place: Milford, Clermont, Ohio; Roll: 1247; Page: 7B; Enumeration District: 0036; FHL #1241247. *Ancestry.com.* Emsly Hill, head; Anna Hill, age 1.

North Carolina. She married (1) **THOMAS POTTER**, son of **JESSE POTTER** and **LOVENIA "LOVEY" HENLEY** on 03 December 1867 in Asheboro, Randolph, North Carolina. He was born in 1823 in Randolph County, North Carolina. She married (2) **JOSEPH EADIE** on 26 December 1888 in Randolph County, North Carolina. He was born in 1844 in Randolph County, North Carolina. She is **buried in Strieby Church Cemetery**. [*See Entry Above*]

a. **THOMAS POTTER** and **MARY JANE HILL** had the following children:
    i. **LAURA A.[3] POTTER** was born in 1869 in Concord, Randolph, North Carolina.[351]
    ii. **DELPHINA ARDILIA POTTER** was born in 1876 in Union, Randolph, North Carolina.[352]
    iii. **LOVIE POTTER** was born in April 1884 in Strieby, Union, Randolph, North Carolina.[353] She died 6 February 1953, in

---

[351] 1870 US Federal Census; Census Place: Concord, Randolph, North Carolina; NARA Roll: M593-1156; Page: 346A; Image: 141; FHL #552655. *Ancestry.com*. Thomas Potter, head; Laura A. Potter, age 1.

[352] 1880 US Federal Census; Census Place: Union, Randolph, North Carolina; NARA Roll: 978; Family History Film: 1254978; Page: 195B; Enumeration District: 224; Image: 0682. *Ancestry.com*. Thomas Potter, head; Ardilia Potter, age 4.

[353] 1900 US Federal Census; Census Place: Cedar Grove, Randolph, North Carolina; NARA Roll: 1212; Page: 2A; Enumeration District: 0082; FHL microfilm: 1241212. *Ancestry.com*. Joseph Eadie, head; Lovey Potter, step daughter, age 16.

Pisgah, Randolph, North Carolina.[354] She married **JAMES A DAVIS**, son of **ANTHONY DAVIS** and **ANN HEARN/CRUMP** on 26 February 1911 in Asheboro, Randolph, North Carolina.[355] He was born in 1866 in Randolph County, North Carolina and died 21 April 1941 in Strieby.[356] They are **both buried in Strieby Church Cemetery**.

b. **JOSEPH EADIE** and **MARY JANE HILL** had the following children:

  i. **ALLER**[3] **EADIE** was born in Oct 1891 in Cedar Grove, Randolph, North Carolina. She died 16 Jul 1921 in Strieby, Union Township, Randolph County, North Carolina and is **buried in Strieby Church Cemetery**.[357] She married **GREELY DAVIS,** son of **WILLIAM DAVIS** and **JANE PARKER** on 22 Dec 1904, in Randolph County, North Carolina.[358] He died on24 Jul 1918 in Strieby, Union,

---

[354] North Carolina, Death Certificates, 1909-1975 [Database on-line]. Ancestry.com. Lovie Davis, 6 Feb 1953.

[355] North Carolina, Marriage Records, 1741-2011 [Database on-line]. *Ancestry.com.* Lovie Potter and James Davis, 26 Feb 1911.

[356] North Carolina, Death Certificates, 1909-1975 [Database on-line]. *Ancestry.com.* James A. Davis, 21 Apr 1941.

[357] North Carolina, Death Certificates, 1909-1975 [Database on-line]. *Ancestry.com.* Allan [sic-original says "Allar"] Davis, 16 Jul 1921.

[358] North Carolina, Marriage Collection, 1741-2004 [Database on-line]. *Ancestry.com.* Allen [*sic*] J Eady and Greely Davis, 22 Dec 1904.

Randolph, North Carolina, and is **buried in Strieby Church Cemetery.**[359]

8. **SARAH "SALLY"**[2] **HILL** (EDWARD "NED"[1]) was born in 1846 in Strieby, Union, Randolph, North Carolina. She married **EDMUND CRANFORD** on 15 Aug 1870 in Asheboro, Randolph, North Carolina. [*See Entry Above*]
    a. **SARAH "SALLY" HILL** had the following child, possibly with **EDMUND CRANFORD:**
        i. **MARY ANN**[3] **HILL** was born in Mar 1868 in the Hill Town area of Randolph County, North Carolina.[360] She died on 29 Jun 1931 in Strieby, Union, Randolph, North Carolina.[361] She married **CHARLES SMITHERMAN**, reported son of **NOAH SMITHERMAN** and **LUCINDA SMITHERMAN** on 29 Jul 1883 in Randolph County, North Carolina.[362] He was born in 1855 in Randolph County, North Carolina. He died before 1900 in Strieby, Union,

---

359 North Carolina, Death Certificates, 1909-1976 [Database on-line]. *Ancestry.com.* Graly [sic] Davis, 24 Jul 1918.

360 1880 US Federal Census; Census Place: Union, Randolph, North Carolina; Roll: 978; Family History Film: 1254978; Page: 195B; Enumeration District: 224; Image: 0682. *Ancestry.com.* Edmond Crawford [*sic* – image reads, "Cranford"], head; Mary Ann Cranford, daughter, age 2.

361 North Carolina, Death Certificates, 1909-1975 [Database on-line]. *Ancestry.com.* Mary Smitherman, 29 Jun 1931.

362 North Carolina, Marriage Collection, 1741-2004 [Database on-line]. *Ancestry.com.* Mary Hill and Charley Smitherman, 29 Jul 1883.

Randolph, North Carolina, when Mary says she is widowed.[363] They are **both buried in Strieby Church Cemetery**.

b. **EDMUND CRANFORD** and **SARAH "SALLY" HILL** had the following children:

   i. **HAL B. CRANFORD** was born about 1877, in Union Township, Randolph County, North Carolina.[364] He died sometime after 1958, most likely in Greensboro, Guilford, North Carolina.[365] He married **BELLE CASSADY** on 12 Jul 1902, in Randolph County.[366] She was born about 1882, the daughter of **STEADMAN** and **LOVIE CASSADY**, from Pleasant Grove, Randolph County, North Carolina.[367] She died in 1960 and is buried in Mount Calvary Cemetery, in

---

[363] 1900 US Federal Census; Census Place: Union, Randolph, North Carolina; Roll: 1213; Page: 6B; Enumeration District: 0099; FHL microfilm: 1241213. *Ancestry.com*. Mary Smitherman, head, "widowed."

[364] 1880 US Federal Census; Census Place: Union, Randolph, North Carolina; Roll: 978; Family History Film: 1254978; Page: 195B; Enumeration District: 224; Image: 0682. *Ancestry.com*. Edmond Crawford [*sic* – image reads, "Cranford"], head; Hally Cranford, son, age 3.

[365] U.S. City Directories, 1821-1989 [Database on-line]. *Ancestry.com*. Hal B. Cranford, 1958.

[366] North Carolina, Marriage Records, 1741-2011 [Database on-line]. *Ancestry.com*. Hal Cranford and Belle Cassady, 12 Jul 1902.

[367] 1900 US Federal Census; Census Place: Pleasant Grove, Randolph, North Carolina; Roll: 1213; Page: 12B; Enumeration District: 0092; FHL microfilm: 1241213. *Ancestry.com*. Steadman Cassady, head; Belle Cassady, age 18.

Asheboro, Randolph, North Carolina.[368]

9. **JULIUS[2] HILL** (EDWARD "NED"[1]) was born in Mar 1854 in Strieby, Union, Randolph, NORTH CAROLINA. He died after 1930 in Strieby, Union, Randolph, North Carolina. He married (1) **MARTHA ANN DUNSON**, daughter of **CALVIN DUNSON** and **NANCY PHILLIPS LASSITER** 24 January 1883 in Wadesboro, Anson, North Carolina. She was born bet 1862-1864 in Lassiter Mill, New Hope, Randolph, North Carolina. She died between 1884-1886 in Lassiter Mill, New Hope, Randolph, North Carolina. He married (2) **ELIZABETH J. DAVIS**, daughter of **ANTHONY DAVIS** and **ANN HEARN/CRUMP** on 09 Sep 1886 in Randolph County, North Carolina. She was born in Jan 1860 in Randolph County, North Carolina. She died on 06 Mar 1940 in Strieby, Union, Randolph, North Carolina and is **buried in Strieby Church Cemetery**. He married (3) **ANNIE** about 1920 in Asheboro, Randolph, North Carolina. She was born in 1901 in North Carolina. [*See Entry Above*]
    a. **JULIUS HILL** and **MARTHA ANN DUNSON** had the following child:
        i. **MAMIE[3] HILL** was born on 04 Mar 1884 in Lassiter Mill, New Hope, Randolph, North Carolina. She died on 23 Nov 1970 in Concord, Cabarrus, North Carolina.[369]

---

[368] U.S., Find A Grave Index, 1700s-Current [Database on-line]. *Ancestry.com*. Belle F. Cranford, 1960.

[369] North Carolina, Death Certificates, 1909-1975 [Database on-line]. *Ancestry.com*. Mamie Poole, 23 Nov 1970. [Note: The death certificate lists Lizzie Hill, Julius' second wife as her mother, but Martha, her birth mother, died when she was an infant. She was raised by Lizzie Hill.]

She married **ARCH POOLE**, son of **BENJAMIN POOL** and **CHARLOTTE** on 27 Dec 1904 in Asheboro, Randolph, North Carolina.[370] He was born about 1879 in Montgomery County, North Carolina. He apparently died sometime before Mamie, since she is listed as a widow on her death certificate.[371]

b. **JULIUS HILL** and **ELIZABETH J. DAVIS** had the following children:

   i. **ETHEL "EFFIE" HILL** was born in May 1891 in Strieby, Union, Randolph, North Carolina.[372] She died 10 Nov 1964, in Winston-Salem, Forsyth, North Carolina.[373] She married (1) **GEORGE WOODING**, son of **ALEX** and **RHODIE WOODING**, 7 Jan 1918, in Danville, Virginia.[374] Effie and George divorced in Feb 1928, also in Virginia.[375] She married

---

[370] North Carolina, Marriage Records, 1741-2011 [Database on-line]. *Ancestry.com*. Mamie Hill and Arch Pool, 27 Dec 1904.
[371] North Carolina, Death Certificates, 1909-1975 [Database on-line]. *Ancestry.com*. Mamie Poole, 23 Nov 1970.
[372] 1900 US Federal Census; Census Place: Union, Randolph, North Carolina; NARA Roll: 1213; Page: 6B; Enumeration District: 0099; FHL microfilm: 1241213. *Ancestry.com*. Julius Hill, head; Effie Hill, age 9.
[373] North Carolina, Death Certificates, 1909-1975 [Database on-line]. *Ancestry.com*. Ethel Woodie Mills, 10 Nov 1964.
[374] Virginia, Select Marriages, 1785-1940 [Database on-line]. *Ancestry.com*. Effie Hill and George Wooding, 7 Jan 1918.
[375] Virginia, Divorce Records, 1918-2014 [Database on-line]. *Ancestry.com*. Ethel Hill Wooding v George Wooding, Feb 1928.

(2) **WILLIE MILLS**, 24 Dec 1936.[376] He died before 1964, according to Ethel's death certificate which listed her as a widow.[377] She was **buried in Strieby Church Cemetery**.

ii. **CARL EDWARD HILL** was born in Jul 1893 in Strieby, Union, Randolph, North Carolina.[378] He died 13 Apr 1942.[379] He married **BERTHA McRAE,** daughter of **JOHN McRAE and LUCY ELLA DENSON**, on 4 May 1916, in Montgomery County, North Carolina.[380]Bertha died 6 May 1936, in Troy, Montgomery County, North Carolina.[381]

iii. **THEODOCIA DELIA HILL** was born in Nov 1894 in Strieby, Union, Randolph,

---

[376] North Carolina, Marriage Records, 1741-2011 [Database on-line]. *Ancestry.com*. Ethel Woods and Willie Mills, 24 Dec 1936.

[377] North Carolina, Death Certificates, 1909-1975 [Database on-line]. *Ancestry.com*. Ethel Woodie Mills, 10 Nov 1964.

[378] 1900 US Federal Census; Census Place: Union, Randolph, North Carolina; NARA Roll: 1213; Page: 6B; Enumeration District: 0099; FHL microfilm: 1241213. *Ancestry.com*. Julius Hill, head; Carl Hill, age 6.

[379] U.S. Social Security Applications and Claims Index, 1936-2007 [Database on-line]. *Ancestry.com*. Charles Edward Hill, 13 Apr 1942.

[380] North Carolina, Marriage Records, 1741-2011 [Database on-line]. *Ancesry.com*. Carl Hill and Burt [sic] McRae, 4 May 1916. [Note: Carl's father, Julius, is called "Jake," in the abstract, but it probably reads "Juke," which was his nickname.]

[381] North Carolina, Death Certificates, 1909-1975 [Database on-line]. *Ancestry.com*. Bertha Hill, 6 May 1936.

North Carolina.[382] She died 14 Feb 1997, in Winston-Salem, Forsyth, North Carolina.[383] Her married name was **WHITE**, but no marriage record to date has been identified. He may be the **THOMAS WHITE** born in North Carolina but living with in Norfolk, Virginia with a wife "Della," in 1930.[384]According to her death index entry she was a widow. She is **buried in Strieby Church Cemetery**.

iv. **ROWENA HILL** was born in Jun 1899 in Strieby, Union, Randolph, North Carolina.[385]

v. **ERNEST MARVIN HILL** was born in 1901 in Strieby, Union, Randolph, North Carolina.[386] He died 23 Mar 1970 in

---

[382] 1900 US Federal Census; Census Place: Union, Randolph, North Carolina; NARA Roll: 1213; Page: 6B; Enumeration District: 0099; FHL microfilm: 1241213. *Ancestry.com*. Julius Hill, head; Theodocia Hill, age 5.

[383] North Carolina, Death Indexes, 1908-2004 [Database on-line]. *Ancestry.com*. Delia Theodocia White, 14 Feb 1997.

[384] 1930 US Federal Census; Census Place: Norfolk, Norfolk (Independent City), Virginia; Roll: 2470; Page: 6A; Enumeration District: 0025; Image: 349.0; FHL microfilm: 2342204. *Ancestry.com*. Thomas White, head; Della White, wife.

[385] 1900 US Federal Census; Census Place: Union, Randolph, North Carolina; NARA Roll: 1213; Page: 6B; Enumeration District: 0099; FHL microfilm: 1241213. *Ancestry.com*. Julius Hill, head; Roena Hill, age 11/12 months.

[386] 1910 US Federal Census; Census Place: Union, Randolph, North Carolina; NARA Roll: T624-1128; Page: 2B; Enumeration District: 0100; FHL microfilm: 1375141. *Ancestry.com*. Julius Hill, head; Marvin Hill, age 7.

Winston-Salem, Forsyth, North Carolina.[387] He was buried at **Strieby Church Cemetery**. He was married to **ANNIE MAE CAVE**, daughter of **WASHNGTON CAVE** and **SYRELLA/SELDREA GRATT**, on 27 May 1923 in Forsyth County, North Carolina.[388] She died on 22 Jun 1973, in Winston-Salem, Forsyth, North Carolina.[389]

vi. **JAMES MARTIN HILL** was born in 1908 in Strieby, Union Township, Randolph, North Carolina.[390] He died 14 Jun 1965, in Durham, Durham, North Carolina and was **buried in Strieby Church Cemetery**.[391] He married **VALLIE MAE GILES**, daughter of **HENRY W. GILES** and **LEORA GRIFFIN**, on 31 Aug 1936, in Wake County, North Carolina.[392]

---

[387] North Carolina, Death Certificates, 1909-1975 [Database on-line]. *Ancestry.com*. Ernest Hill, Sr., 23 Mar 1970.

[388] North Carolina, Marriage Records, 1741-2011 [Database on-line]. *Ancestry.com*. Ernest Hill and Annie Mae Cave, 23 May 1923.

[389] North Carolina, Death Certificates, 1909-1975[Database on-line]. *Ancestry.com*. Annie Mae Hill, 22 Jun 1973.

[390] 1910 US Federal Census; Census Place: Union, Randolph, North Carolina; Roll: T624-1128; Page: 2B; Enumeration District: 0100; FHL microfilm: 1375141. *Ancestry.com*. Julius Hill, head; James Hill, age 2.

[391] North Carolina, Death Certificates, 1909-1975 [Database on-line]. *Ancestry.com*. James Martin Hill, 14 June 1965.

[392] North Carolina, Marriage Records, 1741-2011 [Database on-line]. *Ancestry.com*. James Hill and Vallie Mal [*sic* – original reads, "Mae"] Giles.

According to his death certificate, they divorced.

Generation 3

10. **CLARKSON**[3] **HILL** (NATHAN[2], EDWARD "NED"[1]) was born in Mar 1851 in Union, Randolph County, North Carolina. He married (1) **ELLEN DAVIS** on Dec 1882 in Randolph County, North Carolina. She was born in Randolph County, North Carolina. She apparently died before 1894 in Randolph County, North Carolina, when he married (2) **JANNETTA"NETTIE" KEARNS,** 16 Nov 1894. She was born in Feb 1865 in New Hope, Randolph, North Carolina the daughter of **CLARKSON KEARNS** and his wife **RANAH/RANEY**. Nettie died on 08 Apr 1912 in Randolph County, North Carolina. [*See Entry Above*]
    a. **CLARKSON HILL and ELLEN DAVIS** had the following children:
        i. **CRISSIE**[4] **HILL** was born in Feb 1887 in New Hope, Randolph, North Carolina.[393]
        ii. **MINNIE HILL** was born in Feb 1888 in New Hope, Randolph, North Carolina.[394]
    b. **CLARKSON HILL and JANNETTA "NETTIE" KEARNS** had the following children:

---

[393] 1900 US Federal Census; Census Place: New Hope, Randolph, North Carolina; NARA Roll: 1213; Page: 1B; Enumeration District: 0090; FHL microfilm: 1241213. *Ancestry.com*. Clark J Hill, head; Crissie Hill, age 13.
[394] 1900 US Federal Census; Census Place: New Hope, Randolph, North Carolina; NARA Roll: 1213; Page: 1B; Enumeration District: 0090; FHL microfilm: 1241213. *Ancestry.com*. Clark J Hill, head; Minnie Hill, age 12.

i. **PEARL[4] HILL** was born in 1907 in Asheboro, Randolph County, North Carolina.[395]

ii. **BESSA HILL** was born in 1910 in Asheboro, Randolph County, North Carolina.[396]

11. **WILEY HILL** was born in 1858 in Union, Randolph County, North Carolina. He died on 12 February 1926 in Albemarle, Stanly, North Carolina. He married **IDA STEELE** (called **IDA LITTLE** in the marriage records), daughter of **LOUISA STEELE**, on 2 Oct 1882. She was born Dec 1862 and died 27 Mar 1925 in Albemarle, Stanly, North Carolina. [*See Entry Above*]

a. **WILEY HILL and IDA STEELE** had the following children:

i. **CHARLES[4] S HILL** was born 17 Mar 1884 in Steele, Richmond County, North Carolina.[397] He died 7 Dec 1960, in Albemarle County, North Carolina.[398] He

---

395 1910 US Federal Census; Census Place: Asheboro, Randolph, North Carolina; NARA Roll: T624_1128; Page: 19A; Enumeration District: 0076; FHL microfilm: 1375141. *Ancestry.com.* Clark Hill, head; Pearl Hill, age 3.

396 1910 US Federal; Census Place: Asheboro, Randolph, North Carolina; NARA Roll: T624_1128; Page: 19A; Enumeration District: 0076; FHL microfilm: 1375141. *Ancestry.com*. Clark Hill, head; Bessa Hill, age 0.

397 1900 US Federal Census; Census Place: Steele, Richmond, North Carolina; NARA Roll: 1213; Page: 12A; Enumeration District: 0091; FHL microfilm: 1241213. *Ancestry.com*. Wyley Hill, head; Charles Hill, age 16.

398 North Carolina, Death Certificates, 1909-1975 [Database on-line]. *Ancestry.com*. Charlie S. Hill, 7 Dec 1960.

married **OLIA HARWOOD**, daughter of **FREEMAN HARWOOD and AGNES TURNER**, on 15 Jun 1909.[399]She was born 16 Apr 1890 and died 27 Nov 1958 in Albemarle, Stanly, North Carolina.[400]

ii. **LYSIE HILL** was born Sep 1885, in Steele, Richmond, North Carolina.[401]

iii. **MILTON C HILL** was born 22 Mar 1887, in Steele, Richmond, North Carolina.[402] He died 30 Apr 1945 in Badin, Stanly, North Carolina.[403] He married **ANNA BELL MARSHALL**, daughter of **ANSON WATKINS** and **LOUISE HARRIS**, in Norwood, Stanly, North Carolina.[404] She was born 26 Mar 1901 and died 15 May 1960 in Badin, Stanly, North Carolina.[405]

---

[399] North Carolina, Marriage Records, 1741-2011 [Database on-line]. *Ancestry.com*. Charles Hill and Olia Harwood, 15 Jun 1909.

[400] North Carolina, Death Certificates, 1909-1976 [Database on-line]. *Ancestry.com*. Ola Howard Hill, 27 Nov 1958.

[401] 1900 US Federal Census; Census Place: Steele, Richmond, North Carolina; NARA Roll: 1213; Page: 12A; Enumeration District: 0091; FHL microfilm: 1241213. *Ancestry.com*. Wyley Hill, head; Lysie Hill, age 16.

[402] 1900 US Federal Census; Census Place: Steele, Richmond, North Carolina; NARA Roll: 1213; Page: 12A; Enumeration District: 0091; FHL microfilm: 1241213. *Ancestry.com*. Wyley Hill, head; Milton Hill, age 13.

[403] North Carolina, Death Certificates, 1909-1975 [Database on-line]. *Ancestry.com*. Milton Hill, 30 Apr 1945.

[404] North Carolina, Marriage Records, 1741-2011 [Database on-line]. *Ancestry.com*. Milton Hill and Anna Bell Marshall, 7 Mar 1915.

[405] North Carolina, Death Certificates, 1909-1976 [Database on-line]. *Ancestry.com*. Anna Belle Hill, 15 May 1960.

iv. **SARAH ANN HILL** was born Apr 1891.[406]

v. **BRAXTON "BROCK/BRACK" HILL** was born May 1894. He apparently was the twin to **ANA ELIZA HILL**[407] He died 17 Sep 1974, in Troy, Montgomery, North Carolina.[408] He married **LUCY BARRINGER**, the daughter of **HUBBARD BARRINGER** and **DRUCILLA GAY**, on 1 Oct 1924 in Stanly County, North Carolina,[409] but they later divorced according to Braxton's death certificate.

vi. **ANA ELIZA HILL** was born May 1894 and was apparently the twin of Braxton "Brock" Hill.[410] She died 12 Nov 1973 in Chapel Hill, Orange, North Carolina.[411]

---

[406] 1900 US Federal Census; Census Place: Steele, Richmond, North Carolina; NARA Roll: 1213; Page: 12A; Enumeration District: 0091; FHL microfilm: 1241213. *Ancestry.com*. Wyley Hill, head; Sarah Ann Hill, age 9.
[407] 1900 US Federal Census; Census Place: Steele, Richmond, North Carolina; NARA Roll: 1213; Page: 12A; Enumeration District: 0091; FHL microfilm: 1241213. *Ancestry.com*. Wyley Hill, head; Braxton Hill, age 6.
[408] North Carolina, Death Certificates, 1909-1975 [Database on-line]. *Ancestry.com*. Brack Hill, 17 Sep 1974.
[409] North Carolina, Marriage Records, 1741-2011 [Database on-line]. Ancestry.com. Brack Hill and Lucy Barringer, 1 Oct 1924.
[410] 1900 US Federal Census; Census Place: Steele, Richmond, North Carolina; NARA Roll: 1213; Page: 12A; Enumeration District: 0091; FHL microfilm: 1241213. *Ancestry.com*. Wyley Hill, head; Eliza Hill, age 6.
[411] North Carolina, Death Certificates, 1909-1975 [Database on-line]. *Ancestry.com*. Annie Liza Ingram,

She married **MOSES INGRAM**, son of **BILLY INGRAM** and **MARTHA ELLERBE**, on 4 Aug 1920 in Stanly County, North Carolina.[412] He died 28 May 1967 in Chapel Hill, Orange, North Carolina.[413]

vii. **DOVIE HILL** was born 31 Aug 1903 in Stanly County, North Carolina.[414] She died 13 Nov 1972 in Lexington, Davidson, North Carolina.[415] She married **CRAVEN BROOKS**, son of **THOMAS HENRY BROOKS** and **MARY CARSTEN**, 15 Aug 1919, in Stanly County, North Carolina.[416] Craven Brooks died, 10 Nov 1939 in Badin, Stanly, North Carolina.[417]

12. **MILTON L[3] HILL** (NATHAN[2], EDWARD "NED"[1]) was born in Dec 1865 in Union, Randolph County, North Carolina. He died in 1949 in Jefferson County, Arkansas. He married **SARAH LEAK** on 26 May 1888

---

[412] North Carolina, Marriage Records, 1741-2011 [Database on-line]. *Ancestry.com*. Ana Eliza Hill and Moses Ingram, 4 Aug 1920.

[413] North Carolina, Death Certificates, 1909-1975 [Database on-line]. *Ancestry.com* Moses Ingram.

[414] 1910 US Federal Census; Census Place: Center, Stanly, North Carolina; NARA Roll: T624_1125; Page: 16A; Enumeration District: 0121; FHL microfilm: 1375138. *Ancestry.com*. Wiley H Hill, head; Dorie Hill, age 10.

[415] North Carolina, Death Certificates, 1909-1975 [Database on-line]. *Ancestry.com*. Dovie Hill Brooks, 13 Nov 1972.

[416] North Carolina, Marriage Records, 1741-2011 [Database on-line]. *Ancestry.com*. Dovie Hill and Craven Brooks, 15 Aug 1919.

[417] North Carolina, Death Certificates, 1909-1975 [Database on-line]. *Ancestry.com*. Craven Brooks, 10 Nov 1939.

in Jefferson County, Arkansas. She was born in 1869 in North Carolina. [*See Entry Above*]

a. MILTON L HILL and SARAH LEAK had the following children:

    i. **SADIE[4] HILL** was born in Apr 1890 in Pine Bluff, Jefferson, Arkansas, USA.[418] Her date of death is unknown to this author at this time. She married **JOSHUA MOON**, son of **MADISON MOON** and **LUVENIA WILLIAMS**, 24 May 1908 in Jefferson County, Arkansas.[419] He died in Feb 1950, in Jefferson County, Arkansas.[420]

    ii. **ANDREW MILTON HILL** was born on 07 Sep 1891 in Pine Bluff, Jefferson, Arkansas, USA.[421] He died in Feb 1977, in Arkansas.[422] He married **ALBERTA RAMSEY** on 24 Oct 1915 in Jefferson County, Arkansas.[423] She was born about

---

[418] 1900 US Federal Census; Census Place: Pine Bluff, Jefferson, Arkansas; NARA Roll: 63; Page: 1A; Enumeration District: 0108; FHL microfilm: 1240063. *Ancestry.com*. Milton Hill, head; Satie Hill, age 10.

[419] Arkansas, County Marriages Index, 1837-1957 [Database on-line]. *Ancestry.com*. Joshua Moon and Sadie Hill, 24 May 1908.

[420] Arkansas Death Index, 1914-1950 [Database on-line]. Joshua Moon,

[421] 1900; Census Place: Pine Bluff, Jefferson, Arkansas; NARA Roll: 63; Page: 1A; Enumeration District: 0108; FHL microfilm: 1240063. *Ancestry.com*. Milton Hill, head, Andrew Hill, age 8.

[422] U.S. Social Security Death Index, 1935-Current [Database on-line]. *Ancestry.com*. Andrew Hill, Feb 1977.

[423] Arkansas, County Marriages Index, 1837-1957 [Database on-line]. *Ancestry.com*. Andrew Hill and Alberta Ramsey, 24 Oct 1915.

1897 in Arkansas.[424] Her date of death is not known by this writer at this time. He married **GRACE WOODS**, on 23 Feb 1919 in Jefferson County, Arkansas.[425]

iii. **JAMES R HILL** was born in Sep 1893 in Jefferson County, Arkansas.[426] He married **REBECCA LAMPKINS** on 6 Aug 1922 in Jefferson County, Arkansas.[427]

iv. **WILLIE ERNEST HILL** was born in Jun 1895 in Pine Bluff, Jefferson, Arkansas.[428] He died in Feb 1990 in Pine Bluff, Jefferson, Arkansas.[429] He married **REOLA CHAVIS**, 31 Dec 1922, in Jefferson County, Arkansas.[430]

v. **COLLIER L HILL** was born in Aug 1897 in Pine Bluff, Jefferson, Arkansas.

---

[424] 1900 US Federal Census; Census Place: Pine Bluff, Jefferson, Arkansas; NARA Roll: 63; Page: 1A; Enumeration District: 0108; FHL microfilm: 1240063. *Ancestry.com*. Milton Hill, head; Colure [*sic*] Hill, age 2.

[425] Arkansas, County Marriages Index, 1837-1957 [Database on-line]. *Ancestry.com*. Collier Hill and Gracie Wards [sic], 23 Feb 1919.

[426] 1900 US Federal Census; Census Place: Pine Bluff, Jefferson, Arkansas; NARA Roll: 63; Page: 1A; Enumeration District: 0108; FHL microfilm: 1240063. *Ancestry.com*. Milton Hill, head; James Hill, age 6.

[427] Arkansas, County Marriages Index, 1837-1957 [Database on-line]. *Ancestry.com*. James Hill and Rebecca Lampkins, 6 Aug 1922.

[428] 1900 US Federal Census; Census Place: Pine Bluff, Jefferson, Arkansas; NARA Roll: 63; Page: 1A; Enumeration District: 0108; FHL microfilm: 1240063. *Ancestry.com*. Milton Hill, head; Willie Hill, age 4.

[429] U.S. Social Security Applications and Claims Index, 1936-2007 [Database on-line]. *Ancestry.com*. Willie Earnest Hill, Feb 1990.

[430] Arkansas, County Marriages Index, 1837-1957 [Database on-line]. *Ancestry.com*. Willie Hill and Reola Shafees, 31 Dec 1922.

vi. **LOUIS A HILL** was born in Dec 1898 in Pine Bluff, Jefferson, Arkansas.[431] He married **FANNIE RAMSEY**, daughter of **LULA RAMSEY** on 28 Nov 1925, Jefferson County, Arkansas.[432]

Figure 71: Charles & Martha (Hill) Warren. Photo courtesy of Sharon Shanks.

vii. **MARTHA A HILL** was born in 1901 in Pine Bluff, Jefferson, Arkansas.[433] She died 27 Sep 1997 in Arkansas.[434] She married **CHARLES WARREN** on 19 Dec

---

[431] 1900 US Federal Census; Census Place: Pine Bluff, Jefferson, Arkansas; NARA Roll: 63; Page: 1A; Enumeration District: 0108; FHL microfilm: 1240063. *Ancestry.com*. Milton Hill, head; Luie [sic] Hill, age 2.
[432] Arkansas, County Marriages Index, 1837-1957 [Database on-line]. *Ancestry.com*. Luie Hill and Fannie Ramsey, 28 Nov 1925.
[433] 1910 US Federal Census; Census Place: Washington, Jefferson, Arkansas; NARA Roll: T624-54; Page: 7A; Enumeration District: 0124; FHL microfilm: 1374067. *Ancestry.com*. Milton Hill, head; Martha A Hill, age 9.
[434] U.S. Social Security Applications and Claims Index, 1936-2007 [Database on-line]. *Ancestry.com*. Martha Warren, Death Date: 27 Sep 1997.

1920, in Jefferson County, Arkansas.[435]

Figure 72: DeWtt Hill.
Photo courtesy Sharon Shanks

viii. DEWITT HILL was born in 1903 in Pine Bluff, Jefferson, Arkansas.[436] He died in Jan 1975, in Pine Bluff, Jefferson, Arkansas.[437] He married SUSIE GRAHAM, 29 May 1926, in Jefferson County, Arkansas.[438]

---

[435] Arkansas, County Marriages Index, 1837-1957 [Database on-line]. *Ancestry.com*. Martha Hill and Charley Warren, 19 Dec 1920.
[436] 1910 US Federal Census; Census Place: Washington, Jefferson, Arkansas; NARA Roll: T624-54; Page: 7A; Enumeration District: 0124; FHL microfilm: 1374067. *Ancestry.com*. Milton Hill, head; Dewitt Hill, age 7.
[437] U.S. Social Security Death Index, 1935-Current [Database on-line]. *Ancestry.com*. Dewitt Hill, Jan 1975.
[438] Arkansas, County Marriages Index, 1837-1957 [Database on-line]. *Ancestry.com*. Dewitt Hill and Susie Graham, 29 May 1926.

Figure 73: Dovie D. Hill.
Photo courtesy of Sharon Shanks

ix. **DOVIE D HILL** was born in 1905 in Pine Bluff, Jefferson, Arkansas.[439] She died 20 Feb 1993 in Chicago, Cook, Illinois.[440] She married **JAMES MEYER**, on 26 Dec 1923 in Jefferson County, Arkansas.[441]

x. **HERMAN HILL** is called an "Adopted son" on the 1920 US Census.[442]

---

[439] 1910 US Federal Census; Census Place: Washington, Jefferson, Arkansas; NARA Roll: T624-54; Page: 7A; Enumeration District: 0124; FHL microfilm: 1374067. *Ancestry.com*. Milton Hill, head; Dorie [sic – original appears to read "Dovie" but the "v" is easily misread as "r"] D Hill, age 5.
[440] U.S. Social Security Death Index, 1935-2014 [database on-line].*Ancestry.com*. Dovie Meyer, 20 Feb 1993.
[441] Arkansas, County Marriages Index, 1837-1957 [Database on-line]. *Ancestry.com*. Doris [sic] Hill and James Meyer, 26 Dec 1923.
[442] 1920 US Federal Census; Census Place: Villemont, Jefferson, Arkansas; NARA Roll: T625-68; Page: 6A; Enumeration District: 145; Image: 124. *Ancestry.com*. Milton Hill, head; Herman Hill, adopted son, age 3.

13. **THOMAS JULIUS[3] HILL** (NATHAN[2], EDWARD "NED"[1]) was born on 15 Mar 1871 in Union, Randolph County, North Carolina. He died on 01 Jul 1975 in St Louis, St Louis, Missouri, USA. He married **JULIA ELLA WOODS** on 10 Feb 1894 in Jefferson County, Arkansas. She was born in Aug 1879 in Arkansas. She died in Sep 1961 in Kirkwood, St Louis, Missouri, USA. [*See Entry Above*]

    a. THOMAS JULIUS HILL and JULIA ELLA WOODS had the following children:

        i. **NATHANIEL WOODS[4]** was born in May 1891 in Old River, Jefferson, Arkansas. He is listed as a step-son on the 1900 US Census.[443]

Figure 74: Hannah Laurel Hill. Photo courtesy Sharon Shanks.

        ii. **HANNAH LAURELLA HILL** was born in Feb 1896 in Old River, Jefferson,

[443] 1900 US Federal Census; Census Place: Old River, Jefferson, Arkansas; NARA Roll: 63; Page: 8A; Enumeration District: 0090; FHL microfilm: 1240063. *Ancestry.com*. Tom Hill, head; Nathaniel Hill, step-son, age 9.

Arkansas.[444] She died on 16 Sep 1980 in St Louis, St Louis, Missouri, USA.[445] She married **JOE BURKS**. He was born on 06 May 1891 in Arkansas.[446] He died in 1955 in St Louis, St Louis, Missouri.[447]

Figure 75: Tanner Julius Hill. Photo courtesy of Sharon Shanks.

iii. **TANNER JULIUS HILL** was born on 09 Nov 1897 in Old River, Jefferson,

---

[444] 1900 US Federal Census; Census Place: Old River, Jefferson, Arkansas; NARA Roll: 63; Page: 8A; Enumeration District: 0090; FHL microfilm: 1240063. *Ancestry.com*. Tom Hill, head; Hanah Hill, age 4.
[445] U.S. Social Security Applications and Claims Index, 1936-2007 [Database on-line]. *Ancestry.com*. Hannah Burks, 16 Sept 1980.
[446] U.S. Social Security Applications and Claims Index, 1936-2007 [Database on-line]. *Ancestry.com*. Joe Burks, 6 May 1891.
[447] U.S. Find A Grave Index, 1700s-Current [Database on-line]. Ancestry.com. Joe Burks, 1891-1955.

Arkansas.[448] He died on 17 May 1971, in St Louis, St Louis, Missouri.[449] His wife's first name was reportedly **CORA**.

Figure 76: Edna Hill.
Photo courtesy of Sharon Shanks.

iv. EDNA HILL was born on 13 Nov 1900 in Jefferson, Jefferson, Arkansas, USA.[450] She died on 16 Sep 1974 in St Louis, St Louis, Missouri.[451] She married **1)**

[448] 1900 US Federal Census; Census Place: Old River, Jefferson, Arkansas; NARA Roll: 63; Page: 8A; Enumeration District: 0090; FHL microfilm: 1240063. *Ancestry.com*. Tom Hill, head; Tanner Hill, age 2.
[449] U.S. Social Security Death Index, 1935-Current [Database on-line]. *Ancestry.com*. Tanner Hill, 17 May 1971.
[450] 1910 US Federal Census; Census Place: Jefferson, Jefferson, Arkansas; NARA Roll: T624_54; Page: 8B; Enumeration District: 0099; FHL microfilm: 1374067. *Ancestry.com*. Tom Hill, head; Edna Hill, age 9.
[451] U.S. Social Security Death Index, 1935-2014 [Database on-line]. *Ancestry.com*. Edna Ford, 1901-1974.

GEORGE W WOODMORE;[452] **she married 2) JESSE FORD.**[453]

Figure 77: Virginia Hill.
Photo courtesy of Sharon Shanks.

v. **VIRGINIA HILL** was born on 18 Apr 1903 in Jefferson, Jefferson, Arkansas.[454] She died in Nov 1949 in Chicago, Cook, Illinois. She married **LEANDER HAMPTON**, son of **GEORGE HAMPTON** and **LENORA "NORA"**

---

452 Indiana, Death Certificates, 1899-2011 [Database on-line]. *Ancestry.com*. Thomas J. Woodmore; Parents: George W. Woodmore & Edna Hall [sic]. *See also*: "Edith's Obit" in Sharon Shanks Ancestry Family Tree. *Ancestry.com*. Edith Delores Woodmore.
453 Sharon Shanks Ancestry Family Tree. *Ancestry.com*. Edna Sarah Lenora Hill Ford.
454 1910 US Federal Census; Census Place: Jefferson, Jefferson, Arkansas; NARA Roll: T624-54; Page: 8B; Enumeration District: 0099; FHL microfilm: 1374067. *Ancestry.com*. Tom Hill, head; Virginia Hill, age 7.

LEAK.[455] However, this author has not located the actual marriage record to date. He died 11 Jun 1947, in Chicago, Cook, Illinois.[456]

Figure 78: Dorothy Hill.
Photo courtesy of Sharon Shanks.

vi. **DOROTHY HILL** was born on 12 Jul 1906 in Jefferson, Jefferson,

---

[455] 1930 US Federal Census; Census Place: Chicago, Cook, Illinois; NARA Roll: 482; Page: 6B; Enumeration District: 1535; Image: 906.0; FHL microfilm: 2340217. *Ancestry.com*. Lendra [sic] Hampton, head; Lenora Hampton, mother; George Hampton, father; Virgie Hampton, wife; Bertha Hampton, daughter.

[456] Illinois, Deaths and Stillbirths Index, 1916-1947 [Database on-line]. *Ancestry.com*. Leandrew Hampton, 11 Jun 1947. George Hampton, father; Lenora Leak, mother; Virgie, wife.

Arkansas.[457] She reportedly died in 9 Apr 1959 in Chicago, Cook, Illinois.[458] She married **BOOKER T. WILLIAMS**, son of **JOHN** and **GEORGIA WILLIAMS**, 18 Nov 1922, in Chicago, Cook, Illinois.[459] He died 7 Oct 1987, in Chicago, Cook, Illinois.[460] They divorced. Her second husband's last name was reportedly **JOHNSON**.[461]

vii. **THOMAS JOSEPH HILL** was born on 27 Dec 1908 in Jefferson, Jefferson, Arkansas.[462] He died on 12 Jul 1922 in Jefferson, Jefferson, Arkansas, USA.

---

[457] 1910 US Federal Census; Census Place: Jefferson, Jefferson, Arkansas; NARA Roll: T624-54; Page: 8B; Enumeration District: 0099; FHL microfilm: 1374067. *Ancestry.com*. Tom Hill, head; Dorothy Hill, age 4.

[458] Cook County, Illinois Death Index, 1908-1988 [Database on-line]. *Ancestry.com*. Dorothy Williams, 9 Apr 1959.

[459] Cook County, Illinois Marriage Indexes, 1912-1942 [Database on-line]. *Ancestry.com*. Dartha Hills [*sic*] and Booker T. Williams, 18 Nov 1922.

[460] U.S. Social Security Death Index, 1935-Current [Database on-line]. *Ancestry.com*. Booker T. Williams, 7 Oct 1987.

[461] Sharon Shanks Ancestry Family Tree. *Ancestry.com*. Dorothy Hill.

[462] 1910 US Federal Census; Census Place: Jefferson, Jefferson, Arkansas; NARA Roll: T624-54; Page: 8B; Enumeration District: 0099; FHL microfilm: 1374067. *Ancestry.com*. Tom Hill, head; T J Hill, age 1.

Figure 79: Elmer Hill.
Photo courtesy of Sharon Shanks.

viii. **ELMER HILL** was born about 1914 in Jefferson, Jefferson, Arkansas.[463] He died in March 1985.[464] He married **ERNESTINE STOVALL**.[465]

---

[463] 1930 US Federal Census; Census Place: Bonhomme, St Louis, Missouri; NARA Roll: 1223; Page: 11B; Enumeration District: 0011; Image: 368.0; FHL microfilm: 2340958. *Ancestry.com*. Thomas Hill, head; Elmer Hill, age 16.

[464] U.S. Social Security Death Index, 1935-Current [Database on-line]. *Ancestry.com*. Elmer Hill, Mar 1985.

[465] Missouri, Marriage Records, 1805-2002 [Database on-line]. *Ancestry.com*. Elmer Hill and Earnestine Stovall, 8 Nov 1943.

Figure 80: Carrie Marie Hill.
Photo courtesy of Sharon Shanks.

ix. **CARRIE MARIE HILL** was born on 03 Jul 1916 in Jefferson, Jefferson, Arkansas.[466] She died on 05 Jul 1988 in Union, Missouri.[467] She married **HOWARD D. AITCH**, son of **GEORGE AITCH** and **MAGGIE STANARD**, on 6 Jun 1943.[468]He died

---

[466] 1930 US Federal Census; Census Place: Bonhomme, St Louis, Missouri; NARA Roll: 1223; Page: 11B; Enumeration District: 0011; Image: 368.0; FHL microfilm: 2340958. *Ancestry.com*. Thomas Hill, head; Carrie Hill, age 13.

[467] U.S. Social Security Death Index, 1935-Current [Database on-line]. *Ancestry.com*. Carrie B. Aitch, Jul 1988.

[468] Missouri, Marriage Records, 1805-2002 [Database on-line]. *Ancestry.com*. Carrie Hill and Howard Aitch, 6 Feb 1943.

30 Apr 1991 in St. Louis, Missouri.[469]

Figure 81: Essie Mae Hill. Photo courtesy Sharon Shanks.

x. **ESSIE MAE HILL** was born on 03 Feb 1919 in Jefferson, Jefferson, Arkansas.[470] She died on 27 Dec 1955 in Chicago, Cook, Illinois.[471] She married **LUTHER ASHLEY**.[472] No marriage record has been identified to

---

[469] U.S. Social Security Death Index, 1935-Current [Database on-line]. *Ancestry.com*. Howard Aitch, 30 Apr 1991.

[470] 1930 US Federal Census; Census Place: Bonhomme, St Louis, Missouri; Roll: 1223; Page: 11B; Enumeration District: 0011; Image: 368.0; FHL microfilm: 2340958. *Ancestry.com*. Thomas Hill, head; Essie M Hill, age 11.

[471] Cook County, Illinois Death Index, 1908-1988 [Database on-line]. *Ancestry.com*. Essie Mae Ashley, 27 Dec 1955.

[472] Brigitte Hopkins Hill Family Tree. Ancestry Trees [Database on-line]. *Ancestry.com*. Luther Ashley.

date. He reportedly died Dec 1950, in Chicago, Cook, Illinois.[473]

14. **MARY ELIZA[3] POTTER** (CHARITY[2] HILL, EDWARD "NED" HILL) was born about 1856 in Randolph County, North Carolina. She had an undetermined relationship with a **LEWIS WOOTEN.** *[See Entry Above]*

a. **MARY ELIZA POTTER** and **LEWIS WOOTEN** had the following child:

i. **CHARLIE M.[4] POTTER** was born 17 Sep 1884 most likely in Strieby, Union, Randolph, North Carolina.[474] He died 30 Jul 1968, in Thomasville, Davidson, North Carolina.[475] He was married to **ANNIE CARSON,** the daughter of **ALFRED CARSON** and **ANNIE HARGRAVE,** on 26 Jun 1906, in Davidson County, North Carolina.[476] She died 18 Feb 1953 in Lexington, Davidson, North Carolina.[477]

15. **CALVIN DUCKERY[3] POTTER** (CHARITY[2]HILL, EDWARD "NED"[1]HILL) was born in 1870 in Cedar

---

[473] Brigitte Hopkins Hill Family Tree. Ancestry Trees [Database on-line]. *Ancestry.com*. Luther Ashley.

[474] 1900 US Federal Census; Census Place: Union, Randolph, North Carolina; Roll: 1213; Page: 6B; Enumeration District: 0099; FHL microfilm: 1241213. *Ancestry.com*. Charity Potter, head; Charley Potter, grandson.

[475] North Carolina, Death Certificates, 1909-1975 [Database on-line]. *Ancestry.com*. Charlie M. Potter, 30 Jul 1968.

[476] North Carolina, Marriage Records, 1741-2011 [Database on-line]. *Ancestry.com*. Charlie Potter and Annie Carson, 26 Jun 1906.

[477] North Carolina, Death Certificates, 1909-1975 [Database on-line]. *Ancestry.com*. Annie Potter, 18 Feb 1953.

Grove, Randolph, North Carolina. He died 27 Dec 1940 in Strieby, Randolph County, North Carolina. **He is buried in Strieby Church Cemetery**. He married **ELIZABETH EADY**, daughter of **JOSEPH EADIE** and **JANE KEARNS** on 12 Oct 1895 in Asheboro, Randolph, North Carolina. She was born in 1874 in Cedar Grove, Randolph, North Carolina. She may have died in 1964. [*See Entry Above*]

a. CALVIN DUCKERY POTTER and ELIZABETH EADY had the following children:

   i. **GERTRUDE[4] POTTER** was born in 26 Sep 1898 in Strieby, Union, Randolph, North Carolina.[478] She died 28 Dec 1968 in High Point, Guilford, North Carolina.[479] She married **LACY CHARLES KENDALL** SR.[480] He was born 3 Sep 1894 in Steeles, Richmond, North Carolina to **PINKNEY KENDALL** and **CAROLYN INGRAM.**[481] He died 2 Jan 1956 in High Point, Guilford, North Carolina.[482]

   ii. **HERBERT THOMAS POTTER** was born

---

478 1900 US Federal Census; Census Place: Union, Randolph, North Carolina; NARA Roll: 1213; Page: 6B; Enumeration District: 0099; FHL microfilm: 1241213. *Ancestry.com*. Dock Potter, head; Gertrude Potter, age 1.

479 North Carolina, Death Certificates, 1909-1975 [Database on-line]. *Ancestry.com*. Gertrude Kendall, 28 Dec 1968.

480 North Carolina, Death Certificates, 1909-1975 [Database on-line]. *Ancestry.com*. Gertrude Kendall, 28 Dec 1968.

481 North Carolina, Birth Indexes, 1800-2000 [Database on-line]. *Ancestry.com*. Lacy Kendall, 3 Sep 1894

482 North Carolina, Death Certificates, 1909-1975 [Database on-line]. *Ancestry.com*. Lacy Kendall Sr., 2 Jan 1956.

in 1907 in Strieby, Union, Randolph, North Carolina.[483] He died 14 Feb 1952 in High Point, Guilford, North Carolina.[484]He married **DAISY ESTELLE HILL**, daughter of **CLAUDE** and **ESTELLE HILL**, on 20 Jan 1930 in Guilford County, North Carolina.[485] She was born 6 Mar 1910 and died 7 Nov 1999 in High Point, Guilford, North Carolina.[486]

iii. **LLOYD WATSON POTTER** was born in 12 Apr 1912 in Strieby, Union, Randolph, North Carolina.[487] He died on 27 Feb 1968 in Asheboro, Randolph County, North Carolina.[488] He married **NORMA BOLDING**, daughter of **WILLIAM BOLDING** and **MARY**

---

[483] 1910 US Federal Census; Census Place: Union, Randolph, North Carolina; NARA Roll: T624_1128; Page: 2B; Enumeration District: 0100; FHL microfilm: 1375141. *Ancestry.com*. Dockery C. Potter, head; Herbert Potter, age 1.

[484] North Carolina, Death Certificates, 1909-1975 [Database on-line]. *Ancestry.com*. Herbert Thomas Potter, 14 Feb 1952.

[485] North Carolina, Marriage Records, 1741-2011 [Database on-line]. *Ancestry.com*. Herbert Potter and Daisy E. Hill, 20 Jan 1930.

[486] North Carolina, Death Certificates, 1909-1975 [Database on-line]. Ancestry.com. Daisy Hill Potter, 7 Nov 1999.

[487] 1920 US Federal Census; Census Place: Union, Randolph, North Carolina; Roll: T625_1318; Page: 9A; Enumeration District: 118; Image: 1274. Ancestry.com. Dockery Potter, head; Loyd [sic] Potter, age 12.

[488] North Carolina, Death Certificates, 1909-1975 [Database on-line]. Ancestry.com. Lloyd Watson Potter, 27 Feb 1968.

BYRD. She was born 6 Aug 1912, and died 4 Sep 1965 in Asheboro, Randolph, North Carolina.[489] They are both buried in **Strieby Church Cemetery**.

iv. **ROY POTTER** was born in 1915 in Strieby, Union, Randolph, North Carolina.[490]

v. **JOSEPH FRED POTTER** was born on 28 Jul 1924 in Strieby, Union, North Carolina.[491] He died on 6 Feb 1991, in Lawrence County, Pennsylvania.[492]

16. **MARY LOUISE**[3] **HILL** (CALVIN[2], EDWARD "NED"[1]) was born in 1860 in Strieby, Union, Randolph, North Carolina. [See Entry Above]

a. **MARY LOUISE HILL** reportedly had the following children:

i. **MINERVA**[4] **HILL** was born in Jul 1880 in Strieby, Union, Randolph, North

---

[489] North Carolina, Death Certificates, 1909-1975 [Database on-line]. *Ancestry.com*. Norma B. Potter, 4 Sep 1965.

[490] 1920 US Federal Census; Census Place: Union, Randolph, North Carolina; Roll: T625_1318; Page: 9A; Enumeration District: 118; Image: 1274. *Ancestry.com*. Dockery Potter, head; Roy Potter, age 5.

[491] 1930 US Federal Census; Census Place: Union, Randolph, North Carolina; Roll: 1715; Page: 6A; Enumeration District: 0034; Image: 427.0; FHL microfilm: 2341449. *Ancestry.com*. Dockery Potter head; Joseph Potter, age 6.

[492] Pennsylvania, Veterans Burial Cards, 1777-2012 [Database on-line]. *Ancestry.com*. Fred J Potter, 6 Feb 1991.

Carolina.[493] She died before 1940, in Randolph County, North Carolina.[494] She married **ISRAEL MICHAEL COBLE** on 18 Nov 1897 in Asheboro, Randolph, North Carolina.[495] He was born in Apr 1865 in Alamance County, North Carolina. He died 10 Oct 1945, in Asheboro, Randolph, North Carolina. **He is buried in Strieby Church Cemetery.**[496]

---

[493] 1900 US Federal Census; Census Place: Union, Randolph, North Carolina; NARA Roll: 1213; Page: 6B; Enumeration District: 0099; FHL microfilm: 1241213. *Ancestry.com*. Israel Coble, head; Minerva Coble, age 19.
[494] 1940 US Federal Census; Census Place: Franklinville, Randolph, North Carolina; NARA Roll: T627-2961; Page: 32B; Enumeration District: 76-18. *Ancestry.com*. William P Cable [*sic*] head; Michael I Cable [*sic*] father; Sarah A Cable [sic], step-mother.
[495] North Carolina, Marriage Records, 1741-2011 [Database on-line]. *Ancestry.com*. Nerva Hill and Israel Coble, 18 Nov 1897.
[496] U.S. Find A Grave Index, 1700s-Current [Database on-line]. *Ancestry.com*. Michael I Coble, 10 Oct 1945.

Figure 82: Lester Laughlin (1914-1998), son of Rozina Hill & Thomas E. Laughlin, Strieby Church Trustee.

ii. **ROZINA HILL** was born on 10 Aug 1882 in Strieby, Union, Randolph, North Carolina. She died on 21 Nov 1943 in Randolph County, North Carolina.[497] She married **THOMAS E. LAUGHLIN**, son of **CHESLEY LAUGHLIN** and **SARAH GANAWAY** on 15 Jul 1906 in Asheboro, Randolph, North Carolina.[498] He was born on 10 Sep 1876 in Trinity, Randolph, North Carolina. He died on 09 Jul 1949 in Randolph County, North

---

[497] North Carolina, Death Certificates, 1909-1975 [Database on-line]. *Ancestry.com*. Zina Laughlin, 21 Nov 1943.

[498] North Carolina, Marriage Records, 1741-2011 [Database on-line]. *Ancestry.com*. Zina Hill and T E Laughlin, 15 Nov 1906.

Carolina.[499] They are both **buried in Strieby Church Cemetery.**

17. **DAVID SHERMAN[3] HILL** (CALVIN[2], EDWARD "NED"[1]) was born in 1863 in Strieby, Union, Randolph, North Carolina. He married **IZETTA REDWINE**, daughter of **JAMES REDWINE** and **DIAN JANE STAFFORD**, on 17 Apr 1898 in Asheboro, Randolph, North Carolina. She was born in Nov 1877 in Davidson County, North Carolina. [See Entry Above]
    a. DAVID SHERMAN HILL and IZETTA REDWINE had the following known children:
        i. **ELSIE[4] HILL** was born in Apr 1895.[500]
        ii. **HENRY D. HILL** was born in Jul 1899.[501]
        iii. **SHERMAN W. HILL** was born in 1902.[502]
18. **BARZILLA HARRISON[3] HILL** (CALVIN[2], EDWARD "NED"[1]) was born on 18 Jul 1868 in Strieby, Union, Randolph, North Carolina. He married

---

[499] North Carolina, Death Certificates, 1909-1975 [Database on-line]. *Ancestry.com*. Thomas Edward Laughlin, 8 Jul 1949.

[500] 1900 US Federal Census; Census Place: Union, Randolph, North Carolina; NARA Roll: 1213; Page: 6B; Enumeration District: 0099; FHL microfilm: 1241213. *Ancestry.com*. Sherman Hill, head; Elsie Hill, age 5.

[501] 1900 US Federal Census; Census Place: Union, Randolph, North Carolina; NARA Roll: 1213; Page: 6B; Enumeration District: 0099; FHL microfilm: 1241213. *Ancestry.com*. Sherman Hill, head; Henry D Hill, 10/12 year.

[502] 1910 US Federal Census; Census Place: Union, Randolph, North Carolina; NARA Roll: T624_1128; Page: 2A; Enumeration District: 0100; FHL microfilm: 1375141. *Ancestry.com*. Ulyssus Hill, head; Sherman W Hill, son, age 8. However, Ulysses Hill did not marry Izetta Redwine Hill until 8 Nov 1903. *See*: North Carolina, Marriage Collection, 1741-2004 [Database on-line]. *Ancestry.com*. W [*sic*] G Hill and Isetta Redwine, 8 Nov 1903. Sherman appears to have been named for his father, David Sherman Hill.

ELIZABETH HEARN, the daughter of **ROLLIN HEARN and REBECCA DAVIS** on 01 Jan 1885 in Asheboro, Randolph, North Carolina. She was born in Feb 1865 in Randolph County, North Carolina and died 4 May 1936. **They are both buried in Strieby Cemetery**. [See Entry Above]

a. BARZILLA HARRISON HILL and ELIZABETH HEARN had the following children:

Figure 83: Gurney Calvin Hill. Photo courtesy of Richard Jackson.

i. **GURNEY CALVIN HILL** was born in Oct 1886 in Strieby, Union, Randolph, North Carolina.[503] He died 4 Sep 1947,

[503] 1900 US Federal Census; Census Place: Union, Randolph, North Carolina; NARA Roll: 1213; Page: 6B; Enumeration District: 0099; FHL microfilm: 1241213. *Ancestry.com*. Brayzilla Hill, head; Gurnie Hill, age 13.

Philadelphia, Pennsylvania.[504] He married **SUSAN WHITE**, daughter of **SILAS WHITE** and **MYRA HOWARD**, on 6 Jul 1912 in Springfield, Hampden, Massachusetts.[505] According to Gurney's death certificate, they divorced.

Figure 84: Arthur Hill.
Photo courtesy of Richard Jackson.

ii. **ARTHUR[4] HAZE HILL** was born on 13 Sep 1887 in Hilltown, Union, Randolph, North

---

[504] Pennsylvania, Death Certificates, 1906-1944 [Database on-line]. *Ancestry.com*. Gurnie Calvin Hill, 4 Sep 1947.

[505] Massachusetts Marriages, 1841-1915 [Database on-line].*FamilySearch.org*. Gurnie C Hill and Susan White, 06 Jul 1912; FHL microfilm 2,409,943.

Carolina.[506] He died on 13 Sep 1980 in Strieby, Union, Randolph, North Carolina.[507] He married **ELIZABETH A. LASSITER**, daughter of **AMOS BARZILLA LASSITER** and **HARRIETT PHILLIPS** on 31 Dec 1910 in Asheboro, Randolph, North Carolina.[508] She was born on 17 Oct 1886 in Lassiter Mill, New Hope, Randolph, North Carolina. She died on 16 Dec 1962 in Strieby, Union, Randolph, North Carolina. They are **both buried in Strieby Church Cemetery**.[509]

---

[506] 1900 US Federal Census; Census Place: Union, Randolph, North Carolina; NARA Roll: 1213; Page: 6B; Enumeration District: 0099; FHL microfilm: 1241213. *Ancestry.com*. Brayzilla Hill, head; Arthur H. Hill, age 12.
[507] North Carolina, Death Indexes, 1908-2004 [Database on-line]. *Ancestry.com*. Arthur Haze Hill, 13 Sep 1980.
[508] North Carolina, Marriage Collection, 1741-2004 [Database on-line]. *Ancestry.com*. Arthur Hill and Lizzie Lassiter, 31 Dec 1910.
[509] North Carolina, Death Certificates, 1909-1975 [Database on-line]. *Ancestry.com*. Elizabeth Hill, 16 Dec 1962.

Figure 85: (L) Harriett Glee Hill, daughter & (R) Elizabeth (Lassiter) Hill. Photo courtesy of Richard Jackson.

19. **ULYSSES GRANT[3] HILL** (CALVIN[2], EDWARD "NED"[1]) was born on 30 Jun 1873 in Strieby, Union, Randolph, North Carolina. He died on 20 Aug 1925 in Strieby, Randolph, North Carolina. He married **IZETTA REDWINE**, widow of his brother **DAVID SHERMAN HILL** (*see above*), on 08 Nov 1903 in Randolph County, North Carolina. She was born in Nov 1877 in Randolph County, North Carolina. [*See Entry Above*] He is **buried in Strieby Church Cemetery**.

    a. ULYSSES GRANT HILL and IZETTA REDWINE had the following children:

        i. **LUCRETIA[4] HILL** was born in 1904 in Strieby, Union, Randolph, North Carolina. She died on 25 Jun 1918 in

Strieby, Randolph, North Carolina. She is **buried in Strieby Church Cemetery**.

ii. **DUELLA MAE HILL** was born 20 May 1907 in Strieby, Union, Randolph, North Carolina.[510] She died in Apr 1993, location not identified to date.[511]

iii. **ELIZABETH M. HILL** was born in 1909 in Strieby, Union, Randolph, North Carolina.[512] She died 17 Jan 1993.[513] She was married to **JAMES MERRIWEATHER**, son of **M.C. MERRIWEATHER** and his wife **CALLIE**, on 6 Oct 1935, in Troy, Montgomery, North Carolina.[514]

iv. **CALVIN WORTH HILL** was born in 1912 in Strieby, Union, Randolph, North

---

[510] 1910 US Federal Census; Census Place: Union, Randolph, North Carolina; NARA Roll: T624_1128; Page: 2A; Enumeration District: 0100; FHL microfilm: 1375141. *Ancestry.com*. Ulyssus Hill, head; Duella M Hill, age 6.

[511] U.S. Social Security Applications and Claims Index, 1936-2007 [Database on-line]. *Ancestry.com*. Duella M. Boulware, Apr 1993.

[512] 1910 US Federal Census; Census Place: Union, Randolph, North Carolina; Roll: T624_1128; Page: 2A; Enumeration District: 0100; FHL microfilm: 1375141. *Ancestry.com*. Ulyssus Hill, head; Elizabeth Hill, age 1.

[513] U.S. Social Security Applications and Claims Index, 1936-2007 [Database on-line]. *Ancestry.com*. Elizabeth Merieweather [sic], 17 Jan 1993.

[514] North Carolina, Marriage Records, 1741-2011[Database on-line]. *Ancestry.com*. Elizabeth Hill and James Merriweather, 6 October 1935, in Troy, Montgomery, North Carolina.

Carolina.[515]He died 15 Nov 1998 in Manning, Clarendon, South Carolina.[516]

v. **JOHN CARSON HILL** was born in 1914 in Strieby, Union, Randolph, North Carolina.[517]

vi. **WALTER HOWARD HILL** was born on 4 Apr 1916 in Strieby, Union, Randolph, North Carolina.[518] He died in New York on 21 Jul 1979.[519]

vii. **MILTON REID HILL** was born in 1919 in Strieby, Union, Randolph, North Carolina.[520] He died 26 Jun 1993,[521]

---

[515] 1920 US Federal Census; Census Place: Union, Randolph, North Carolina; NARA Roll: T625_1318; Page: 9A; Enumeration District: 118; Image: 1274. *Ancestry.com*. Ulysses Hill, head; Worth Hill, age 8.

[516] U.S. Social Security Applications and Claims Index, 1936-2007 [Database on-line]. *Ancestry.com*. Calvin Hill, 15 Nov 1998.

[517] 1920 US Federal Census; Census Place: Union, Randolph, North Carolina; NARA Roll: T625_1318; Page: 9A; Enumeration District: 118; Image: 1274. *Ancestry.com*. Ulysses Hill, head; Floyd Hill, age 6. See also: U.S. WWII Draft Cards Young Men, 1940-1947 [Database on-line]. *Ancestry.com*. John Carson Hill, 4 Sep 1914; and 1940; Census Place: Union, Randolph, North Carolina; NARA Roll: T627_2962; Page: 2A; Enumeration District: 76-15. *Ancestry.com*. John C Hill, head, age 25; Howard Hill, brother, age 22; Milton Hill, brother, age 18.

[518] 1920 US Federal Census; Census Place: Union, Randolph, North Carolina; NARA Roll: T625_1318; Page: 9A; Enumeration District: 118; Image: 1274. *Ancestry.com*. Ulysses Hill, head; Walter H Hill, age 4.

[519] U.S. Veterans Gravesites, ca.1775-2006 [Database on-line]. *Ancestry.com*. Walter Howard Hill, 21 Jul 1979.

[520] 1920 US Federal Census; Census Place: Union, Randolph, North Carolina; NARA Roll: T625_1318; Page: 9A; Enumeration District: 118; Image: 1274. *Ancestry.com*. Ulysses Hill, head; Milton R Hill, age 1.

possibly in Halifax County, Virginia.[522]

viii. **EDWARD[4] HILL** was born in 1922 in Strieby, Union, Randolph, North Carolina.[523]

ix. **JAMES HILL** was born in 1924 in Strieby, Union, Randolph, North Carolina.[524]

20. **ELIZABETH[3] HILL** (BETHANA[2], EDWARD "NED"[1]) was born in 1861 in Strieby, Union, Randolph, North Carolina. She married **WILLIAM FISHER**. He was born in 1858 in North Carolina. [*See Entry Above*]

a. ELIZABETH HILL and WILLIAM FISHER had the following children:

i. **MARY ELIZABETH[4] FISHER** was born in 1889 in Strieby, Union, Randolph, North Carolina.[525]She died 2 Oct 1933, in High Point, Guilford, North Carolina. She is **buried in Strieby Church Cemetery**. She married **WILLIAM HOLT** on 31 Dec 1914 in Randolph County, North

---

[521] U.S. Social Security Applications and Claims Index, 1936-2007 [Database on-line]. *Ancestry.com.* Milton Reid Hill, 26 Jun 1993.

[522] Virginia, Death Records, 1912-2014 [Database on-line]. *Ancestry.com.* Milton Hill, 26 Jun 1993.

[523] 1930 US Federal Census; Census Place: Union, Randolph, North Carolina; NARA Roll: 1715; Page: 6B; Enumeration District: 0034; Image: 428.0; FHL microfilm: 2341449. *Ancestry.com.* Izetta Hill, head; Edward Hill, age 8.

[524] 1930 US Federal Census; Census Place: Union, Randolph, North Carolina; NARA Roll: 1715; Page: 6B; Enumeration District: 0034; Image: 428.0; FHL microfilm: 2341449. *Ancestry.com.* Izetta Hill, head; James Hill, age 6.

[525] 1900 US Federal Census; Census Place: Union, Randolph, North Carolina; NARA Roll: 1213; Page: 6B; Enumeration District: 0099; FHL microfilm: 1241213. *Ancestry.com.* William Fisher, head; Mary E. Fisher, age 13.

Carolina.[526]

ii. **CALVIN C. FISHER** was born in Strieby, Union, Randolph, North Carolina.[527]

iii. **ESTELLE FISHER** was born in 1895 in Strieby, Union, Randolph, North Carolina.[528] She married **JOHN WESLEY CARTER**, the son of **HENRY CARTER** and **LULA MILLER**, 16 Jun 1918 in Guilford County, North Carolina.[529] He was born 3 Oct 1895 and died 24 Nov 1971, in High Point, Guilford, North Carolina.[530]

21. **WILLIAM JULIUS[3] HILL** (EMSLEY[2], EDWARD "NED"[1]) was born on 17 Dec 1871 in Strieby, Union, Randolph, North Carolina. He died on 28 May 1925 in Mt. Washington, Hamilton, Ohio. He married **FLORA ELIZABETH SETTLES** on 02 Nov 1898 in Ohio. She was

---

[526] North Carolina, Marriages, 1759-1979 [Database on-line]. *FamilySearch.com*. Wm. A. Holt and Mary Fisher, 31 Dec 1914; citing Randolph, North Carolina, reference 125 & 126; FHL microfilm 475,239.accessed 18 September 2015: https://familysearch.org/ark:/61903/1:1:FZYY-ZY9

[527] 1900 US Federal Census; Census Place: Union, Randolph, North Carolina; NARA Roll: 1213; Page: 6B; Enumeration District: 0099; FHL #1241213. *Ancestry.com*. William Fisher, head; Calvin C. Fisher, age 10.

[528] 1900 US Federal Census; Census Place: Union, Randolph, North Carolina; NARA Roll: 1213; Page: 6B; Enumeration District: 0099; FHL #1241213. *Ancestry.com*. Estella Fisher, age 5.

[529] North Carolina, Marriage Records, 1741-2011 [Database on-line]. *Ancestry.com*. Estella Fisher and John W. Carter, 16 Jun 1918.

[530] North Carolina, Death Certificates, 1909-1975 [Database on-line]. *Ancestry.com*. John Wesley Carter, 24 Nov 1971.

born on 22 Sep 1877 in Brah Hill, Clermont, Ohio, USA. She died on 01 Mar 1949 in Cleveland, Cuyahoga, Ohio, USA. [*See Entry Above*]

a. WILLIAM JULIUS HILL and FLORA ELIZABETH SETTLES had the following child:

   i. **JOHN G.[4] HILL** was born 17 Jan 1899 in Milford, Clermont, Ohio. He died 7 May 1899, most likely in Milford, Clermont, Ohio.[531]

   ii. **ROMAINE HILL** was born 29 Jul 1900 in Dayton, Montgomery, Ohio.[532] She reportedly died on 23 July 1972, in San Bernardino, San Bernardino, California.[533]

   iii. **LULA MAE HILL** was born about 1906, in Cincinnati, Clermont, Ohio.[534] She reportedly died 1 May 1950, in Boston, Suffolk, Massachusetts.[535]

   iv. **SARAH LUCRETIA HILL** was born about 5 Nov 1908, in Cincinnati,

---

[531] Asaptraveler. (n.d.) Brigitte Hopkins Hill Family Tree. *Ancestry.com*. John G. Hill, born 17 Jan 1899; died 7 May 1899.

[532] Ohio, Births and Christenings Index, 1800-1962 [Database on-line]. *Ancestry.com*. Romaine Hill, 29 Jul 1900.

[533] Family Data Collection - Individual Records [Database on-line]. *Ancestry.com*. Romaine Hill, 23 Jul 1972.

[534] 1910 US Federal Census; Census Place: Cincinnati Ward 1, Hamilton, Ohio; NARA Roll: T624_1188; Page: 6A; Enumeration District: 0019; FHL #1375201. *Ancestry.com*. William J. Hill, head; Lulu M. Hill, age 6.

[535] Asaptraveler. (n.d.) Brigitte Hopkins Hill Family Tree. *Ancestry.com*. Lula Mae Hill, 1 May 1950.

Clermont, Ohio.[536] She died 22 Nov 1991, in Cincinnati, Clermont, Ohio.[537] She was married to **ROSCOE ANDERSON FULTZ**, son of **JOHN** and **LIZZIE FULTZ**.[538] He was born Dec 1897, in Ohio.[539] He reportedly died 29 Jan 1954 in Cuyahoga County, Ohio.[540]

v. **DORA ELISE HILL** was born 22 Jul 1911 in Hamilton County, Ohio.[541] She reportedly died 7 Dec 1984, in Cincinnati, Hamilton, Ohio.[542]

vi. **CATHERINE ELIZABETH HILL** was born 5 Jan 1916 in Hamilton County,

---

[536] 1910 US Federal Census; Census Place: Cincinnati Ward 1, Hamilton, Ohio; NARA Roll: T624_1188; Page: 6A; Enumeration District: 0019; FHL #1375201. *Ancestry.com*. William J. Hill, head; Sarah L. Hill, age 1.
[537] Ohio Deaths, 1908-1932, 1938-2007 [Database on-line]. *Ancestry.com*. Sarah Lucretia Fultz, 22 Nov 1991.
[538] U.S. City Directories, 1821-1989 [Database on-line]. *Ancestry.com*. Sarah Fultz and Roscoe Fultz, Cincinnati, Ohio, 1942.
[539] 1900 US Federal Census; Census Place: Williamsburg, Clermont, Ohio; NARA Roll: 1247; Page: 2A; Enumeration District: 0056; FHL #1241247. *Ancestry.com*. John Fultz, head, Roscoe Fultz, age 2.He reportedly died 29 Jan 1954 in Cuyahoga County, Ohio.
[540] U.S. Find A Grave Index, 1700s-Current [Database on-line]. *Ancestry.com*. Roscoe Fultz, 29 Jan 1954.
[541] Ohio Birth Index, 1908-1964 [Database on-line]. *Ancestry.com*. Dora E. Hill, 22 Jul 1911.
[542] Asaptraveler. (n.d.) Brigitte Hopkins Hill Family Tree. *Ancestry.com*. Dora Elise Hill, 7 Dec 1984.

Ohio.[543] She reportedly died 1 Aug 1965, in Cleveland, Cuyahoga, Ohio.[544]

vii. **FLORA MAMIE HILL** was born Aug 1917, in Cincinnati, Hamilton, Ohio. She died 2 Feb 1918, in Cincinnati, Hamilton, Ohio.[545]

viii. **WILLIAM ROBERT HILL** was born about 9 Jul 1919, in Hamilton County, Ohio.[546] He died 27 Sep 1999, in Cleveland, Cuyahoga, Ohio.[547]

ix. **EVIE RUTH[4] HILL** was born on 05 Mar 1925 in Cincinnati, Hamilton, Ohio.[548] She died on 30 Jan 1998 in Cincinnati,

---

[543] 1920 US Federal Census; Census Place: Anderson, Hamilton, Ohio; NARA Roll: T625_1388; Page: 4B; Enumeration District: 2; Image: 37. *Ancestry.com*. William J Hill, head; Catherine E Hill, age 4.

[544] Asaptraveler. (n.d.) Brigitte Hopkins Hill Family Tree. *Ancestry.com*. Catherine Elizabeth Hill, 1 Aug 1965.

[545] Asaptraveler. (n.d.) Brigitte Hopkins Hill Family Tree. *Ancestry.com*. Flora Mamie Hill, born 1917; died 2 Feb 1918, in Cincinnati, Hamilton, Ohio.

[546] 1920 US Federal Census; Census Place: Anderson, Hamilton, Ohio; NARA Roll: T625_1388; Page: 4B; Enumeration District: 2; Image: 37. *Ancestry.com*. William J Hill, head; William R Hill, age 0. *See also*: U.S. Social Security Applications and Claims Index, 1936-2007 [Database on-line]. *Ancestry.com*. William Robert Hill, born 9 Jul 1919.

[547] Ohio Deaths, 1908-1932, 1938-2007 [Database on-line]. *Ancestry.com*. William Robert Hill, 27 Sep 1999. *See also*: U.S., Social Security Applications and Claims Index, 1936-2007 [Database on-line]. *Ancestry.com*. William Robert Hill, died 27 Sep 1999.

[548] Ohio Birth Index, 1908-1964 [Database on-line]. *Ancestry.com*. Eva R. Hill, 5 Mar 1925.

Hamilton, Ohio.[549] She married **DANIEL GRADY**. He died on 24 Nov 1987, Cincinnati, Hamilton, Ohio.[550]

22. **ISLAY THOMAS[3] HILL** (EMSLEY[2] HILL, NED HILL) was born 1877 in Union Township, Randolph County, North Carolina. He died 4 Aug 1970 in Dayton, Montgomery, Ohio. He married first **MARY CARROLL**. He married second, **MARGARET SUE** (maiden name unknown). [*See Entry Above*]
    a. ISLAY THOMAS HILL and MARY CARROLL had the following children:
        i. **WILLIAM[4] HILL** was born May 1897 in Cincinnati, Hamilton, Ohio.[551]
        ii. **STANLEY HILL** was born about 1901, in Cincinnati, Hamilton, Ohio[552] and died 12 May 1969, in Cincinnati, Hamilton, Ohio.[553]
        iii. **CORNELIUS HILL** was born about 1905

---

[549] Ohio Deaths, 1908-1932, 1938-2007 [Database on-line]. *Ancestry.com.* Evie Ruth Grady, 30 Jan 1998.
[550] Ohio Deaths, 1908-1932, 1938-2007 [Database on-line]. *Ancestry.com.* Daniel Grady, 24 Nov 1987.
[551] 1900 US Federal Census; Census Place: Dayton Ward 7, Montgomery, Ohio; Roll: 1307; Page: 10A; Enumeration District: 0063; FHL #1241307. *Ancestry.com.* Iolay [sic – original reads Islay] Hill, head; William Hill, age 3.
[552] 1920 US Federal Census; Census Place: Cincinnati Ward 9, Hamilton, Ohio; Roll: T625_1390; Page: 9A; Enumeration District: 153; Image: 803. *Ancestry.com.* T Isley Hill, head; Stanley Hill, age 19.
[553] Ohio Deaths, 1908-1932, 1938-2007 [Database on-line]. *Ancestry.com.* Stanley Hill, born 1901, died 12 May 1969.

in Cincinnati, Hamilton, Ohio.[554] He died 15 Feb 1960 in Cincinnati, Hamilton, Ohio.[555] He married **GRACIE BATES**, the daughter of **CHARLES BATES** and **HATTIE BAKER**, 28 Jan 1924, in Cincinnati, Hamilton, Ohio.[556] She was born about 1905 in Alabama.[557] She died the 2 Oct 1925 in Kenton County, Kentucky.[558] Her death certificate notes that she was divorced.

23. **DELPHINA ARDILIA**[3] **"DELLA" POTTER** (MARY JANE[2] HILL, EDWARD "NED"[1] HILL) was born 2 Apr 1876 in Union, Randolph, North Carolina. She died 17 Mar 1944, in New Hope, Randolph, North Carolina. **ARDILIA POTTER** also went by the name of **DELPHINA WILSON**. Her father's name was listed as **LEZE/LEGE (?-sp, Elijah?) WILSON** on her death certificate. She married **JOHN W D McCRAY/McRAE** on 12 Oct 1895 in Randolph County. *[See Entry Above]*

---

[554] 1920 US Federal Census; Census Place: Cincinnati Ward 9, Hamilton, Ohio; Roll: T625_1390; Page: 9A; Enumeration District: 153; Image: 803. Ancestry.com. T Isley Hill, head; Cornelius Hill, age 15.

[555] Ohio Deaths, 1908-1932, 1938-2007 [Database on-line]. *Ancestry.com*. Cornelius Hill, 15 Feb 1960.

[556] Ohio Marriages, 1800-1958," database, *FamilySearch*. Cornelius Hill and Gracie Bates, 28 Jan 1924; citing Hamilton, Ohio, reference 2:3R97NMX; FHL #384,184.

[557] 1920 US Federal Census; Census Place: Cincinnati Ward 16, Hamilton, Ohio; NARA Roll: T625_1392; Page: 10B; Enumeration District: 279; Image: 756. *Ancestry.com*. Hattie Bates, head; Gracie Bates, age 15.

[558] Kentucky Death Records, 1852-1963 [Database on-line]. *Ancestry.com*. Grace Hill, 2 Oct 1925, "Divorced".

a. DELPHINA ARDILIA POTTER and JOHN D McRAE had the following children:

i. **PAROLEE[4] MCRAE** was born 15 May 1897 in Union, Randolph, North Carolina,[559] and died 31 May 1949, in Cedar Grove, Randolph, North Carolina.[560] Her death certificate says was buried in the "Congregational church cemetery, Farmer, NC," which is probably a reference to *Salem* Congregational Church, *not* Strieby. She married (1), **WILLIAM McKINLEY CHANDLER**, the son of **THOMAS** and **MARTITIA CHANDLER**, on 7 Jun 1919, in Greensboro, Guilford, North Carolina.[561] They apparently divorced. She married (2), **JOHN MATTHEWS**, son of **ERWIN MATTHEWS** and wife **MATTIE HARRIS**, on 7 Jun 1928, in Greensboro, Guilford, North Carolina.[562] He died 13 Sep 1993 in Wilson, Wilson, North Carolina.[563]

---

[559] 1900 US Federal Census; Census Place: Union, Randolph, North Carolina; NARA Roll: 1213; Page: 5B; Enumeration District: 0099; FHL #1241213. *Ancestry.com*. John Mcray, head; Parrow L Mcray, age 3.

[560] North Carolina, Death Certificates, 1909-1975 [Database on-line]. *Ancestry.com*. Parolee Matthews, 31 May 1949.

[561] North Carolina, Marriage Records, 1741-2011 [Database on-line]. *Ancestry.com*. Paralee McCray and McKinley Chandler, 7 Jun 1919.

[562] North Carolina, Marriage Records, 1741-2011 [Database on-line]. *Ancestry.com*. Pearline [sic] and John Matthews, 7 Jun 1928.

[563] U.S. Social Security Death Index, 1935-Current [Database on-line]. *Ancestry.com*. John A. Matthews, 13 Sep 1993. See also: North Carolina, Death Indexes, 1908-2004 [Database on-line]. *Ancestry.com*. John Alstons Matthews, 13 Sep 1993. Note: the Social Security Index give his last place of

ii. **PEARLIE A McRAE** was born in Dec 1899, in Union, Randolph, North Carolina.[564]

iii. **EDWARD S McRAE** was born in 1902 in Union, Randolph, North Carolina.[565] He died 19 Feb 1919, in Asheboro, Randolph, North Carolina and is **buried in Strieby Cemetery.**[566]

iv. **ROWENA McRAE** was born about 1905, in Union, Randolph, North Carolina.[567] Her date of death has not been identified to date. She married **HENRY LLOYD CHAMBERS**, son of **NOAH KING** and **ANGELETTE CHAMBERS** between 1920

---

residence as Greensboro. The birthdate therein agrees with his Draft record which is different from the NC death index. The Social Security numbers for both death records are identical. Although the NC death index record lists his father's name as "Harris," that was his mother's maiden name. The NC death index also indicates he was divorced. The author believes these records are for the same person.

[564] 1900 US Federal Census; Census Place: Union, Randolph, North Carolina; NARA Roll: 1213; Page: 5B; Enumeration District: 0099; FHL #1241213. *Ancestry.com*. John Mcray, head; Pearlie A. Mcray, age 5/12.

[565] 1910 US Federal Census; Census Place: Union, Randolph, North Carolina; NARA Roll: T624_1128; Page: 1A; Enumeration District: 0100; FHL #1375141. *Ancestry.com*. John W Mcray, head; Eddie S Mcray, age 8.

[566] North Carolina, Death Certificates, 1909-1975 [Database on-line]. *Ancestry.com*. Edward McRae, 19 Feb 1919.

[567] 1910 US Federal Census; Census Place: Union, Randolph, North Carolina; NARA Roll: T624_1128; Page: 1A; Enumeration District: 0100; FHL #1375141. *Ancestry.com*. John W Mcray, head; Roena M Mcray, age 5.

and 1930.[568] They divorced before 1940.[569] He died 4 Nov 1953 in Asheboro, Randolph, North Carolina.[570]

v. **ETHEL McRAE** was born about 1907 in Union, Randolph, North Carolina. [571]

vi. **CURTIS McRAE** was born about 1908, in Union, Randolph, North Carolina.[572]

vii. **ELSIE McRAE** was born about 1910 in Union, Randolph, North Carolina.[573]

viii. **LUGENIA McRAE** was born about 1912 in Union, Randolph, North Carolina.[574]

---

[568] 1930 US Federal Census; Census Place: Cedar Grove, Randolph, North Carolina; NARA Roll: 1714; Page: 5A; Enumeration District: 0008; Image: 925.0; FHL #2341448. *Ancestry.com*. Angelette Chambers, head; Roena Chambers, daughter-in-law.

[569] 1940 US Federal Census; Census Place: Cedar Grove, Randolph, North Carolina; NARA Roll: T627_2961; Page: 10B; Enumeration District: 76-8. *Ancestry.com*. Angelette Chamless [*sic*-original says Chambers] head; Lloyd Chamless [*sic*], son, "divorced."

[570] North Carolina, Death Certificates, 1909-1975 [Database on-line]. *Ancestry.com*. Henry Lloyd Chambers, 4 Nov 1953.

[571] 1910 US Federal Census; Census Place: Union, Randolph, North Carolina; NARA Roll: T624_1128; Page: 1A; Enumeration District: 0100; FHL #1375141. *Ancestry.com*. John W Mcray, head; Ethel Mcray, age 3.

[572] 1910 US Federal Census; Census Place: Union, Randolph, North Carolina; NARA Roll: T624_1128; Page: 1A; Enumeration District: 0100; FHL #1375141. *Ancestry.com*. John W Mcray, head; Curtis Mcray, age 2.

[573] 1920 US Federal Census; Census Place: Union, Randolph, North Carolina; NARA Roll: T625_1318; Page: 10A; Enumeration District: 118; Image: 1276. *Ancestry.com*. John Mcrae, head; Elsie Mcrae, age 10.

[574] 1920 US Federal Census; Census Place: Union, Randolph, North Carolina; NARA Roll: T625_1318; Page: 10A; Enumeration District: 118; Image: 1276. *Ancestry.com*. John Mcrae, head; Lugene, age 8.

She died in 1992 and is **buried in Strieby Church Cemetery**.[575]

ix. **ELZEVAN McRAE** was born 28 Mar 1914, in Strieby (Union), Randolph, North Carolina[576] and died 13 Jan 1978 in Rowan County, North Carolina.[577] He never married.

x. **ELNORA McRAE** was born about 1917 in Strieby (Union), Randolph, North Carolina.[578]

---

[575] U.S. Find A Grave Index, 1700s-Current [Database on-line]. *Ancestry.com*. Lugenia McRae, 1992.

[576] 1920 US Federal Census; Census Place: Union, Randolph, North Carolina; NARA Roll: T625_1318; Page: 10A; Enumeration District: 118; Image: 1276. *Ancestry.com*. John Mcrae, head; Elzevan Mcrae, age 5.

[577] North Carolina, Death Indexes, 1908-2004 [Database on-line]. *Ancestry.com*. Elzevan McRae, 13 Jan 1978.

[578] 1920 US Federal Census; Census Place: Union, Randolph, North Carolina; NARA Roll: T625_1318; Page: 10A; Enumeration District: 118; Image: 1276. *Ancestry.com*. John Mcrae, head; Elnora Mcrae, age 3.

**Figure 86: (L) Edgar Raymond McRae.
(R) Ivy (Walden) McRae.
Photos courtesy of Lettice (McRae) Tate.**

xi. **EDGAR RAYMOND McRAE** was born 16 Jul 1918 in Strieby (Union), Randolph, North Carolina.[579] He died 21 Mar 2004 in Asheboro, Randolph, North Carolina.[580] He married **IVY JANE WALDEN,** daughter of **HENRY C WALDEN** and **ETTA RUSH.** She was born 14 Feb 1912 and died 15 May 1996 in Asheboro,

---

[579] 1920 US Federal Census; Census Place: Union, Randolph, North Carolina; NARA Roll: T625_1318; Page: 10A; Enumeration District: 118; Image: 1276. *Ancestry.com*. John Mcrae, head; Ramond Mcrae, age 1. *See also*: North Carolina, Birth Indexes, 1800-2000 [Database on-line]. *Ancestry.com*. Mcrae, Male, Colored, 16 Jul 1918, Delphina O Potter, mother and John Wellens Duckery McRae, father.

[580] North Carolina, Death Indexes, 1908-2004 [Database on-line]. *Ancestry.com*. Edgar Raymond McRae, 21 Mar 2004.

Randolph, North Carolina.[581]**They are both buried in Strieby Cemetery.**

xii. **EVELENA McRAE** was born 13 Mar 1921, in Strieby (Union), Randolph, North Carolina.[582]

xiii. **GENEVA McRAE** was born 21 Apr 1923.[583] She died 21 Jun 1932, in Cedar Grove, Randolph, North Carolina. **She is buried in Strieby Cemetery.**[584]

xiv. **JERALD WINFORD McRAE** was born about 1926, in Strieby (Union), Randolph, North Carolina[585] He died 3 Jan 1974 in

---

[581] U.S. Social Security Applications and Claims Index, 1936-2007 [Database on-line]. *Ancestry.com*. Ivy Jane McRae, 15 May 1996. See also: North Carolina, Death Indexes, 1908-2004 [Database on-line]. *Ancestry.com*. Ivy Jane McRae, 24 May 1996.

[582] 1930 US Federal Census; Census Place: New Hope, Randolph, North Carolina; NARA Roll: 1715; Page: 1B; Enumeration District: 0020; Image: 150.0; FHL #2341449. *Ancestry.com*. John Mcray, head; Evelena Mcray, age 9. *See also*: North Carolina, Birth Indexes, 1800-2000 [Database on-line]. *Ancestry.com*. McRae, Female, Birth – 13 Mar 1921; John W D McRae, father; Delphinie Potter, mother.

[583] 1930 US Federal Census; Census Place: New Hope, Randolph, North Carolina; NARA Roll: 1715; Page: 1B; Enumeration District: 0020; Image: 150.0; FHL #2341449. *Ancestry.com*. John Mcray, head; Geneva Mcray, age 6.

[584] North Carolina, Death Certificates, 1909-1975 [Database on-line]. *Ancestry.com*. Geneva McRae, 21 Jun 1932.

[585] 1930 US Federal Census; Census Place: New Hope, Randolph, North Carolina; Roll: 1715; Page: 1B; Enumeration District: 0020; Image: 150.0; FHL #2341449. *Ancestry.com*. John Mcray, head; J W Mcray, age 4.

Asheboro, Randolph, North Carolina.[586] He married **OUIDA WALDEN** on 8 Oct 1947 in Asheboro, Randolph, North Carolina.[587] He is **buried in Strieby Church Cemetery.**

24. LOVIE[3] POTTER (MARY JANE[2]HILL, EDWARD "NED"[1]HILL) was born Apr 1884 in Union, Randolph, North Carolina. She died 6 Feb 1953 in Pisgah, Randolph, North Carolina. She married **JAMES A DAVIS**, the son of **ANTHONY DAVIS** and **ANNIE CRUMP/HEARN**, 26 Feb 1911 in Randolph County. They are **both buried in Strieby Church Cemetery**. *[See Entry Above]*

a. **LOVIE POTTER** may have had the following child:

   i. **NETTY[4] POTTER** was born in Dec 1895, in Cedar Grove, Randolph, North Carolina.[588]

b. LOVIE POTTER and JAMES DAVIS had the following *adopted* child:

   i. **EARNEST DAVIS** was born about 1924 in Strieby (Union), Randolph, North

---

[586] North Carolina, Death Certificates, 1909-1975. [Database on-line]. *Ancestry.com*. Jerald Winfod Mcrae, 3 Jan 1974.

[587] North Carolina, Marriage Records, 1741-2011 [Databse on-line]. *Ancestry.com*. Gerald McRae and Oneita [*sic*-original says Ouita] Walden, 8 Oct 1947.

[588] 1900 US Federal Census; Census Place: Cedar Grove, Randolph, North Carolina; NARA Roll: 1212; Page: 2A; Enumeration District: 0082; FHL #1241212. *Ancestry.com*. Netty Potter, age 4.

Carolina.[589]

25. ALLER[3] EADIE (MARY JANE[2] HILL, EDWARD "NED"[1]HILL) was born in Oct 1891 in Cedar Grove, Randolph, North Carolina. She died 16 Jul 1921 in Strieby, Union township, Randolph County. She married **GREELY DAVIS,** the son of **WILLIAM DAVIS** and **JANE PARKER,** on 22 Dec 1904 in Randolph County. He died 24 Jul 1918 in Strieby, Union township, Randolph, North Carolina. They are **both buried in Strieby Church Cemetery**. [*See Entry Above*]

a. GREELEY DAVIS and ALLER EADIE had the following children:

- **i. CATHELINE[4] DAVIS** was born in 1908 in Strieby, Union, Randolph, North Carolina.[590] She may be the **CATHERINE DAVIS** living in New York in 1940, along with possible sister **NANCY (DAVIS) BENDER.**[591] No additional information has been identified by this author to date.
- **ii. ERNEST DAVIS** was born in 1909 in Strieby, Union, Randolph, North Carolina.[592]

---

[589] 1900 US Federal Census; Census Place: Cedar Grove, Randolph, North Carolina; NARA Roll: 1212; Page: 2A; Enumeration District: 0082; FHL #1241212. *Ancestry.com*. James Davis, head; Earnest Davis, age 6.

[590] 1910 US Federal Census; Census Place: New Hope, Randolph, North Carolina; NARA Roll: T624_1128; Page: 4B; Enumeration District: 0087; FHL #1375141. *Ancestry.com*. Greeley D Davis, head; Cathlene Davis, age 2.

[591] 1940 US Federal Census; Census Place: New York, New York, New York; NARA Roll: T627_2660; Page: 13A; Enumeration District: 31-1531. *Ancestry.com*. Catherine Davis, age 32; Nancy Bender, age 28.

[592] 1910 US Federal Census; Census Place: New Hope, Randolph, North Carolina; NARA Roll: T624_1128; Page: 4B; Enumeration District: 0087; FHL #1375141. *Ancestry.com*. Greeley D Davis, head; Ernest Davis, age 1.

iii. **ELLA MAE DAVIS** was born in 1912 in Strieby, Union, Randolph, North Carolina.[593]

iv. **NANCY JANE DAVIS** was born in 6 Nov 1912 in Strieby, Union, Randolph, North Carolina.[594] She died in Apr 1979, in the Bronx, New York.[595] Her married name was **BENDER**, but the identity of her husband has not been determined by this researcher to date.

v. **LOURINA "LURA" ANN DAVIS** was born in 1914 in Strieby, Union, Randolph, North Carolina.[596]

vi. **CALLIE DAVIS** was born in 15 Apr 1918 in Strieby, Union, Randolph, North Carolina.[597] She died 30 Oct 1987 in Asheboro, Randolph, North

---

[593] 1920 US Federal Census; Census Place: Union, Randolph, North Carolina; NARA Roll: T625_1318; Page: 9A; Enumeration District: 118; Image: 1274. *Ancestry.com*. Allie Davis, head; Ella M Davis, age 8.

[594] 1920 US Federal Census; Census Place: Union, Randolph, North Carolina; NARA Roll: T625_1318; Page: 9A; Enumeration District: 118; Image: 1274. *Ancestry.com*. Allie Davis, head; Nannie Davis, age 7.

[595] U.S. Social Security Applications and Claims Index, 1936-2007 [Database on-line]. *Ancestry.com*. Nancy Jane Bender, born 6 Nov 1912, Strieby, North Carolina; died Apr 1979. *See also*: U.S. Social Security Death Index, 1935-Current [Database on-line]. *Ancestry.com*. Nancy Bender, Apr 1979, New York.

[596] 1920 US Federal Census; Census Place: Union, Randolph, North Carolina; NARA Roll: T625_1318; Page: 9A; Enumeration District: 118; Image: 1274. *Ancestry.com*. Allie Davis, head; Lura Davis, age 6.

[597] 1920 US Federal Census; Census Place: Union, Randolph, North Carolina; NARA Roll: T625_1318; Page: 9A; Enumeration District: 118; Image: 1274. *Ancestry.com*. Allie Davis, head; Callie Davis, age 5.

Carolina.[598] She married (1) **GEORGE HENLEY Jr.**, son of **GEORGE HENLEY** and **MARTHA "METTA" COTTON**, on 19 Sep 1946, in Randolph County.[599] He died 27 Mar 1962 in Asheboro, Randolph, North Carolina and is **buried in Strieby Church Cemetery**.[600] She married (2) **WILLIAM PENSA "PENN" COBLE**, son of **ISRAEL MICHAEL COBLE** and her cousin **MINERVA A HILL**, on 18 Dec 1978, in Randolph County.[601] He died on 10 Apr 1995.[602]

vii. **LEWIS CLARENCE DAVIS** was born in 14 Mar 1918 in Strieby, Union, Randolph, North Carolina.[603] He died 19 Feb 2006 in North Carolina.[604]

24. **MARY ANN[3] HILL** (SARAH "SALLY"[2], EDWARD "NED"[1]) was born in Mar 1868 in Randolph County, North

---

[598] North Carolina, Death Indexes, 1908-2004 [Database on-line]. *Ancestry.com*. Callie Davis Coble, 30 Oct 1987.
[599] North Carolina, Marriage Records, 1741-2011 [Database on-line]. *Ancestry.com*. Callie Davis and Geo Henley Jr 19 Sep 1946.
[600] North Carolina, Death Certificates, 1909-1975 [Database on-line]. *Ancestry.com*. George Henley Jr., 27 Mar 1962.
[601] North Carolina, Marriage Collection, 1741-2004 [Database on-line]. *Ancestry.com*. Callie Henely and William Penn Coble, 18 Dec 1978.
[602] North Carolina, Death Indexes, 1908-2004 [Database on-line]. *Ancestry.com*. William Penn Coble, 10 Apr 1995.
[603] 1920 US Federal Census; Census Place: Union, Randolph, North Carolina; NARA Roll: T625_1318; Page: 9A; Enumeration District: 118; Image: 1274. *Ancestry.com*. Allie Davis, head; Louis Davis, age 1. See also: North Carolina, Birth Indexes, 1800-2000 [Database on-line]. *Ancestry.com*. Lewis Davis, 14 Mar 1918.
[604] U.S. Social Security Applications and Claims Index, 1936-2007 [Database on-line]. *Ancestry.com*. Lewis Clarence Davis, 19 Feb 2006.

Carolina. She died on 29 Jun 1931 in Strieby, Union, Randolph, NORTH CAROLINA. She married **CHARLES SMITHERMAN**, believed to be the (probable) son of **NOAH SMITHERMAN** and **LUCINDA SMITHERMAN** on 29 Jul 1883 in Randolph County, North Carolina. He was born in 1855 in Randolph County, North Carolina. He may have died in early 1900, before June, in Strieby, Union, Randolph, North Carolina. He is most likely buried in Strieby Church Cemetery. Mary Ann is **buried in Strieby Church Cemetery**.[*See Entry Above*]

a. CHARLES SMITHERMAN and MARY ANN HILL had the following children:

Figure 87: Bertis Smitherman.
Photo courtesy of Richard Jackson

i. **BERTIS[4] SMITHERMAN** was born on 21 Jun 1884 in Strieby, Union, Randolph, North

Carolina.[605] He died on 09 Jan 1982 in Strieby, Union, Randolph, North Carolina and is **buried in Strieby Church Cemetery**.[606] He never married.

ii. **ROY SMITHERMAN** was born on 20 Oct 1887 in Strieby, Union, Randolph, North Carolina. He died on 03 Sep 1889 in Strieby, Union, Randolph, North Carolina, and is **buried in Strieby Church Cemetery**.[607]

iii. **HARRISON SMITHERMAN** was born in Jul 1890 in Strieby, Randolph, North Carolina.[608] He died on 14 Jun 1977 in Strieby, Union, Randolph, North Carolina. He met and had a relationship with **LAURA EDNA NETTIE LASSITER**. She was born in May 1900 in Lassiter Mill, New Hope, Randolph, North Carolina. She died on 24 Jun 1980 in North Carolina.[609] They are **both buried in Strieby**

---

[605] 1900 US Federal Census; Census Place: Union, Randolph, North Carolina; NARA Roll: 1213; Page: 6B; Enumeration District: 0099; FHL #1241213. *Ancestry.com*. Mary Smitherman, head; Burtis Smitherman, age 14.

[606] North Carolina, Death Indexes, 1908-2004 [Database on-line]. *Ancestry.com*. Birtis Smitherman, 9 Jan 1982. *See also*: U.S. Find A Grave Index, 1700s-Current [Database on-line]. *Ancestry.com*. Bertis Smitherman, 9 Jan 1982.

[607] U.S. Find A Grave Index, 1700s-Current [Database on-line]. *Ancestry.com*. Roy Smitherman, 20 Oct 1887 – 3 Sep 1889.

[608] 1900 US Federal Census; Census Place: Union, Randolph, North Carolina; NARA Roll: 1213; Page: 6B; Enumeration District: 0099; FHL #1241213. *Ancestry.com*. Mary Smitherman, head; Harrison Smitherman, age 9.

[609] North Carolina, Death Indexes, 1908-2004 [Database on-line]. *Ancestry.com*. Edna Lassiter Everett, 9 May 1900-24 Jun 1980. *See also*: U.S.

Church Cemetery.

Figure 88: Winston Smitherman.
Photo courtesy of Richard Jackson.

iv. **WINSTON SMITHERMAN** was born on 01 Sep 1893 in Strieby, Union, Randolph, North Carolina.[610] He died on 24 Jul 1980 in Asheboro, Randolph, North Carolina and is **buried in Strieby Church Cemetery.**[611]

Find A Grave Index, 1700s-Current [Database on-line]. *Ancestry.com.* Edna Everett, 24 Jun 1980.

[610] 1900 US Federal Census; Census Place: Union, Randolph, North Carolina; NARA Roll: 1213; Page: 6B; Enumeration District: 0099; FHL #1241213. *Ancestry.com.* Mary Smitherman, head; Winston Smitherman, age 6.

[611] North Carolina, Death Indexes, 1908-2004 [Database on-line]. *Ancestry.com.* Winston Smitherman, 24 Jul 1980. *See also*: U.S. Find A Grave Index, 1700s-Current [Database on-line]. *Ancestry.com.* Winston Smitherman, 24 Jul 1980.

iv. **SARAH "SALLIE" M. SMITHERMAN** was born on 06 May 1898 in Strieby, Union, Randolph, North Carolina.[612] She died on 27 Mar 1961 in Strieby, Union, Randolph, North Carolina and is **buried in Strieby Church Cemetery**.[613]

Figure 89: Sarah Juanita Smitherman.

v. **SARAH JUANITA SMITHERMAN** was born on 09 Jan 1901 in Strieby, Union, Randolph, North Carolina.[614] She died on 29 Jul 1975 in

---

[612] 1900 US Federal Census; Census Place: Union, Randolph, North Carolina; NARA Roll: 1213; Page: 6B; Enumeration District: 0099; FHL #1241213. *Ancestry.com*. Mary Smitherman, head; Sarah Smitherman, age 4.
[613] North Carolina, Death Certificates, 1909-1975 [Database on-line]. *Ancestry.com*. Sallie Smitherman, 27 Mar 1961.
[614] 1910 US Federal Census; Census Place: Union, Randolph, North Carolina; NARA Roll: T624_1128; Page: 2B; Enumeration District: 0100; FHL #1375141. *Ancestry.com*. Mary Smitherman, head; Sary J Smitherman, age 9.

Asheboro, Randolph, North Carolina and is **buried in Strieby Church Cemetery.**[615] She married **GEORGE ULYSSES "GRANT" LASSITER**, son of **ULYSSES WINSTON LASSITER** and **ORA CLARA KEARNS** on 20 Apr 1946 in Asheboro, Randolph, North Carolina.[616] He was born on 18 Dec 1901 in Lassiter Mill, New Hope, Randolph, North Carolina and died 25 Jan 1989 in Lassiter Mill, New Hope, Randolph, North Carolina. He is also **buried in Strieby Church Cemetery.**[617]

26. **HAL[3] B. CRANFORD** (SARAH "SALLY"[2] HILL, EDWARD "NED"[1] HILL, EDMUND). He was born in Strieby, Union, Randolph, North Carolina about 1877. He died sometime after 1958. He married **BELLE CASSADY**, the daughter of **STEADMAN** and **LOVIE CASSADY** on 12 June 1902. She died in 1960. [*See Entry Above*]
    a. **HAL CRANFORD** and **BELLE CASSADY** had the following children:
        i. **(LUCY) ODESSA[4] M CRANFORD** was born about 1901 in Strieby, Union, Randolph, North

---

[615] North Carolina, Death Certificates, 1909-1975 [Database on-line]. *Ancestry.com*. Sarah Smitherman Lassiter, 29 Jul 1975.
[616] North Carolina, Marriage Records, 1741-2011 [Database on-line]. *Ancestry.com*. Sarah Juanita Smitherman and George U Lassiter, 20 Apr 1946.
[617] U.S. Find A Grave Index, 1700s-Current [Database on-line]. *Ancestry.com*. George Ulysses Lassiter, 18 Dec 1902 – 25 Jan 1989.

Carolina.[618] Her date of death has not been identified, but appears to be after 1990. She married **ERNEST GRANT** 22 Jul 1925 in Randolph County.[619] He died before 1940 when Odessa says she is a "widow."[620]

ii. **HAROLD BENSON CRANFORD** was born about 1904 in Strieby, Union, Randolph, North Carolina.[621] His date of death has not been learned. He married **HILDA CRAVEN**, on 13 Jan 1934, in Randolph County.[622]

iii. **CLARA BELLE CRANFORD** was born about 1906, in Strieby, Union, Randolph, North Carolina.[623] She was most likely the Clara Cranford who was a **teacher at Strieby School** in

---

[618] 1910 US Federal Census; Census Place: Asheboro, Randolph, North Carolina; Roll: T624_1128; Page: 19A; Enumeration District: 0076; FHL #1375141. *Ancestry.com*. Hall Cranford, head; Odessa Cranford, age 10.

[619] North Carolina, Marriage Records, 1741-2011 [Database on-line]. *Ancestry.com*. Lucy Odena [sic- original says Odessa] Cranford and Ernest Grant, 22 Jul 1925.

[620] 1940 US Federal Census; Census Place: Asheboro, Randolph, North Carolina; NARA Roll: T627_2961; Page: 15B; Enumeration District: 76-1. *Ancestry.com*. Odessa Grant, head.

[621] 1910 US Federal Census; Census Place: Asheboro, Randolph, North Carolina; NARA Roll: T624_1128; Page: 19A; Enumeration District: 0076; FHL #1375141. *Ancestry.com*. Hall Cranford, head; Benson Cranford, age 6.

[622] North Carolina, Marriage Records, 1741-2011 [Database on-line]. *Ancestry.com*. Benson Cranford and Hilda Craven, 13 Jan 1934.

[623] 1910 US Federal Census; Census Place: Asheboro, Randolph, North Carolina; NARA Roll: T624_1128; Page: 19A; Enumeration District: 0076; FHL #1375141. *Ancestry.com*. Hall Cranford, head; Clara Cranford, age 4. *See also*: North Carolina, Birth Indexes, 1800-2000 [Database on-line]. *Ancestry.com*. Clara Belle Cranford, Delayed Birth.

the 1920s.

iv. **ALBERT CRANFORD** was born about 1910, in Strieby, Union, Randolph, North Carolina.[624]

v. **JOHN OSCAR CRANFORD** was born about 1911, in Strieby, Union, Randolph, North Carolina.[625]

vi. **KATE BEATRICE PAULINE CRANFORD** was born about 1913 in Strieby, Union, Randolph, North Carolina.[626] She died 23 Oct 1990, in Greensboro, Guilford, North Carolina.[627] She married **WHIT MANLEY**, son of **RUFUS MANLEY** and **ANN RICHARDSON**, on 17 Dec 1946, in Guilford County, North Carolina.[628] He was born 9 Aug 1909 in Halifax County, North

[624] 1910 US Federal Census; Census Place: Asheboro, Randolph, North Carolina; NARA Roll: T624_1128; Page: 19A; Enumeration District: 0076; FHL #1375141. *Ancestry.com*. Hall Cranford, head; Albert Cranford, age 0.

[625] 1920 US Federal Census; Census Place: Asheboro, Randolph, North Carolina; NARA Roll: T625_1318; Page: 24A; Enumeration District: 96; Image: 692. *Ancestry.com*. Hall Cranford, head; Oscar Cranford, age 10. *See also*: North Carolina, Birth Indexes, 1800-2000 [Database on-line]. *Ancestry.com*. John Oscar Cranford, Delayed Birth.

[626] 1920 US Federal Census; Census Place: Asheboro, Randolph, North Carolina; NARA Roll: T625_1318; Page: 24A; Enumeration District: 96; Image: 692. *Ancestry.com*. Hall Cranford, head; Pauline Cranford, age 7. *See also*: North Carolina, Birth Indexes, 1800-2000 [Database on-line]. *Ancestry.com*. Katie Beatrice Pauline Cranford, Delayed Birth.

[627] North Carolina, Death Indexes, 1908-2004 [Database on-line]. *Anceestry.com*. Pauline Cranford Manley, 23 Oct. 1990.

[628] North Carolina, Marriage Records, 1741-2011 [Database on-line]. *Ancestry.com*. Pauline Cranford and Whit Manley, 17 Dec 1946.

Carolina.[629] He died 30 Dec 1991 in Greensboro, Guilford, North Carolina.[630]

vii. **JEWEL CRANFORD** was born about 1919 in Strieby, Union, Randolph, North Carolina. [631] She died in Feb 1986, in Wadesboro, Anson, North Carolina.[632]

27. **MAMIE[3] HILL** (JULIUS[2], EDWARD "NED"[1]) was born on 04 Mar 1884 in Lassiter Mill, New Hope, Randolph, North Carolina. She died on 23 Nov 1970 in Concord, Cabarrus, North Carolina. She married **ARCH POOLE**, son of **BENJAMIN POOLE** and **CHARLOTTE POOLE**, 27 Dec 1904, in Randolph County. He was born about 1879 in Montgomery County, North Carolina. He died in Tyson, Stanly County, North Carolina. *[See Entry Above]*

a. ARCH POOLE and MAMIE HILL had the following children:

i. **EMMA[4] POOLE** was born on 15 Nov 1906 in Davidson, North Carolina.[633] She died on 10 Nov 1987 in Albemarle, Stanly, North

---

[629] 1910 US Federal Census; Census Place: Brinkleyville, Halifax, North Carolina; NARA Roll: T624_1115; Page: 4B; Enumeration District: 0041; FHL #1375128. *Ancestry.com*. Rufus L Manly, head; Whit Manly, age 0.

[630] North Carolina, Death Indexes, 1908-2004 [Database on-line]. *Ancestry.com*. Whit Manley, 30 Dec 1991.

[631] 1920 US Federal Census; Census Place: Asheboro, Randolph, North Carolina; NARA Roll: T625_1318; Page: 24A; Enumeration District: 96; Image: 692. *Ancestry.com*. Hall Cranford, head; Jewel Cranford, age 1.

[632] U.S. Social Security Death Index, 1935-Current. *Ancestry.com*. Jewell Cranford, Feb 1986.

[633] 1910 US Federal Census; Census Place: Emmons, Davidson, North Carolina; NARA Roll: T624_1106; Page: 2A; Enumeration District: 0023; FHL #1375119. Archie Pool, head; Emma Pool, age 5.

Carolina.[634] She married **CLARENCE SMITH,** son of **LEROY SMITH** and **MAGGIE SMITH** on 11 Dec 1939, in Cabarrus County, North Carolina.[635] He died before Emma according to her death record where she was listed as "widowed."[636]

ii. **WILLIAM HOLTON POOLE** was born on 11 Jan 1909 in Davidson, North Carolina.[637] He died in Aug 1979 in Seagrove, Randolph, North Carolina.[638]

iii. **VELLON POOLE** was born in 1911 in North Carolina.[639]

iv. **COLON POOLE** was born about 1912 in North Carolina.[640]

v. **WOODROW WILSON POOLE** was born on

---

634 North Carolina, Death Indexes, 1908-2004 [Database on-line]. *Ancestry.com*. Emma Poole Smith, 10 Nov 1987.

635 North Carolina, Marriage Records, 1741-2011 [Database on-line]. *Ancestry.com*. Clarence Smith and Emma Pool, 11 Dec 1939.

636 North Carolina, Death Indexes, 1908-2004 [Database on-line]. *Ancestry.com*. Emma Poole Smith, 10 Nov 1987.

637 1910 US Federal Census; Census Place: Emmons, Davidson, North Carolina; NARA Roll: T624_1106; Page: 2A; Enumeration District: 0023; FHL #1375119. *Ancestry.com*. Archie Pool, head; William H. Pool, age 1.

638 U.S. Social Security Death Index, 1935-Current [Database on-line]. *Ancestry.com*. William Poole, Aug 1979.

639 1920 US Federal Census; Census Place: Union, Randolph, North Carolina; NARA Roll: T625_1318; Page: 10A; Enumeration District: 118; Image: 1276. *Ancestry.com*. Arch Poole, head; Vellon Poole, age 9.

640 1930 US Federal Census; Census Place: Tyson, Stanly, North Carolina; NARA Roll T635_1721; FHL #23441455; Page 240; Sheet 16A; Enumeration District 84-22; Image 1061. *Ancestry.com*. Arch Poole, head; Colon Poole, age 18.

26 Mar 1913 in Stanly County, North Carolina.[641] He died in 5 Jul 1987 in Charlotte, Mecklenburg, North Carolina.[642]

vi. **LACY POOLE** was born on 03 Sep 1915 in New Hope, Randolph, North Carolina.[643]

vii. **RALPH POOLE** was born on 30 Apr 1918 in North Carolina.[644] He died on 30 Apr 1918 in Charlotte, Mecklenburg, North Carolina.[645] He married **MARGARET KLUTZ**, daughter of **RAYMOND KLUTZ** and **LULA TURNER**, on 5 May 1945 in Stanly County, North Carolina.[646]

viii. **MARY POOLE** was born on 09 Mar 1921 in Concord, Randolph, North Carolina. She died on 17 Mar 1921 in Concord, Randolph, North

---

641 1920 US Federal Census; Census Place: Union, Randolph, North Carolina; NARA Roll: T625_1318; Page: 10A; Enumeration District: 118; Image: 1276. *Ancestry.com*. Arch Poole, head; Wilson Poole, age 7.

642 North Carolina, Death Indexes, 1908-2004 [Database on-line]. *Ancestry.com*. Woodrow Poole, 5 Jul 1987.

643 1920 US Federal Census; Census Place: Union, Randolph, North Carolina; NARA Roll: T625_1318; Page: 10A; Enumeration District: 118; Image: 1276. *Ancestry.com*. Arch Poole, head; Lacy [sic] Poole, age 4. *See also*: North Carolina, Birth Indexes, 1800-2000, [Database on-line]. *Ancestry.com*. Poole, male, colored, 3 Sep 1915; Archie Poole and Mamie Hill.

644 1920 US Federal Census; Census Place: Union, Randolph, North Carolina; NARA Roll: T625_1318; Page: 10A; Enumeration District: 118; Image: 1276. *Ancestry.com*. Arch Poole, head; Ralph Poole, age 1.

645 North Carolina, Death Indexes, 1908-2004 [Database on-line]. *Ancestry.com*. Ralph Poole, 28 Feb 1989.

646 North Carolina, Marriage Records, 1741-2011 [Database on-line]. *Ancestry.com*. Ralph Poole and Margaret Klutz, 5 May 1945.

Carolina.[647]

ix. **UNNAMED GIRL (LOUISA) POOLE** was born on 15 Apr 1923 in Concord, Randolph, North Carolina. She died on 15 Apr 1923 in New Hope, Randolph, North Carolina. She was **buried in Strieby Church Cemetery.**[648]

28. **CARL**[3] **HILL** (JULIUS[2], EDWARD "NED"[1]) was born in Jul 1893 in Strieby, Union, Randolph, North Carolina. He married **BERTHA McRAE,** daughter of **JOHN McRAE and LUCY ELLEN DENSON,** 4 May 1916, in Montgomery County, North Carolina. [*See Entry Above*]

   a. CARL HILL and BERTHA McRAE had the following children:

Figure 90: John Chester "JC" Hill. Photo courtesy of London Hill.:

---

[647] North Carolina, Death Certificates, 1909-1975 [Database on-line]. *Ancestry.com*. Mary Pool 17 Mar 1921.

[648] North Carolina, Death Certificates, 1909-1975 [Database on-line]. *Ancestry.com*. Unnamed (female) Pool. 15 Apr 1923. See also: Randolph County Death Book 10:677.

i. **JOHN CHESTER.[4] HILL** was born 22 Jul 1916, in Troy, Montgomery, North Carolina.[649] "JC" died on 6 Aug 1981, in Montgomery County, North Carolina.[650] He was divorced.

ii. **DAVID EDWARD HILL** was born 17 Jul 1918 in Randolph County, North Carolina.[651] He died 27 Jun 1958 in Asheboro, Randolph, North Carolina. According to his Death Certificate he was married to **MARIE RUSH**.[652] He is **buried in Strieby**

---

[649] 1920; Census Place: Troy, Montgomery, North Carolina; NARA Roll: T625_1311; Page: 4A; Enumeration District: 80; Image: 853. *Ancestry.com.* Carl E Hill, head; J Carl Hill, age 3. *See also*: U.S. WWII Draft Cards Young Men, 1940-1947 [Database on-line]. *Ancestry.com.* John Chester Hill, 22 Jul 1916. His home contact person was Ellen Handy, his grandmother who had married James Handy after John McRae had died, on 12 Nov 1938, in Montgomery County, North Carolina (North Carolina, Marriage Records, 1741-2011 [Database on-line: *Ancestry.com*], James Handy and Ellen McCrae, 12 Nov 1938).

[650] North Carolina, Death Indexes, 1908-2004 [Database on-line]. *Ancestry.com.* John Chester Hill, 6 Aug 1981. (Note: a different birth date is listed that is not supported by the records. However, his SSN is the same as his SSDI information. His SSDI information agrees with his Draft record's birth date and is consistent with the 1920 census information, *See*: U.S. Social Security Death Index, 1935-Current, [Database on-line]. *Ancestry.com.* John Hill, Aug 1981; SSN: 245-05-1333.)

[651] North Carolina, Birth Indexes, 1800-2000 [Database on-line]. *Ancestry.com.* Davie Edward Hill, 17 Jul 1918. *See also*: 1920; Census Place: Troy, Montgomery, North Carolina; NARA Roll: T625_1311; Page: 4A; Enumeration District: 80; Image: 853. *Ancestry.com.* Carl E Hill, head; David E Hill, age 1.

[652] North Carolina, Death Certificates, 1909-1975 [Database on-line]. *Ancestry.com.* David Edward Hill, 27 Jun 1958; wife: Marie Rush.

Church Cemetery.

iii. **SAMUEL HILL** was born 23 Oct 1922 in Troy, Montgomery, North Carolina.[653] He died 16 Apr 2002 in Charleston, Charleston, South Carolina. [654]

iv. **UNNAMED GIRL HILL**, was born 28 Dec 1924 and died on 30 Dec 1924, in Strieby, Union Township, Randolph, North Carolina. She is **buried in Strieby Church Cemetery**. [655]

v. **BERTHA MAE HILL** was born 3 Feb 1926 in Randolph County, North Carolina.[656] She married **LEROY HARVIN**, son of **MOSES HARVIN and BEULAH EPPS**, on 2 Mar 1946 in Forsyth County, North Carolina.[657]

vi. **ETHEL ALLENE HILL** was born 3 Aug 1928, in Randolph County, North Carolina.[658]She died in

---

[653] 1930 US Federal Census; Census Place: Troy, Montgomery, North Carolina; NARA Roll: 1708; Page: 7A; Enumeration District: 0014; Image: 317.0; FHL #2341442. *Ancestry.com*. John Mcray, head; Samuel Hill, age 7, "Grandson." *See also*: U.S. Social Security Applications and Claims Index, 1936-2007 [Database on-line]. *Ancestry.com*. Samuel Leroy Hill, b: 23 Oct 1922.

[654] U.S. Social Security Applications and Claims Index, 1936-2007 [Database on-line]. *Ancestry.com*. Samuel Leroy Hill, d: 16 Apr 2002.

[655] North Carolina, Deaths, 1906-1930 [Database on-line]. *Ancestry.com*. Unnamed Infant Hill (Female), b: 28 Dec 1924; d: 30 Dec 1924.

[656] North Carolina, Birth Indexes, 1800-2000 [Database on-line]. *Ancestry.com*. Bertha May Hill, 3 Feb 1926.

[657] North Carolina, Marriage Records, 1741-2011 [Database on-line]. *Ancestry.com*. Bertha Mae Hill and Leray [*sic*] Harvin, 2 Mar 1946.

[658] North Carolina, Birth Indexes, 1800-2000 [Database on-line]. *Ancestry.com*. Ethel Hill, 3 Aug 1928.

April 1995.[659] Her Social Security and North Carolina Death records indicate that her married name was "**DAVIS**."[660]

29. **THEODOCIA[3] DELIA HILL** (JULIUS[2], EDWARD "NED"[1]) was born in Nov 1894 in Strieby, Union, Randolph, North Carolina. She died 14 Feb 1997 in Winston-Salem, Forsyth, North Carolina. Her married name was "**WHITE**." She may have been married to **THOMAS WHITE**, and lived in Norfolk, Virginia, until her last years when she apparently moved with family in Winston-Salem. She is **buried in Strieby Church Cemetery**. [*See Entry Above*].
    a. THEODOCIA HILL reportedly had the following children:
        i. **JOHN CLIFTON[4] HILL** was born in 1914 in Strieby, Union, Randolph, North Carolina.[661] He died 7 Nov 1988, in Winston-Salem, Forsyth, North Carolina.[662]

---

[659] U.S. Social Security Applications and Claims Index, 1936-2007 [Database on-line]. *Ancestry.com*. Ethel Allene Hill (Claim on 3 May 1995 listed name as Ethel Davis). *See also*: North Carolina, Death Indexes, 1908-2004 [Database on-line]. *Ancestry.com*. Ethel Hill Davis, 24 Apr 1995.

[660] U.S. Social Security Applications and Claims Index, 1936-2007 [Database on-line]. *Ancestry.com*. Ethel Allene Hill (Claim on 3 May 1995 listed name as Ethel Davis). *See also*: North Carolina, Death Indexes, 1908-2004 [Database on-line]. *Ancestry.com*. Ethel Hill Davis, 24 Apr 1995.

[661] 1920 US Federal Census; Census Place: Union, Randolph, North Carolina; NARA Roll: T625_1318; Page: 8B; Enumeration District: 118; Image: 1273. *Ancestry.com*. Julius Hill, head; Clifton Hill, age 6, "grandson." His World War II Draft registration listed "Theodoshan Hill" as his mother. *See*: U.S. WWII Draft Cards Young Men, 1940-1947 [Database on-line]. *Ancestry.com*. John Clifton Hill, born 20 Mar 1914.

[662] North Carolina, Death Indexes, 1908-2004 [Database on-line]. *Ancestry.com*. John Clifton Hill, 7 Nov 1988.

ii. **CHARLIE[4] HILL** was born in 1916 in Strieby, Union, Randolph, North Carolina.[663]

iii. **DOROTHY (HELEN?) HILL** was born about 1918 in Strieby, Union, Randolph, North Carolina.[664] She may be the **HELEN HILL** born 7 Jun 1918 in Randolph County, North Carolina to a **HENRY HILL and DELIA THEODOCIA HILL**.[665]

30. **ERNEST MARVIN[3] HILL** (JULIUS[2], EDWARD "NED"[1]) was born about 1903 in Strieby, Union, Randolph, North Carolina.[666] He died 23 Mar 1970 in Winston-Salem, Forsyth, North Carolina.[667] He married **ANNIE MAE CAVE**, daughter of **WASHINGTON CAVE and SELDREA/SYRELLA GRATT** of Farmville, South Carolina, on 27 May 1923 in Winston-Salem, Forsyth, North Carolina.[668] **ANNIE MAE** was born 28 Oct 1905 in South Carolina and died on 22 Jun 1973 in Winston-Salem,

---

[663] 1920 US Federal Census; Census Place: Union, Randolph, North Carolina; NARA Roll: T625_1318; Page: 8B; Enumeration District: 118; Image: 1273. *Ancestry.com*. Julius Hill, head; Charlie Hill, age 5, "grandson."

[664] 1920 US Federal Census; Census Place: Union, Randolph, North Carolina; NARA Roll: T625_1318; Page: 8B; Enumeration District: 118; Image: 1273. *Ancestry.com*. Julius Hill, head; Dorthy Hill, age 1½, "granddaughter."

[665] North Carolina, Birth Indexes, 1800-2000 [Database on-line]. *Ancestry.com*. Helen Hill, 7 Jun 1918.

[666] 1910 US Federal Census; Census Place: Union, Randolph, North Carolina; NARA Roll: T624_1128; Page: 2B; Enumeration District: 0100; FHL #1375141. *Ancestry.com*. Julius Hill, head; Ernest Hill, age 7.

[667] North Carolina, Death Certificates, 1909-1975 [Database on-line]. *Ancestry.com*. Ernest Hill Sr., 23 Mar 1970.

[668] North Carolina, Marriage Records, 1741-2011 [Database on-line]. *Ancestry.com*. Ernest Hill and Annie Mae Cave, 27 May 1923.

Forsyth, North Carolina.[669] She was a **teacher at Strieby School** during the 1920s. [*See Entry Above*]

a. ERNEST MARVIN HILL and ANNIE MAE CAVE had the following child:
   i. **ERNEST MARVIN (JR.)[4] HILL** was born about 1928 in Winston-Salem, Forsyth, North Carolina.[670]

---

[669] North Carolina, Death Certificates, 1909-1975 [Database on-line]. *Ancestry.com*. Annie Mae Hill, 22 Jun 1923.

[670] 1930 US Federal Census; Census Place: Winston-Salem, Forsyth, North Carolina; NARA Roll: 1690; Page: 39A; Enumeration District: 0051; Image: 1213.0; FHL #2341424. *Ancestry.com*. Ernest M. Hill, head; Ernest M. Hill, age 2.

Figure 91: Clarence Hays Hill (1917-1958), Grandson of Arthur Haze Hill. Photo courtesy of Christine Hill.

Figure 92: Katherine (Polk) "Granny Kate" Lassiter. Photo courtesy of Patrice Lassiter Bryant.

Descendants of MILES and HEALY LASSITER

Generation 1

1. **MILES[1] LASSITER** was born between 1775 and 1777 in Lassiter Mill, New Hope, Randolph, North Carolina.[671] He died on 22 June 1850 in Lassiter Mill, New Hope,

[671] 1850 US Federal Census, Free Schedule, Southern Division, Randolph, North Carolina; Census Place: Southern Division, Randolph, North Carolina; Roll: M432_641; Page: 136; Image: 285. *Ancestry.com*. Miles Lassiter.

Randolph, North Carolina.[672] He married **HEALY PHILLIPS** about 1810 in New Hope, Randolph, North Carolina.[673] She was born in 1780 in North Carolina. She died in 1845 in Lassiter Mill, New Hope, Randolph, North Carolina.[674]

a. MILES LASSITER and HEALY PHILLIPS had the following children:

   i. **EMSLEY PHILLIPS**[2] **LASSITER/LASTER** was born on 01 May 1811 in Lassiter Mill, New Hope, Randolph, North Carolina.[675] He died on 10 March 1892 in Indianapolis, Marion, Indiana.[676] He married **ELIZABETH WINBURN**, daughter of **THOMAS WINBURN and ANNIE JAMES**[677] on 03 April 1845 in Rush County,

---

[672] Miles Lassiter Obituary, *Friends Review*, 1850, iii: 700.

[673] Statement of J. Worth, 21 January 1851, Original Letter is in the possession of Patrice Lassiter Bryant, Greensboro, North Carolina. *See also*, Randolph County, North Carolina, Record of Deeds Book 22, 1839-1841, FHL #19368, pp. 356-357. John Newsom to Ezekiel Lassiter (Deed of Trust), 20 June 1840: "Helley Phillips & her heirs or children had by Miles Lassiter..."

[674] Statement of J. Worth, 21 January 1851. Worth states that "Helia" died about five years before.

[675] Handwritten birth record in possession of Patrice Lassiter Bryant.

[676] Indiana Deaths, 1882-1920 [Database on-line].*Ancestry.com.* Enssly Laster, 10 March 1892, County Board of Health: Indianapolis.

[677] Emsley Lassiter. (n.d.). *Lawrence Carter Papers*. Carthage Public Library, Carthage, Indiana.

Indiana.[678] She was born on 24 July 1818 in Halifax County, North Carolina. She died on 21 April 1908 in Center (Marion), Grant, Indiana.[679]

ii. **ABIGAIL PHILLIPS LASSITER** was born in September 1812 in Lassiter Mill, New Hope, Randolph, North Carolina.[680] She died in 1920, at home in Lassiter Mill, New Hope, Randolph, North Carolina. She is **buried in an unmarked grave in Strieby Church Cemetery**.[681]

iii. **COLIER PHILLIPS LASSITER** was born on 06 November 1815 in Lassiter Mill, New Hope, Randolph, North Carolina.[682] He died about 1887 in New

---

[678] Rush County, Indiana, Marriage Records, 1845, p. 152. Emsley Lassiter and Elizabeth Winburn: License, 28 March 1845; Marriage, 3 April 1845 (incorrectly transcribed as 8 April in index; Emsley's name incorrectly transcribed in index). General index to marriages, 1822-1907, FHL#1630369 Items 3-4; Marriage records v. 6-8, 1843-1861, FHL#1630189.

[679] Find A Grave Memorial# 85281546, *Findagrave.com*, Elizabeth Laster. Birth: Jul. 24, 1829 [*sic*-however, by reviewing all census records and marriage record she was more likely born about 1818]; Death: Apr. 21, 1908; Burial: Estates of Serenity, Marion, Grant County, Indiana; Plot: B26 L23.

[680] Handwritten birth record in possession of Patrice Lassiter Bryant.

[681] Information provided by Kate Lassiter Jones, in September 1982.

[682] Handwritten birth record in possession of Patrice Lassiter Bryant.

Hope, Randolph, North Carolina.[683] He married **KATHERINE POLK**, (probably) the daughter of **MARY POLK** and granddaughter of **CHARITY (POLK?) LASSITER**, on 26 September 1854 in Asheboro, Randolph, North Carolina.[684] She was born on 07 March 1832 most likely in either Davidson County or Randolph County, North Carolina.[685] She died on 19 December 1906 in Lassiter Mill, New Hope, Randolph, North Carolina.[686] She is

---

683 *Randolph County, North Carolina, Deeds,* 1887, *38*:288. "Abigail, Colier and Kate Lassiter to Jenny Lassiter." This is the last known record of Colier Lassiter. By 1893 his land was embroiled in a lawsuit and divided and distributed to his heirs in "*Anderson Smitherman et al v. Solomon Kearns et Ux.*" Deed Book 248:156.

684 North Carolina, Marriages, 1759-1979, index. *FamilySearch*, Calier Lassiter and Catharine Polk, 26 Sep 1854; Randolph, North Carolina. FHL #6,330,307.

685 1850 US Federal Census; Census Place: Southern Division, Randolph, North Carolina; Roll: M432_641; Page: 136A; Image: 278. *Ancestry.com*. Jack Lassiter, head; Charity Lassiter, age Catherine Lassiter, age 19. *See also*: 1870 US Federal Census; Census Place: New Hope, Randolph, North Carolina; Roll: M593_1156; Page: 407B; Image: 264; Family History Library Film: 552655. *Ancestry.com*. Collier Lassiter, head; Catharine Lassiter, age 38; & Charity Lassiter, age 75. *Also*: 1880 US Federal Census; Census Place: New Hope, Randolph, North Carolina; Roll: 978; Family History Film: 1254978; Page: 184A; Enumeration District: 223; Image: 0659. *Ancestry.com*. Calier Lassiter, head; Catherine Lassiter, wife, age 44; Mary Polk, relationship not specified, age 72.

686 Tombstone, Strieby Congregational United Church of Christ Cemetery, Strieby Church Road, Asheboro, North Carolina,

buried in Strieby Church Cemetery. He also had a relationship with **LAURA ANN E. WILLIAMS**. She was born on 07 January 1831 in Randolph County, North Carolina.[687]

iv. **SUSANNAH PHILLIPS LASSITER** was born on 03 October 1817 in New Hope, Randolph, North Carolina.[688] She died after 1854 in New Hope, Randolph, North Carolina.

v. **WILEY PHILLIPS LASSITER** was born on 13 May 1820 in New Hope, Randolph, North Carolina.[689] He died after 1860, most likely in Fayetteville, Cumberland, North Carolina.[690] He married **ELIZABETH RIDGE** about 1845 in Asheboro, Randolph, North

---

"Katie, wife of Calier Lassiter. Birth March 7, 1832, death December 19, 1906".

[687] Vidales. (Spring 1999). Randolph County, North Carolina Apprentice Bonds, 1840-1841, The *Genealogical Journal* by the Randolph County Genealogical Society, pp. XXIII(2): 7-8. Nov 1840: "Sheriff to bring children of color, Laure Ann Williams, -10, & Martiba Williams, -8; 1 Feb 1841: Commissioner Drake, Master: Wm Burney, bond with Jesse Walker not to remove from county; child: Laura Ann E. Williams, orphan 10, 7th last month.

[688] Handwritten birth record in possession of Patrice Lassiter Bryant.

[689] Handwritten birth record in possession of Patrice Lassiter Bryant.

[690] Wiley Lassiter is last found living with his family in Fayetteville in 1860 census, Year: 1860; Census Place: Fayetteville, Cumberland, North Carolina; Roll: M653_894; Page: 248; Image: 498.

Carolina.[691] She was born about 1830 in Randolph County, North Carolina. She died after 1870 in Randolph County, North Carolina.

vi. **NANCY PHILLIPS LASSITER** was born in February 1823 in New Hope, Randolph, North Carolina.[692] She died about 1890 in New Hope, Randolph, North Carolina.[693] She married **CALVIN DUNSON** about 1852 in Randolph

---

[691] 1850 US Census, Free Schedule, Southern Division, Randolph, North Carolina; NARA Roll: M432_641, *Ancestry.com*, Page: 136; Image: 285; Family 816: Willie Lassiter, head. There is no county marriage record for this couple, however, the marriage record of their daughter Nancy Jane Lassiter and Thomas Bryant records her mother's maiden name as "Betsy Ridge." *See*: Randolph County Marriage Registers 3:42, Jane Lassiter to Thomas Bryant.

[692] Handwritten birth record in possession of Patrice Lassiter Bryant.

[693] Vidales. (Summer 2011).*The Genealogical Journal* by the Randolph County Genealogical Society, pp. XXXV(2): 45-46. Carol Lawrence Vidales, "William Dunston-1892," Randolph County Estates: Diffee-Dumas. Petition for sale of land for division, filed 23 Nov 1892. Solomon Kearns & wife Adelaide Kearns vs Anderson Smitherman & wife Ellen Smitherman, Mamie Hill, Wm Dunston. Calvin Dunston died intestate about ten years ago, leaving a widow who has since died. Dunston left surviving your petitions Adalade Kearns, wife of Solomon, Ellen Smitherman, wife of Anderson, Martha Dunston who intermarried with Julius Hill and died, leaving surviving the deft. Mamie Hill, now aged 8 or 9 years, Rebecca Dunston, who died leaving surviving Wm Dunston, now about 16 years, and Harris Dunston, his children and only heirs at law. Harris Dunston sold his interest to Anderson Smitherman. Land in New Hope Township by J.T. Thornburg, Clark Loflin & other, 52 acres. Includes affidavit of J.W. Birkhead that partition could not be made without injury to the parties. J.W. Birkhead was appointed *guardian ad litem* of Mamie Hill & Wm Dunston.

County, North Carolina.[694] He was born about 1818 in Wake County, North Carolina.[695] He died about 1879 in New Hope, Randolph, North Carolina.[696] She also had an unknown relationship with **J. G. HOAGIN** that landed her in court where she charged him in a bastardy case.

vii. **JANE PHILLIPS LASSITER** was born on 07 January 1825 in New Hope, Randolph, North Carolina.[697] She died after 1893 in Randolph County, or possibly Davidson or Rowan County,

[694] 1860 US Federal Census, free schedule, Randolph County, North Carolina (NARA #M653-910), p.148. Calvin Dunson, head. There is no county marriage record for this couple. *See also*: Vidales. (Summer 2011). *The Genealogical Journal by the Randolph County Genealogical Society,* pp. XXXV(2): 45-46. Carol Lawrence Vidales, "William Dunston-1892," Randolph County Estates: Diffee-Dumas. Petition for sale of land for division, filed 23 Nov 1892.

[695] 1840; Census Place: Wake, North Carolina; NARA Roll: 374, *Ancestry.com*, Page: 136; Image: 761; FHL #0018098. Name: Calvin Burson [image says Calvin Dunson]

[696] 1880 US Census, population schedule, Randolph County, North Carolina, New Hope Township (NARA #T9-978), *Ancestry.com*, p. 1. Nancy Dunson, "Wid," head of household. *See also*: Vidales. (Summer 2011).*The Genealogical Journal by the Randolph County Genealogical Society,* pp. XXXV(2):45-46. "William Dunston-1892," Randolph County Estates: Diffee-Dumas. Petition for sale of land for division, filed 23 Nov 1892.

[697] Handwritten birth record in possession of Patrice Lassiter Bryant.

North Carolina.[698]

Generation 2

2. **EMSLEY PHILLIPS[2] LASSITER/LASTER** (MILES[1]) was born on 01 May 1811 in New Hope, Randolph, North Carolina. Hedied on 10 March 1892 in Indianapolis, Marion, Indiana. He married **ELIZABETH WINBURN**, daughter of **THOMAS WINBURN** and **ANNIE JAMES** on 03 April 1845 in Rush County, Indiana. She was born on 24 July 1818 in Halifax County, North Carolina. She died on 21 April 1908 in Center (Marion), Grant, Indiana. *[See Generation 1, above]*
   a. EMSLEY PHILLIPS LASSITER and ELIZABETH WINBURN had the following children:
      i. **SARAH A[3] LASSITER** was born in 1848 in Ripley, Rush, Indiana.[699]
      ii. **MARY ELISABETH LASSITER** was born in 1849 in Ripley, Rush, Indiana.[700]
      iii. **CHRISTINA LASSITER/LASTER** was

---

[698] Randolph County, North Carolina Superior Court Orders and Decrees 2:308-309; FHL #0475265. Jane is listed to receive a share of the land. No record of her has been found after this date.
[699] 1860 US Federal Census; Census Place: Ripley, Rush, Indiana; NARA Roll: M653_294, *Ancestry.com*, Page: 710; Image: 214; FHL #803294. Erusly Lasitur (Image says Emsly Lasitur).
[700] 1860 US Federal Census; Census Place: Ripley, Rush, Indiana; NARA Roll: M653_294, Page: 10; Image: 214; FHL #803294. *Ancestry.com*. Erusly Lasitur (Image says Emsly Lasitur).

born in June 1850 in Ripley, Rush, Indiana.[701] She died after 1910 in Marion, Grant, Indiana.[702] She married **JOSEPH T. OVERMAN** on 01 May 1881 in Rush County, Indiana.[703] He was born in July 1859 in Indiana. He died between 1900 and 1910 in Marion, Grant, Indiana.[704]

iv. **NANCY LASSITER/LASTER** was born in 1851 in Ripley, Rush, Indiana.[705] She married **WILLIAM PETTIFORD** on 07 November 1888 in Grant County, Indiana.[706] He was born in Indiana.

v. **MICA LASSITER** was born in 1852 in

---

[701] 1860 US Federal Census; Census Place: Ripley, Rush, Indiana; NARA Roll: M653_294, Page: 710; Image: 214; FHL #803294.*Ancestry.com.* Erusly Lasitur (Image says Emsly Lasitur).

[702] 1910 US Federal Census; Census Place: Marion Ward 2, Grant, Indiana; NARA Roll: T624_352, Page: 7B; Enumeration District: 0051; Image: 145; FHL #1374365.*Ancestry.com.*Christina Overman, 46, widowed, servant. This is the last census where she was identified.

[703] Indiana Marriage Collection, 1800-1941 [Database on-line]. *Ancestry.com.* Name: Joseph T. Overman; Spouse Name: Christina Laster; Marriage Date: 1 May 1881; Marriage County: Rush; Marriage Book 11: 462.

[704] 1910 US Federal Census; Census Place: Marion Ward 2, Grant, Indiana; NARA Roll: T624_352, Page: 7B; Enumeration District: 0051; Image: 145; FHL #1374365. *Ancestry.com.* Christina Overman, 46, widowed, servant.

[705] 1860 US Federal Census; Census Place: Ripley, Rush, Indiana; NARA Roll: M653_294, Page: 710; Image: 214; FHL: #803294. *Ancestry.com.* Erusly Lasitur (Image says Emsly Lasitur).

[706] Indiana Marriage Collection, 1800-1941 [Database on-line *Ancestry.com.* Name: Wm Pettiford; Spouse Name: Nancy Laster; Marriage Date: 7 Nov 1888; Marriage County: Grant; Marriage Book 8: 351.

Ripley, Rush, Indiana.[707]

vi. **WYLEY LASSITER/LASTER** was born in March 1852 in Ripley, Rush, Indiana.[708] He married (1) **ANNIE JONES** on 10 November 1877 in Indianapolis, Marion, Indiana.[709]Annie and Wiley appear to have separated by 1880.[710]He married (2) **CARRIE BROWN** on 11 October 1884 in Chicago, Cook, Illinois. She was born in 1855 in Chicago, Cook, Illinois.[711] She appears to

---

[707] 1860 US Federal Census; Census Place: Ripley, Rush, Indiana; NARA Roll: M653_294, Page: 710; Image: 214; FHL #803294. *Ancestry.com*. Erusly Lasitur (Image says Emsly Lasitur).

[708] 1860 US Federal Census; Census Place: Ripley, Rush, Indiana; NARA Roll: M653_294, Page: 710; Image: 214; FHL #803294. *Ancestry.com*. Erusly Lasitur (Image says Emsly Lasitur).

[709] Indiana, Marriages, 1780-1992 [Database on-line] *FamilySearch* spouse: Annie Jones; groom's name: Wiley Laster; bride's name: Annie Jones; marriage date: 10 Nov 1877; marriage place: Indianapolis, Marion, Indiana; indexing project (batch) number: M01331-4; system origin: Indiana-EASy source film number: 499373.

[710] R L Polk and Co.'s Indianapolis Directory 1880, p 228 [Database on-line]. *Ancestry.com*. Annie Laster (col'd, wid Wiley) res 120 Tremont. Although she lists herself as a widow, this may simply be an attempt to avoid publically admitting to a separation and *de facto* divorce. Wiley is shown living at 962 N Mississippi. There is no evidence that there is any other contemporary Wiley who would have in fact died.

[711] Cook County, Illinois, Marriages Index, 1871-1920 [Database on-line]. *Ancestry.com*. FHL #1030142. Name: Wiley Laster; Age: 31; Gender: Male; Birth Year: about 1853; Birth Place: Chicago, Cook, Illinois; Marriage Type: Marriage; Marriage Date: 11 Oct 1884; Spouse Name: Carrie Brown; Spouse

have died by 1900.[712]He married (3) **EMMA (LNU)** about 1904, place unidentified.[713] She was born about 1855 in Indiana. She apparently died between 1910 and 1920.[714] He also had a relationship with **WINNIE** or **MINNIE ADAMS WASHINGTON**.[715]

Age: 30; Spouse Gender: Female; Spouse Birth Place: Chicago, Cook, Illinois; Spouse Marital Status: Married.

[712] 1900 US Federal Census; Census Place: Indianapolis, Marion, Indiana; NARA Roll: T623_388, *Ancestry.com*, Page: 5A; Enumeration District: 53. Wiley Laster, 48, boarder, "Widowed."

[713] 1910 US Federal Census; Census Place: Indianapolis Ward 3, Marion, Indiana; NARA Roll: T624_367, Page: 1A; Enumeration District: 0070; Image: 204; FHL #1374380. *Ancestry.com*. Wriley Loster (sic-Wiley Laster); 56 -- Married (3) - this marriage - 6 years; Emma Loster (sic-Emma Laster) 55 -- Married (2) - mother of 1 child 0 living.

[714] 1920 US Federal Census; Census Place: Indianapolis Ward 3, Marion, Indiana; NARA Roll: T625_451, Page: 16B; numeration District: 64; Image: 743.*Ancestry.com.* Name: Willy Laster, 60 – widowed.

[715] The marriage of Wyley/Wiley's son Wiley, lists his mother in one record as Winnie Washington and in another as Minnie Adams. Winnie Adams married a George Washington in 1904. *See*: Indiana, Marriages, 1780-1992, index [Database on-line]. *FamilySearch.* Wiley Laster in entry for Wiley Laster and Minnie E Cowan, 12 Nov 1918; citing reference 193; FHL #499,415. Winnie Washington is named as the mother.
See also: Indiana, Marriages, 1780-1992, index, *FamilySearch.* Wiley Laster in entry for Wiley Laster and Minnie E. Cowan, Nov 1918; citing reference p. 225; FHL #413,547, Minnie Adams is named as mother in this record.
In 1904, Winnie Adams married George Washington: Indiana, Marriages, 1780-1992, index: George Washington and Winnie Adams, 23 Mar 1904; citing reference p. 270; FHL #499,383. *FamilySearch.*
In the 1900 census, Winnie Adams, "Widowed," lists a son Wiley Adams, age 16. Wiley Laster, "Widowed," is also living in the household. Since there is

vii. **PENINA LASSITER/LASTER** was born in May 1854 in Ripley, Rush, Indiana.[716] She died sometime between 1931 and 1940, in Marion, Grant, Indiana.[717] She married **TURNER A NEWSOM**, son of **WILLIAM H NEWSOM and MARTHA BROWN** on 03 August 1880 in Rush County, Indiana.[718] He was born in February 1855 in Indiana. Turner and Penina appear to have separated around 1907, after which she reports being a "widow,"[719] and Turner returns to Carthage to live with his brother as "single."[720] Turner died between 1910

---

no identified marriage record for this couple, it is understandable that Wiley would be listed under his mother's last name. As many do once reaching adulthood, Wiley apparently took the Laster name and can be found living with his father briefly later on.

716 1860 US Federal Census; Census Place: Ripley, Rush, Indiana; NARA Roll: M653_294, Page: 710; Image: 214; FHL #803294. *Ancestry.com*. Erusly Lasitur (Image says Emsly Lasitur).

717 US City Directories, 1822-1995 [Database on-line]. Marion, Indiana, City Directory, 1931. *Ancestry.com*. Penina Newsome (wid Turner), h 1202 S Nebraska.

718 Indiana Marriage Collection, 1800-1941 [Database on-line], *Ancestry.com*, Name: Turner A. Newsom Spouse Name: Pennina Laster; Marriage Date: 3 Aug 1880; Marriage County: Rush; Source Title 1: Rush County, Indiana Book: 11: 381.

719 1910 US Federal Census; Census Place: Marion Ward 2, Grant, Indiana; Roll: T624_352; Page: 11A; Enumeration District: 0051; FHL microfilm: 1374365. *Ancestry.com*. Penina Newsome, "widowed."

720 1910 US Federal Census; Census Place: Carthage Ward 6, Rush, Indiana; Roll: T624_377; Page: 10B; Enumeration District: 0116; FHL microfilm:

and 1920 in Carthage, Rush, Indiana.[721] He's buried in Riverside Cemetery, Carthage, Rush, Indiana.[722]

viii. **WILLIAM "QUIT" LASSITER/LASTER** was born in 1857 in Ripley, Rush, Indiana.[723] He married **MARTHA WATKINS** on 31 December 1912 in Detroit, Oakland, Michigan.[724] She was born in 1867.

ix. **MARY ANNA LASSITER** was born about 1859 in Ripley, Rush, Indiana.[725] She married **JAMES N WEAVER**, son

---

1374390. *Ancestry.com*. Thomas Newsom, head; Turner Newsom, brother, "single."

[721] Turner was last found in the 1920 US Federal Census (*See above). See also*: Find A Grave Memorial #31143643, *Findagrave.com*, Turner Newsom. Death: unknown; Burial: Riverside Cemetery, Carthage, Rush County, Indiana.

[722] U.S., Find A Grave Index, 1700s-Current (2012) [Database on-line]. Riverside Cemetery, Carthage, Indiana. *Ancestry.com*. Turner Newsom, n.d. Find A Grave Memorial# 31143643.

[723] 1860 US Federal Census; Census Place: Ripley, Rush, Indiana; NARA Roll: M653_294, Page: 710; Image: 214; FHL #803294. *Ancestry.com.* Erusly Lasitur (Image says Emsly Lasitur).

[724] Michigan, Marriages, 1868-1925, *FamilySearch.org*. Groom's name: Wm. Laster; groom's age: 49 years; groom's birth date: 1863; groom's birthplace: Indiana; bride's name: Martha Watkins; bride's age: 45 years; bride's birth date: 1867; marriage date: 31 Dec 1912; marriage place: Detroit, Oakland, Michigan; groom's father: Ensley [*sic*] Laster; groom's mother: Elizabeth Limber [*sic*]; digital folder number: 42.

[725] 1860 US Federal Census; Census Place: Ripley, Rush, Indiana; NARA Roll: M653_294, Page: 710; Image: 214; FHL #803294. *Ancestry.com*. Erusly Lasitur (Image says Emsly Lasitur).

of **HENRY WEAVER** and **SARAH BURDEN** on 17 March 1894 in Grant County, Indiana.[726] He was born in 1856 in Mill, Grant, Indiana. He died in 1943 in Weaver, Grant, Indiana.[727]

x. **ANNIE LASSITER** was born in 1867 in Ripley, Rush, Indiana.[728]

3. **COLIER PHILLIPS[2] LASSITER** (MILES[1]) was born on 06 November 1815 in Lassiter Mill, Randolph, North Carolina. He died about 1887 in New Hope, Randolph, North Carolina. He married **KATHERINE POLK,** (probably) the daughter of **MARY POLK** and granddaughter of **CHARITY (POLK?) LASSITER** on 26 September 1854 in Asheboro, Randolph, North Carolina. She was born on 07 March 1832 in North Carolina. She died on 19 December 1906 in Lassiter Mill, New Hope, Randolph, North Carolina. He also had a relationship with **LAURA ANNE WILLIAMS.** She was born on 07 January 1831 in Randolph County, North Carolina. **KATHERINE (POLK) LASSITER** is **buried in Strieby Church Cemetery.** (*See above entry*)

    a. COLIER PHILLIPS LASSITER and LAURA ANN E. WILLIAMS had the following child:

---

[726] Indiana Marriage Collection, 1800-1941 [database on-line], *Ancestry.com.* Name: James M Weaver; Spouse Name: Mary Lassiter; Marriage Date: 25 Jul 1883; Marriage County: Grant; Marriage Book: 7: 199.

[727]The Pettiford Family of North Carolina - Past & Present, *Tribalpages.com.* Admin: Susan Hall, Edited: October 23 2013. Retrieved from: http://pettifordsofnc.tribalpages.com

[728] 1880 US Census, population schedule, Rush County, Indiana, Ripley, (NARA #T9-0308), 62. Emsley Lasiter, head.

i. **BOY[3] WILLIAMS** was born in November 1850 in Randolph County, North Carolina.[729]

b. COLIER PHILLIPS LASSITER and KATHERINE POLK (POPE) had the following children:

i. **BETHANA MARTITIA[3] LASSITER** was born in February 1856 in Lassiter Mill, New Hope, Randolph, North Carolina.[730] She died on 11 July 1917 in Cedar Grove, Randolph, North Carolina.[731] She married **POSTELL HENLEY**, son of **EASTER HENLEY** on 20 March 1879 in Asheboro, Randolph, North Carolina.[732] He was born in April 1854 in Randolph, North Carolina.[733] He died on 07 June 1925 in Cedar Grove,

---

[729] Calyer Phillips Bastardy Bond. (May Term 1851) *Minutes of the Court of Common Pleas and Quarter Sessions, Randolph County, North Carolina.* FHL #0019652 or #0470212. *See also*: Vidales. (1999). Bastardy Bonds, 1850-1859. *The Genealogical Journal* by the Randolph County Genealogical Society, Volume XVIII(2):16. North Carolina State Archives call number, C.R. 081.102.5. "Mother Lorey Ann Williams."

[730] 1860 US Federal Census; Census Place: Western Division, Randolph, North Carolina; NARA Roll: M653_910; Page: 212; Image: 429; FHL #803910. *Ancestry.com*. Cal Lassiter, head; Bethana Lassiter, age 4.

[731] Randolph County, North Carolina Deaths, Book 4:204. Martitia Henley.

[732] North Carolina, Marriage Records, 1741-2011 [Database on-line]. *Ancestry.com*. Marriage Register 4:69. J. P. Henley and Martitia Lassiter.

[733] 1900 US Federal Census; Census Place: New Hope, Randolph, North Carolina; NARA Roll: 1213; Page: 1B; Enumeration District: 0090; FHL #1241213. *Ancestry.com*. Postell Henley, head.

Randolph, North Carolina.[734]

ii. **SPINKS LASSITER** was born in 1858 in Lassiter Mill, New Hope, Randolph, North Carolina.[735] He died before 1870 in Lassiter Mill, New Hope, Randolph, North Carolina.[736]

iii. **AMOS BARZILLA LASSITER** was born on 04 December 1861 in Lassiter Mill, New Hope, Randolph, North Carolina. He died on 16 December 1930 in Lassiter Mill, New Hope, Randolph, North Carolina.[737]

---

[734] North Carolina, Death Certificates, 1909-1975 [Database on-line]. *Ancestry.com*. Pastelle [*sic*] Henley, 7 Jun 1925. Index erroneously says he is "white;" certificate says he is "black."

[735] 1860 US Federal Census; Census Place: Western Division, Randolph, North Carolina; NARA Roll: M653_910; Page: 212; Image: 429; FHL #803910. *Ancestry.com*. Cal Lassiter, head; Spinks, age 2.

[736] 1870 US Federal Census; Census Place: New Hope, Randolph, North Carolina; NARA Roll: M593_1156; Page: 407B; Image: 264; FHL #552655. *Ancestry.com*. Collier Lassiter, head. Spinks' name not found in 1870 or any census thereafter.

[737] North Carolina, Death Certificates, 1909-1975 [Database on-line]. *Ancestry.com*. Barzillai Lassiter, 16 Dec 1930. *See also*: Strieby Cemetery Tombstone.

Figure 93: Harriett Phillips.
Photo courtesy of Richard Jackson.

He married **HARRIETT PHILLIPS**, daughter of **REUBEN PHILLIPS and MARY SCOTT** on 11 May 1882 in Asheboro, Randolph, North Carolina.[738] She was born on 01 February 1862 in Cedar Grove, Randolph, North Carolina. She died on 01 March 1942 in Lassiter Mill, New Hope, Randolph, North Carolina.[739] They are **both buried in Strieby Church Cemetery**.

[738] North Carolina, Marriage Records, 1741-2011 [Database on-line]. *Ancestry.com*. Amos B. Lassiter and Harriett Phillips, 11 May 1882.
[739] North Carolina, Death Certificates, 1909-1975 [Database on-line]. *Ancestry.com*. Harriett Lassiter, 1 Mar 1942. *See also*: Strieby Cemetery Tombstone.

Figure 94: Rhodemia Charity Lassiter. Photo courtesy of Ruth M. Howard.

iv. **RHODEMIA CHARITY LASSITER** was born in 1866 in Lassiter Mill, New Hope, Randolph, North Carolina.[740] She died after 1930 in New York, New York.[741] She married **ALEXANDER ADDERTON**, son of **JENNYADDERTON** on 20 September 1883 in Asheboro, Randolph, North

[740] 1870 US Federal Census; Census Place: New Hope, Randolph, North Carolina; NARA Roll: M593_1156; Page: 407B; Image: 264; FHL #552655. *Ancestry.com*. Collier Lassiter, head; Charity Lassiter, age 4.

[741] 1930 US Federal Census; Census Place: Manhattan, New York, New York; Roll: 1563; Page: 9B; Enumeration District: 888; Image: 934.0. *Ancestry.com*. Adderton.

Carolina.[742] He was born in 1854 In North Carolina. He died on 01 June 1917 in Asheboro, Randolph, North Carolina.[743] He is **buried** in **Strieby Church Cemetery.**

Figure 95: Ulysses Winston Lassiter. Photo courtesy of Patrice Lassiter Bryant.

v. **ULYSSES WINSTON LASSITER** was born on 30 December 1869 in Lassiter Mill, New Hope, Randolph, North Carolina.[744] He died on 26 November

---

[742] North Carolina, Marriage Records, 1741-2011[Database on-line].*Ancestry.com.* Alex Adderton and Rudema Lassiter, 20 Sep 1883.
[743] North Carolina, Death Certificates, 1909-1975 [Database on-line], *Ancestry.com.* Alex Aderton, 1 Jun 1917.
[744] 1900 US Federal Census; Census Place: New Hope, Randolph, North Carolina; NARA Roll: 1213; Page: 1B; Enumeration District: 0090; FHL #1241213. *Ancestry.com.* Winson Lassiter, head.

1937 in Lassiter Mill, New Hope, Randolph, North Carolina.[745]

Figure 96: (L) Ora Clara Kearns. (R) Ora ca. 1950. Photos courtesy of Patrice Lassiter Bryant.

He married **ORA CLARA KEARNS**, daughter of **CLARKSON KEARNS** and **ABIGAIL HEAD** on 08 September 1892 in Asheboro, Randolph, North Carolina.[746] She was born on 29 April 1874 in New Hope, Randolph, North Carolina. She died on 12 September 1951 in Lassiter Mill, New Hope,

---

[745] North Carolina, Death Certificates, 1909-1975 [Database on-line]. *Ancestry.com*. Winston Lassiter, 26 Nov 1937. *See also*: U.S. Find A Grave Index, 1700s-Current [Database on-line]. *Ancestry.com*. Ulysses Winston Lassiter.

[746] North Carolina, Marriage Collection, 1741-2004 [Database on-line]. *Ancestry.com*. N.W. [*sic*] Lassiter and Ora Kearns, Marriage Register 5:79, 8 Sep 1892.

Randolph, North Carolina.[747] They are **both buried in Strieby Church Cemetery**.

4. **SUSANNAH PHILLIPS[2] LASSITER** (MILES[1]) was born on 03 Oct 1817 in New Hope, Randolph, North Carolina. She died after 1854 in New Hope, Randolph, North Carolina. *[See above entry]*
   a. SUSANNAH PHILLIPS LASSITER may have had the following child:
      i. **JOHN PHILLIPS[3]** (?) was born in 1836 in Lassiter Mill, Randolph, North Carolina.[748]
5. **WILEY PHILLIPS[2] LASSITER** (MILES[1]) was born on 13 May 1820 in New Hope, Randolph, North Carolina. He died after 1860 in Fayetteville, Cumberland, North Carolina. He married **ELIZABETH "BETSY" RIDGE** about 1845 in Asheboro, Randolph, North Carolina. She was born in 1830 in Randolph County, North Carolina. She died between 1870 and 1880 in Randolph County, North Carolina. [*See above entry*]
   a. WILEY PHILLIPS LASSITER and ELIZABETH

---

[747] North Carolina, Death Certificates, 1909-1975 [Database on-line]. *Ancestry.com.* Ora Lassiter, 12 Sep 1951, Book 38:207. *See also*: U.S. Find A Grave Index, 1700s-Current, Ora Lassiter.

[748] 1850 US Federal Census, Free Schedule, Southern Division, Randolph, North Carolina; NARA Roll: M432_641, Census Place: Southern Division, Randolph, North Carolina, NARA Roll: M432_641; Page: 136; Image: 285.*Ancestry.com*. Miles Lassiter, head; John Phillips. He was probably a grandson of Miles, and may have been a son of Susannah's. He also may be the "Emsley" in the house of Nancy and her husband Calvin Dunson in 1860.

"BETSY" RIDGE had the following children:

i. **PARTHANIA[3] LASSITER** was born in 1845 in Lassiter Mill, Randolph, North Carolina.[749] She may be the same Parthana living in Miles' home in 1850.[750]

ii. **ABAGAIL[3] LASSITER** (WILEY PHILLIPS[2], MILES[1]) was born in 1846 in Lassiter Mill, New Hope, Randolph, North Carolina.[751] She died 27 April 1931, in Friendship, Guilford, North Carolina.[752] She married **JESSE L SMITH** 14 Feb 1869.[753] He was born about 1846in North Carolina.[754] He apparently died between 1928 and 1931 in Guilford County, North

---

[749] 1860 US Federal Census Fayetteville, Cumberland, North Carolina, NARA Roll: M653_894, Page: 248; Image: 498, FHL #803894. *Ancestry.com*. "Wriley Sprister" [*sic* – index; original reads Wiley Lassiter], head.

[750] 1850 US Federal Census, Free Schedule, Southern Division, Randolph, North Carolina; Census Place: Southern Division, Randolph, North Carolina; NARA Roll: M432_641; Page: 136; Image: 285, *Ancestry.com*. Miles Lassiter, head.

[751] 1850 US Federal Census, Free Schedule, Southern Division, Randolph, North Carolina; NARA Roll: M432_641, Page: 136; Image: 285; Family 816. *Ancestry.com*. Willie Lassiter, head.

[752] North Carolina, Death Certificates, 1909-1975 [Database on-line]. *Ancestry.com*. Abbie Smith, 26 Apr 1931.

[753] North Carolina, Marriage Records, 1741-2011 [Database on-line]. *Ancestry.com*. Abia Lassiter [*sic*] and Jesse Smith, 14 Feb 1869.

[754] 1870 U.S. Federal Census; Census Place: Friendship, Guilford, North Carolina. NARA Roll: M593_1140; Page: 67B; Image: 366; FHL#552639. *Ancestry.com*. Jesse Smith, head.

Carolina, when he was last identified with Abbey [*sic*] (1928) and she was reportedly a widow (1931).[755]

iii. **NANCY JANE[3] LASSITER** was born in [756] February 1848 in Lassiter Mill, New Hope, Randolph, North Carolina.[757] She died after 1900 in Randolph County, North Carolina.[758] She married **THOMAS BRYANT** on 01 October 1868 in Asheboro, Randolph, North Carolina.[759] He was born in August 1842 in North Carolina. He died after 1900 in Randolph County, North Carolina.[760]

---

[755] U.S. City Directories, 1821-1989 [Database on-line]. *Ancestry.com*. Jesse L Smith (Abbey), 1928, p. 416. *See also*: North Carolina, Death Certificates, 1909-1975 [Database on-line]. *Ancestry.com*. Abbie Smith, 26 April 1931.
[756] North Carolina, Death Certificates, 1909-1975 [Database on-line]. *Ancestry.com*. Abbie Smith, 26 April 1931.
[757] 1850 US Census, Free Schedule, Southern Division, Randolph, North Carolina; NARA Roll: M432_641, *Ancestry.com*, Page: 136; Image: 285; Family 816: Willie Lassiter, head.
[758] Last found: 1900 US Federal Census; Census Place: Cedar Grove, Randolph, North Carolina; NARA Roll: T623_1212; Page: 4A; Enumeration District: 82.*Ancestry.com*. Nancy J. Bryant.
[759] North Carolina, Marriage Records, 1741-2011 [Database on-line]. *Ancestry.com*. Jane Lassiter and Thomas Bryant, 1 Oct 1868; Register 3:42.
[760] Last found: 1900 US Federal Census; Census Place: Cedar Grove, Randolph, North Carolina; NARA Roll: T623_1212; Page: 4A; Enumeration District: 82. *Ancestry.com*. Thomas Bryant.

Figure 97: Julia Anna Lassiter & brother, Thomas Lassiter. Photo courtesy Martha Brooks.

iv. **JULIA ANN[3] LASSITER** was born in May 1852 in Lassiter Mill, New Hope, Randolph, North Carolina.[761] She died on 31 January 1921 in Cedar Grove, Randolph, North Carolina.[762] She married

---

[761] 1860 US Census Fayetteville, Cumberland, North Carolina, NARA Roll: M653_894, Page: 248; Image: 498, Family History Library Film: 803894. *Ancestry.com*. "Wriley Sprister" [*sic* – index; original reads Wiley Lassiter], head. Julie A. Sanders' tombstone at St. Mark United Methodist Church Cemetery, Mechanic, Concord Township, Asheboro, Randolph County, records her birthdate.

[762] North Carolina, Deaths, 1906-1930 [Database on-line]. *Ancestry.com*. Julia Anna Sanders, 31 Jan 1921; Book 8:59.

HENRY B. W. SANDERS on 18 January 1877 in Asheboro, Randolph, North Carolina.[763] He was born in September 1853 in North Carolina. He died after 1900 in Cedar Grove, Randolph, North Carolina.[764]

v. **MARTHA LASSITER** was born in 1854 in Lassiter Mill, Randolph, North Carolina.[765]

vi. **JOHN LASSITER** was born in 1857 in Lassiter Mill, Randolph, North Carolina.[766]

vii. **ADDISON B.**[3] **LASSITER** was born in 1862 in Fayetteville, Cumberland, North Carolina.[767] He died after 1930 most likely

---

[763] North Carolina, Marriage Records, 1741-2011 [Database on-line]. *Ancestry.com.* H. B. Sanders and Julia Lassiter, 18 Jan 1877; Book 4:45.
[764] 1900 US Federal Census; Randolph County, North Carolina, Census place, Cedar Grove. NARA Roll 1212 page 3 B, ED 0082, FHL #1241212. *Ancestry.com.* Henry Saunder [*sic*], head.
[765] 1860 US Federal Census; Fayetteville, Cumberland, North Carolina, Roll: M653_894, Page: 248; Image: 498, FHL#803894.*Ancestry.com*. "Wriley Sprister" [*sic* – index; original reads Wiley Lassiter], head.
[766] 1860 US Federal Census; Fayetteville, Cumberland, North Carolina, Roll: M653_894, Page: 248; Image: 498, FHL#803894.*Ancestry.com*. "Wriley Sprister" [*sic* – index; original reads Wiley Lassiter], head.
[767] 1870 US Federal Census; Census Place: Asheboro, Randolph, North Carolina; Roll: M593_1156, Page: 287B; Image: 24; Family History Library Film: 552655. *Ancestry.com*. Elizabeth Lassiter, head – "Wd"

in Union, Ocean, New Jersey.[768] He married (1) **ADELAIDE FREEMAN**, daughter of **ISAAC FREEMAN** and **MARY STITH** on 22 September 1883 in Randolph County, North Carolina.[769] She was born in 1866 in Trinity, Randolph, North Carolina. She may have died in the early 1890s. According to the 1900 census, Addison, now living in Galloway, Atlantic County, New Jersey, had married (2) "**ANNIE (LNU)**," in 1896.[770] Galloway is not far from either the Jersey shore or Philadelphia. In 1905, he married (3) **HENRIETTA STANTON**, in Philadelphia, Pennsylvania.[771] She was born about 1885 in Maryland. She may have died between 1920 and 1930 in Philadelphia, Pennsylvania, when Addison is found "widowed," living in

---

[768] 1930 US Federal Census; Census Place: Union, Ocean, New Jersey; Roll: 1375, Page: 3B; Enumeration District: 43; Image: 760.0. *Ancestry.com*. Addison Lasiter, 65 -Roomer - "Wd".

[769] North Carolina Marriage Collection, 1741-2004 [Database on-line], Marriage Book 4:117. *Ancestry.com*. Addison Lassiter and Adalade Freeman, 22 Sep 1883.

[770] 1900 US Federal Census, Atlantic County, New Jersey, Census place, Galloway. NARA Roll # 954, Page 14A. FHL #1240954. *Ancestry.com*. Addeson Laster, head.

[771] Pennsylvania, Philadelphia Marriage Indexes, 1885-1951, index and images [Database on-line]. *FamilySearch*. Clerk of the Orphan's Court, License #189132. Addison Lastier [*sic*] and Henriette Stanton..

Union, Ocean County, New Jersey.[772]

viii. **THOMAS EMERY[3] LASSITER** was born in 1865 in Fayetteville, Cumberland, North Carolina.[773] He died after 1930 in Washington, DC, the last known entry in the census.[774]According to the 1930 census, he married **ALICE (LNU)** about 1929 in Washington, DC; she was born in 1870 in Virginia.[775] However, various family members believed he lived in Atlantic City, Monmouth County, New Jersey. On 24 September 1895, a **THOMAS E. LASSITER** married a **MARTHA P. HICKS** in Atlantic City, Monmouth, New Jersey.[776] She may be the same

---

[772] 1930 US Federal Census, Ocean County, New Jersey, Census place, Union. NARA Roll: 1375, Page: 3B; Enumeration District: 43; Image: 760.0. *Ancestry.com*. Addison Lasiter, 65 -Roomer - "Wd".

[773] 1870 US Federal Census; Census Place: Asheboro, Randolph, North Carolina; NARA Roll: M593_1156, Page: 287B; Image: 24; FHL#552655.*Ancestry.com*. Elizabeth Lassiter, head.

[774] 1930 US Census; Washington, District Of Columbia; NARA Roll: 294; Page: 20A; Enumeration District: 77; Image: 243.0. *Ancestry.com*. Thomas E. Lassiter.

[775] 1930 US Federal Census; Washington, District Of Columbia; NARA Roll: 294; Page: 20A; Enumeration District: 77; Image: 243.0. *Ancestry.com*. Thomas E. Lassiter.

[776] New Jersey Marriages, 1678-1985, index [Database on-line]. *FamilySearch,* FHL #495721. Thos. E. Lassiter and Martha P. Hicks, 24 Sep 1895.

MARTHA P. HICKS LASSITER, married to a **THOMAS LASSITER**, who died on 8 January 1922 in Washington, DC. She was the daughter of **DAVID HICKS** and **JULIA SEYMOUR**, born in Pennsylvania.[777]

6. **NANCY PHILLIPS[2] LASSITER** (MILES[1]) was born in February 1823 in New Hope, Randolph, North Carolina. She died about 1890 in New Hope, Randolph, North Carolina. She married **CALVIN DUNSON**, about 1852 in Randolph County, North Carolina. He was born about 1818 in Wake County, North Carolina. He died about 1879 in New Hope, Randolph, North Carolina. She identified and charged **J. G. HOAGIN** in court as the father of an unborn child. [*See above entry*]
    a. J. G. HOAGIN and NANCY PHILLIPS LASSITER had the following child:[778]
        i. **J. RICHARD[3] DUNSON** was born in 1859 in New Hope, Randolph, North Carolina.[779] He died between 1860 and 1870 in New Hope,

[777] District of Columbia Deaths, 1874-1959, index and images [Database on-line]. FHL #2115942. *FamilySearch.* Martha P. Lassiter, 8 January 1922.
[778] Minutes of the Court of Common Pleas and Quarter Sessions, Nancy Dunson v. J. G. Hoagin, February 1859. FHL #047212 or #0019653.
[779] 1860 US Federal Census; Census Place: Western Division, Randolph, North Carolina; NARA Roll: M653_910; Page: 212; Image: 429; FHL#803910. *Ancestry.com.* Calvin Dunson, head; Richd Dunson.

Randolph, North Carolina.[780]

b. CALVIN DUNSON and NANCY PHILLIPS LASSITER had the following children:

   i. **ELLEN[3] DUNSON** was born on 08 August 1852 in New Hope, Randolph, North Carolina. She died on 12 June 1920 in Asheboro, Randolph, North Carolina.[781] She married (1) **ANDERSON SMITHERMAN,** reported son of **NOAH SMITHERMAN** and **LUCINDA SMITHERMAN** on 23 September 1865 in Asheboro, Randolph, North Carolina.[782] He was born in November 1848 in Union, Randolph, North Carolina.[783] He died in 1909 in Asheboro, Randolph, North Carolina.[784] She married (2) **CHARLES**

---

[780] 1870 US Federal Census; Census Place: New Hope, Randolph, North Carolina; NARA Roll: M593_1156; Page: 400B; Image: 250; FHL #552655.*Ancestry.com*. Calvin Dunson, head, J. A. [*sic*] Dunson, age 11.J. Richard does not appear again in any census.

[781] North Carolina Bureau of Vital Statistics, Standard Death Certificate, #16225, 404. Ellen Mayo.

[782] Randolph County, North Carolina Marriage Registers, Marriage Book 2:71. Anderson Smitherman and Ellen Dunson.

[783] 1900 US Federal Census; Census Place: Asheboro, Randolph, North Carolina; NARA Roll: 1212; Page: 3B; Enumeration District: 0079; FHL #1241212. *Ancestry.com*. Anderson Smotherman [*sic*], "servant."

[784] There is no death certificate and no probate, but he deeded his Asheboro home to his second wife Victoria (Bell) Smitherman (Marriage Book 5:197) on 21 January 1909, (recorded in 1920); she took out a mortgage on the property in November 1909 (Deed Book 138:36). Anderson was not in the 1910 census.

MAYO in 1895 in North Carolina.[785]

ii. **SARAH REBECCA[3] DUNSON** was born in 1857 in New Hope, Randolph, North Carolina.[786] She died between 1881 and 1892 in New Hope, Randolph, North Carolina.[787]

iii. **J. HARRIS DUNSON** was born in 1860 in New Hope, Randolph, North Carolina.[788] He died after 1920 in New Hope, Randolph, North Carolina.[789] He married **PHOEBE FARMER** on 03 April 1890 in Asheboro, Randolph, North

---

[785] 1900 US Federal Census; Census Place: Morehead, Guilford, North Carolina; NARA Roll: 1198; Page: 4B; Enumeration District: 0065; FHL # 1241198. *Ancestry.com*. Charles Mays [*sic*], head.

[786] 1860 US Federal Census; Census Place: Western Division, Randolph, North Carolina; NARA Roll: M653_910; Page: 212; Image: 429; FHL#803910. *Ancestry.com*. Calvin Dunson, head; Sarah Dunson, age 3.

[787] 1880 US Census, population schedule, Randolph County, North Carolina, New Hope Township, p. 1. NARA #T9-978. *Ancestry.com*. Nancy Dunson, head. Sarah Rebecca last appears in this census. She is not named in the division of the land of Miles Lassiter. *See also*: Vidales. (Summer 2011). Randolph County Estates, Dunbar-Duty: William Dunston. *Genealogical Journal* by the Randolph County Genealogical Society.

[788] 1870 US Federal Census; Census Place: New Hope, Randolph, North Carolina; NARA Roll: M593_1156; Page: 400B; Image: 250; FHL#552655. *Ancestry.com*. Calvin Dunson, head, S A R Dunson, age 13.

[789] 1920; Census Place: Concord, Randolph, North Carolina; NARA Roll: T625_1318; Page: 10B; Enumeration District: 103; Image: 897. *Ancestry.com.* Salomon J. Kearns, head. Harris Dunson has not been found after this.

Carolina.[790] She was very likely the younger sister of **ELEANORA W. (FARMER) WALDEN,**[791] identified as the **"P. FARMER"** who helped **ISLAY WALDEN** with his Students' Mission, in New Brunswick, New Jersey.[792] She died after 1891, when she was last identified in a deed transferring land from her and her husband HARRIS DUNSON to her sister-in-law, **ELLEN DUNSON SMITHERMAN.**[793]

iv. **M. ADELAIDE DUNSON** was born in 1861 in New Hope, Randolph, North Carolina.[794] She died on 09 May 1929 in Concord, Randolph, North Carolina.[795] She married **SOLOMON KEARNS**, son of **LINDSAY INGRAM** and **LYDIA "LETTIE" KEARNS**, on 17 April 1890 in

---

[790] Randolph County, North Carolina Marriage Registers, Book 5:13, FHL #0475241.Harris Dunson and Phoebe Farmer.

[791] 1880 US Federal Census; Census Place: New Brunswick, Middlesex, New Jersey; Roll: 789; Family History Film: 1254789; Page: 79B; Enumeration District: 122; Image: 0586. *Ancestry.com*. John V. Farmer, head; Phoebia A. Farmer, daughter, age 14.

[792] *The Daily Times*, 3 January, 1879, p. 3; & 4 January 1879, p. 3.

[793] Randolph County, North Carolina, Deeds, Deed Book 144:216. FHL #0470278. J. H. and Phoebe A. Dunson to Ellen Smitherman.

[794] 1870 US Federal Census; Census Place: New Hope, Randolph, North Carolina; NARA Roll: M593_1156; Page: 400B; Image: 250; FHL#552655. *Ancestry.com*. Calvin Dunson, head, H A Dunson, age 9.

[795] Randolph County, North Carolina, Deaths, Book 16:161. FHLM #0475244. Adelaide Kearns.

Asheboro, Randolph, North Carolina.[796] He was born on 01 May 1853 in Farmer, Randolph, North Carolina and died on 11 September 1942 in Thomasville, Davidson, North Carolina.[797]

v. **MARTHA ANN DUNSON** was born in 1864 in Lassiter Mill, New Hope, Randolph, North Carolina.[798] She died between 1884-1886 in Lassiter Mill, New Hope, Randolph, North Carolina.[799] She married **JULIUS HILL**, son of **EDWARD "NED" HILL and PRISCILLA MAHOCKLY** 24 January 1883 in Wadesboro, Anson, North Carolina.[800] He was born in March 1854 in Hill Town, Union, Randolph, North Carolina.[801] He

---

[796] Randolph County, North Carolina Marriage Registers, Book 5:17. FHLM #0475241. Solomon Kearns and Adelaide Dunson.

[797] North Carolina Death Certificates, 1909-1975 [Database on-line], *Ancestry.com*. Registration District 28-80; Certificate 80-17. Solomon J Kearns.

[798] 1870 US Federal Census; Census Place: New Hope, Randolph, North Carolina; Roll: M593_1156; Page: 400B; Image: 250; FHL #552655. *Ancestry.com*. Calvin Dunson, head; M Ann Dunson, age 7.

[799] Vidales, C. (2011). Randolph County Estates, Dunbar-Duty: William Dunston. *The Genealogical Journal by the Randolph County Genealogical Society,* Volume XXXV(2): 45-46.

[800] North Carolina Marriages, 1759-1979, index. *FamilySearch.* FHL #296692. Julius Hill and Martha Dunson, 24 January 1883.

[801] 1900 US Federal Census; Census Place: Union, Randolph, North Carolina; NARA Roll: 1213; Page: 6B; Enumeration District: 0099; FHL #1241213. *Ancestry.com*. Julius Hill, head.

died after 1930, most likely in Strieby, Union, Randolph, North Carolina.[802]

Generation 3

7. **WYLEY[3] LASSITER** (EMSLEY PHILLIPS[2], MILES[1]) was born in March 1852 in Ripley, Rush, Indiana. He married (1) **ANNIE JONES** on 10 November 1877 in Indianapolis, Marion, Indiana. He married (2) **CARRIE BROWN** on 11 October 1884 in Chicago, Cook, Illinois. She was born in 1855 in Chicago, Cook, Illinois. He married (4) **EMMA** (LNU) about 1904. She was born about 1855 in Indiana. He also had a relationship with **WINNIE** or **MINNIE ADAMS WASHINGTON**.*[See entry above]*
   a. WYLEY LASSITER and MINNIE ADAMS (not married) had the following child:
      i. **WILEY[4] LASTER** was born on 25 March 1876 in Indiana. He married (1) **MARIETTA CHATTMAN** on 10 November 1908 in Chicago, Cook, Illinois.[803] She was born in 1880 in Canada. He married (2) **MINNIE COWAN** on 12 November 1918 in

[802] 1930 US Census, Randolph County, North Carolina. Census place: Union Township, NARA Roll: 1715; Page: 6A; Enumeration District: 34; Image: 427.0. *Ancestry.com*. Julius Hill.

[803] Cook County, Illinois, Marriages Index, 1871-1920, FHL #1030449. *Ancestry.com*. Wiley Laster and Maretta Chattman, 10 Nov 1908.

Indianapolis, Marion, Indiana.[804] She was born about 1880 in Ohio.

8. **PENINA[3] LASSITER/LASTER** (EMSLEY PHILLIPS[2], MILES[1]) was born in May 1854 in Ripley, Rush, Indiana, and died sometime between 1931 and 1940, in Marion, Grant, Indiana. She married **TURNER A NEWSOM**, son of **WILLIAM H NEWSOM and MARTHA BROWN** on 03 August 1880 in Rush County, Indiana. He was born in February 1855 in Indiana. He died between 1910 and 1920, in Carthage, Rush, Indiana. *[See entry above]*
   a. TURNER A NEWSOM and PENINA LASSITER/LASTER had the following children:
      i. **ARMETA[4] NEWSOM** was born 27November 1881 in Carthage, Rush, Indiana, USA. She died in Sep 1976 in Marion, Grant, Indiana.[805] She married **OTTO PETTIFORD**, son of **YOUNG PETTIFORD** and **NARCISSA WEAVER** on 18 Feb 1904 in Grant County, Indiana.[806] He was born on 15 Oct 1883 in Weaver, Grant, Indiana.[807]

---

[804] Indiana Marriage Collection, 1800-1941 [Database on-line]. *Ancestry.com.* Wiley Laster and Minnie E Cowan, 12 Nov 1918, Marion County.

[805] US Social Security Death Index, 1935-2014 [Database on-line]. *Ancestry.com.* Armeto Pettiford.

[806] Indiana Marriage Collection, 1800-1941 [Database on-line], *Ancestry.com*, Otto Pettiford and Armeto Newsom, 18 Feb 1904, Grant County.

[807] U.S. World War II Draft Registration Cards, 1942, *Ancestry.com*, Otto Pettiford, Birth Date: 15 Oct 1883, Birth Place: Weaver, Indiana, Residence: Grant, Indiana.

Figure 98: Lawrence "Bucky" Pettiford (1939-2010), grandson of Armeta Newsom and Otto Pettiford. Photo courtesy of Tiffany Pettiford.

ii. **HERMAN NEWSOM** was born on 27 Mar 1883 in Carthage, Rush, Indiana, USA.[808] He died 9 Jul 1921, in Marion, Grant, Indiana.[809] He is buried in Estates of Serenity Cemetery, Marion, Grant, Indiana.[810] He married **BELLE**

---

[808] World War I Draft Registrations, FHL #1503894.[Database on-line]. *Ancestry.com*. Name: Herman Newsom, Grant County, Indiana, Birth Date: 27 Mar 1881.

[809] Web: Indiana, Marion Public Library Death Index, 1812 – 2011 [Database on-line}. *Ancestry.com*. Herman Newsom, 9 Jul 1921.

[810] U.S., Find A Grave Index, 1700s-Current (2012) [Database on-line]. Ancestry.com. Herman Newsom. 9 Jul 1921.

BRIMBEE in Aug 1914 in Grant County, Indiana. She was born in 1881 in Ohio.[811]

iii. **ALLIE F NEWSOM** was born in Aug 1885 in Carthage, Rush, Indiana, USA.[812]

iv. **MERLE NEWSOM** was born on 02 Mar 1887 in Carthage, Rush, Indiana, USA. She died in Jun 1979 in Indianapolis, Marion, Indiana, USA.[813] She married **ISUM THOMAS REED** on 06 Aug 1915 in Indianapolis, Marion, Indiana, USA.[814] He was born on 20 Feb 1889 in Lexington, Fayette, Kentucky, USA. He died in Oct 1961 in Indianapolis, Marion, Indiana, USA.[815]

v. **EVA A NEWSOM** was born in Jul 1890 in

---

[811] Indiana Marriage Collection, 1800-1941 [Database on-line]. *Ancestry.com*. Herman Newsom and Belle Brimbee, August 1914, Grant County, Indiana

[812] US Census, 1910, index and images, Marion Ward 2, Grant, Indiana, sheet 11A, family 331, NARA Series T624, FHL #1374365 *FamilySearch.org*, Allie Newsome in household of Penina Newsome.

[813] 187 U. S. Social Security Death Index, 1935-Current, [Database on-line]. *Ancestry.com*. Merle Reed, Born: 2 Mar 1887, Died: Jun 1979.

[814] Indiana, Marriages, 1780-1992, *FamilySearch.org*. Groom's name: Isum Reed, groom's birth date: 20 Feb 1889, groom's birthplace: Lexington, KY; bride's name: Merle Newsome, bride's birth date: 02 Mar 1887, bride's birthplace: Carthage, Indiana; marriage date: 06 Aug 1915.

[815] Find A Grave Memorial# 45999400, *Findagrave.com*, Isum Thomas Reed. Birth: unknown, Death: 1961, burial: OCT 21,1961, Burial: Crown Hill Cemetery, Indianapolis, Marion, Indiana, USA

Carthage, Rush, Indiana, USA.[816] She may have died around 1919.[817]

vi. **FLOYD RAYMOND NEWSOM** was born on 09 May 1893 in Carthage, Rush, Indiana, USA.[818] He died in Mar 1957, in Marion, Grant, Indiana.[819] He married **OCTA JONES**, daughter of **SILAS JONES** and **OLIVE A BURDEN** on 26 Jun 1920 in Grant County, Indiana.[820] She was born on 11 Oct 1893 in Franklin, Grant, Indiana and died 09 January 1991.[821] They are both buried at Estates of Serenity Cemetery, Marion, Grant, Indiana.[822]

9. **MARY ANNA[3] LASSITER** (EMSLEY PHILLIPS[2],

---

[816] US Federal Census, 1910,Marion Ward 2, Grant, Indiana; index and images, sheet 11A, family 331, NARA microfilm publication T624, FHL #1374365.*FamilySearch.org*, Eva Newsome in household of Penina Newsome.

[817] U.S. City Directories, 1821-1989 [Database on-line]. Marion, Indiana City Directory, 1919. *Ancestry.com*. Eva Newsom, h443 E 3rd.

[818] World War I Draft Registrations, FHL #1503894. *Ancestry.com*. Name: Floyd R Newsom, Grant County, Indiana. Birth Date: 9 May 1892.

[819] Web: Grant County, Indiana, Marion Public Library Death Index, 1812-2015 [Database on-line]. *Ancestry.com*. Floyd R Newsome, Mar 1957.

[820] Indiana Marriage Collection, 1800-1941 [Database on-line], *Ancestry.com*. Floyd R. Newson and Octa Jones, 26 Jun 1920, Grant County, Indiana.

[821] US Social Security Death Index, 1935-Current. [Database on-line]. *Ancestry.com*. Octa Newsome, Marion, Grant, Indiana. Born: 11 Oct 1894, Died: 9 Jan 1991.

[822] US Findagrave Index, 1600s-Current. [Database on-line]. *Ancestry.com*. Floyd R Newsom, 1892-Mar 1957, Plot: B36 L12 G6; and Octa Newsom, 11 Oct 1894- 9 Jan 1991, Plot: B36 L12 G5.

MILES[1]) was born about 1859 in Ripley, Rush, Indiana. She married **JAMES M WEAVER**, son of **HENRY WEAVER and SARAH BURDEN** on 17 Mar 1894 in Grant County, Indiana. He was born in 1856 in Mill, Grant, Indiana, USA. He died in 1943 in Weaver, Grant, Indiana. *[See Entry Above]*

a. JAMES M WEAVER and MARY ANNA LASSITER had the following children:

   i. **WILBERT P[4] WEAVER** was born in 1889 in Marion, Grant, Indiana, USA. He married **ELLEN McMATH** on 12 Jun 1919 in Grant County, Indiana.[823] She was born in Jan 1870 in Indiana.

   ii. **BENJAMIN HARRISON[4] WEAVER** was born on 02 Feb 1889 in Marion, Grant, Indiana, USA. He married (1) **ELIZABETH MCMATH**, daughter of **ELISHA McMATH and ELLEN** on 25 Feb 1910 in Grant County, Indiana.[824] She was born in Nov 1890 in Center, Grant, Indiana, USA.[825] She apparently died

---

[823] Indiana Marriage Collection, 1800-1941 [Database on-line], *Ancestry.com*. Name: Wilbur P. Weaver and Ellen McMath; Marriage Date: 12 Jun 1919; Marriage County: Grant.

[824] Indiana Marriage Collection, 1800-1941 [Database on-line]. *Ancestry.com*. Name: Benjamin H. Weaver and Elizabeth McMath. Marriage Date: 25 Feb 1910; Grant County, Indiana.

[825] 1900 US Federal Census, Grant County, Indiana. Census Place: Center, Grant, Indiana. Page: 10B; Enumeration District: 31. NARA #T623_373, *Ancestry.com*. Elisha McMath, head; Ellen McMath, wife; Lizzie McMath, daughter (other children are also listed).

between 1918 and 1920 in Marion, Grant, Indiana, USA. He married (2) **RUTH E JONES VENTERS** on 22 Mar 1921 in Grant County, Indiana.[826]

iii. **ELIZABETH[4] WEAVER.**[827]

10. **BETHANA MARTITIA[3] LASSITER** (COLIER PHILLIPS[2], MILES[1]) was born in Feb 1856 in Lassiter Mill, New Hope, Randolph, North Carolina. She died on 11 Jul 1917 in Cedar Grove, Randolph, North Carolina. She married **POSTELL HENLEY**, son of **EASTER HENLEY** on 20 Mar 1879 in Asheboro, Randolph, North Carolina. He was born in Apr 1854 in Randolph, North Carolina. He died on 07 Jun 1925 in Cedar Grove, Randolph, North Carolina. *[See Entry Above]*

a. POSTELL HENLEY and BETHANA MARTITIA LASSITER had the following child:

i. **GEORGE[4] HENLEY** was born in August 1882 in Lassiter Mill, New Hope, Randolph, North Carolina.[828] He died on 31 December 1943 in New Hope,

---

[826] Indiana Marriage Collection, 1800-1941 [Database on-line], *Ancestry.com.* Harrison Weaver and Ruth Venters, 22 Mar 1921, Grant County, Indiana.

[827] 1910 US Federal Census; Census Place: Marion Ward 4, Grant, Indiana; NARA Roll: T624_352. Page: 1A; Enumeration District: 0057; Image: 332; FHL #1374365. *Ancestry.com.* Mary Weaver, head – divorced; Elizabeth Weaver.

[828] 1900 US Federal Census; Census Place: New Hope, Randolph, North Carolina; NARA Roll: 1213; Page: 1B; Enumeration District: 0090; FHL #1241213. *Ancestry.com.* Postell Henley, head; Georg Henley, age 17.

Randolph, North Carolina.[829] He married **METTA COTTON**, daughter of **WEBSTER "WEBBE" COTTON** and **ROSETTA (ETTA) SHORT** on 10 June 1917 in Asheboro, Randolph, North Carolina.[830] She was born in August 1899 in Randolph, North Carolina. She died on 04 February 1930 in Lassiter Mill, New Hope, Randolph, North Carolina.[831]They are **both buried in Strieby Church Cemetery**.

11. **AMOS BARZILLA[3] LASSITER** (COLIER PHILLIPS,[2] MILES[1]) was born on 04 Dec 1861 in Lassiter Mill, New Hope, Randolph, North Carolina. He died on 16 Dec 1930 in Lassiter Mill, New Hope, Randolph, North Carolina. He married **HARRIETT PHILLIPS**, daughter of **REUBEN PHILLIPS and MARY SCOTT** on 11 May 1882 in Asheboro, Randolph, North Carolina. She was born on 01 Feb 1862 in Cedar Grove, Randolph, North Carolina. She died on 01 Mar 1942 in Lassiter Mill, New Hope, Randolph, North Carolina. They are **both buried in Strieby Church Cemetery**.[*See Entry Above*]
    a. AMOS BARZILLA LASSITER and HARRIETT PHILLIPS had the following children:

---

[829] Randolph County, North Carolina, Deaths [Database on-line]. *Ancestry.com*. George Henley, 31 Dec 1943; Book 30:225.
[830] Randolph County, North Carolina Marriage Registers, 7:175. George Henley and Metta Cotton, 10 June 1917.
[831] North Carolina Death Certificates, 1909-1975 [Database on-line]. *Ancestry.com*. Mettie Henley, 04 February 1930.

Figure 99: Blanche Lassiter.
Photo courtesy of Shirley (Birkhead) Green.

i. **BLANCHE[4] LASSITER** was born in 31 March 1883 in Lassiter Mill, New Hope, Randolph, North Carolina. She died in 20 March 1954 in Asheboro, Randolph, North Carolina.[832]

[832] North Carolina Death Certificates, 1909-1975 [Database on-line]. *Ancestry.com*. Blanche Burkhead, 20 March 1954.

Figure 100: Columbus "Lum" Birkhead.
Photo coutesy of Shirley Birkhead Green.

She married **COLUMBUS "LUM" BIRKHEAD**, son of **SAMUEL BIRKHEAD** and **JANE WALDEN CALLICUTT** on 22 Sep 1901 in Asheboro, Randolph, North Carolina.[833] He was born on 12 Sep 1876 in Concord, Randolph County, North Carolina. He died on 22 Nov 1947 in Randolph, North Carolina.[834]

---

[833] Randolph County, North Carolina Marriage Index. [Database on-line]. *Ancestry.com*. Blanche Lassiter and Lum Birkhead, 22 September 1901, Marriage Book 6:15.

[834] North Carolina Death Certificates, 1909-1975 [Database on-line]. *Ancestry.com*. Columbus Birkhead, 6 January 1948.

Figure 101: Elizabeth Lassiter. Photo courtesy of Christine Hill.

ii. **ELIZABETH A. LASSITER** was born on 17 October 1886 in Lassiter Mill, New Hope, Randolph, North Carolina. She died on 16 December 1962 in Strieby, Union, Randolph, North Carolina.[835] She married **ARTHUR HAZE HILL**, son of **BARZILLA HARRISON HILL and ELIZABETH "LIZZIE" HEARN** on 31 Dec 1910 in Asheboro, Randolph, North Carolina.[836] He was born on 13

[835] North Carolina Death Certificates, 1909-1975 [Database on-line]. *Ancestry.com*. Elizabeth Hill, 16 December 1962.

[836] North Carolina Marriage Index, 1741-2004. [Database on-line]. *Ancestry.com*. Lizzie Lassiter and Arthur Hill, 31 December 1910.

September 1887 in Hilltown, Union, Randolph, North Carolina. He died on 13 September 1980 in Strieby, Union, Randolph, North Carolina.[837]They are **both buried in Strieby Church Cemetery**.

**Figure 102: Harris Lassiter.
Photo courtesy of Elbert Lassiter, Jr.**

iii. **HARRIS STOCKTON LASSITER** was born on 07 Feb 1889 in Lassiter Mill, New Hope, Randolph, North Carolina.[838] He died on 31 Jan 1964 in Lassiter Mill,

---

[837] North Carolina Death Indexes, 1908-2004. [Database on-line]. *Ancestry.com*. Arthur Haze Hill, 13 September 1980.

[838] 1900 US Federal Census; Census Place: New Hope, Randolph, North Carolina; NARA Roll: 1213; Page: 1B; Enumeration District: 0090; FHL #1241213. *Ancestry.com*. Amos Lassiter, head; Harris Lassiter, age 10.

New Hope, Randolph, North Carolina.[839]

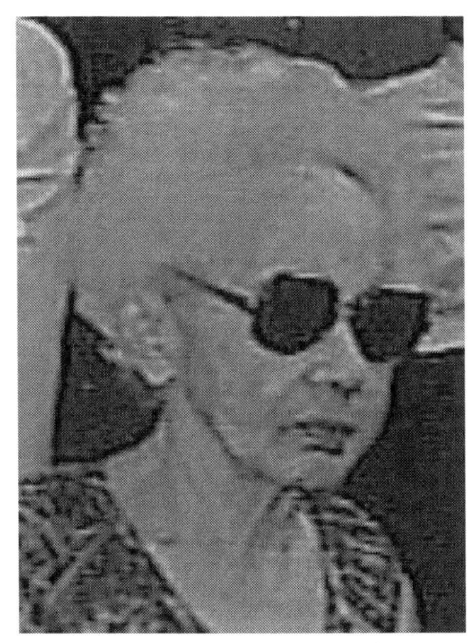

Figure 103: Cora Henley Lassiter, 1987. Photo courtesy of Margo Lee Williams.

He married **CORA KATHERINE HENLEY**, daughter of **THOMAS HENLEY and MARY FAULS,** on 25 Dec 1920 in Asheboro, Randolph, North Carolina.[840] She was born in August 1897 in Cedar Grove, Randolph, North Carolina. She died on 01 Jan 1990 in

[839] North Carolina Death Certificates, 1909-1975 [Database on-line], *Ancestry.com*. Certificate #2758, Harris S. Lassiter, 7 Feb 1889.
[840] North Carolina Marriage Index, 1741-2004 [Database-on-line]. *Ancestry.com*. Marriage Book 7:254. Harris Lassiter and Cora Henley, 25 Dec 1920.

Asheboro, Randolph, North Carolina.[841] They are **both buried in Strieby Church Cemetery**.

Figure 104: Spinks Lassiter.
Photo courtesy of Jerry Laughlin.

iv. **SPINKS LASSITER** was born in Jun 1894 in Lassiter Mill, New Hope, Randolph, North Carolina.[842] He died

---

[841] North Carolina, Death Indexes, 1908-2004. [Database on-line]. *Ancestry.com*. Cora Katherine Lassiter, 01 Jan 1990.

[842] 1900 US Federal Census; Census Place: New Hope, Randolph, North Carolina; NARA Roll: 1213; Page: 1B; Enumeration District: 0090; FHL #1241213.*Ancestry.com*. Amos Lassiter, head; Spinks Lassiter, age 5.

about between 1910-1920, in Lassiter Mill, New Hope, Randolph, North Carolina.

Figure 105: Alice Ruth Lassiter. Photo courtesy of Jerry Laughlin.

v. **ALICE RUTH LASSITER** was born in Apr 1897 in Lassiter Mill, New Hope, Randolph, North Carolina.[843] She died on 17 Nov 1986 in Lassiter Mill, New Hope, Randolph, North Carolina.[844] She married **HARRY SPEED** on 19 Oct 1935

[843] 1900 US Federal Census; Census Place: New Hope, Randolph, North Carolina; NARA Roll: 1213; Page: 1B; Enumeration District: 0090; FHL #1241213.*Ancestry.com*. Amos Lassiter, head; Alice Lassiter, age 3.
[844] North Carolina, Death Indexes, 1908-2004 [Database on-line]. *Ancestry.com*. Alice Ruth Speed, 16 Nov 1986.

in Asheboro, Randolph, North Carolina.[845] He died on 06 Jul 1941 in Asheboro, Randolph, North Carolina.[846] They are **both buried in Strieby Church Cemetery.**

vi. **EDNA NETTIE LASSITER** (also called **LAURA EDNA LASSITER**) was born in May 1900 in Lassiter Mill, New Hope, Randolph, North Carolina. She died on 24 Jun 1980 in North Carolina.[847] She had a brief relationship with **WILLIAM TOMM** in 1926 (no other information about him is known),[848] as well as one with **HARRISON SMITHERMAN** in 1933.[849] Harrison was born in Jul 1890 in Strieby, Randolph, North Carolina. He died on 14 Jun 1977 at the VA Hospital in Durham, Durham, North Carolina.[850]

---

[845] Randolph County, North Carolina Marriage Registers, Book 7:406. Harry Speed and Alice Lassiter.

[846] North Carolina, Death Indexes, 1908-2004 [Database on-line]. *Ancestry.com.* Harry Speed, 6 Jul 1941.

[847] North Carolina, Death Indexes, 1908-2004 [Database on-line]. *Ancestry.com.* Edna Lassiter Everett, 24 Jun 1980.

[848] North Carolina Birth Indexes1800-2000 [Database on-line], *Ancestry.com.* William Tomm, Father, Nettie Aline Lassiter, born 1 Dec 1926.

[849] North Carolina, Birth Indexes, 1800-2000 [Database on-line]. *Ancestry.com.* Harris Smitheron [*sic*], Father: Thomas Avern Lassiter, born 2 Aug 1933.

[850] North Carolina Death Indexes, 1908-2004 [Database on-line]. *Ancestry.com.* Harrison Smitherman, 14 June 1977.

She married **NEWTON EVERETT** sometime after 1933. No details about this marriage are known by this author. **Both she and HARRISON SMITHERMAN** are **buried in Strieby Church Cemetery.**

RHODEMIA CHARITY[3] LASSITER (COLIER PHILLIPS[2], MILES[1]) was born in 1866 in Lassiter Mill, New Hope, Randolph, North Carolina. She died after 1930 in New York, New York. She married **ALEXANDER ADDERTON**, son of **JENNY ADDERTON** on 20 Sep 1883 in Asheboro, Randolph, North Carolina. He was born in 1854 in North Carolina. He died on 01 Jun 1917 in Asheboro, Randolph, North Carolina and is **buried in Strieby Church Cemetery**. *[See Entry Above]*

b. ALEXANDER ADDERTON and RHODEMIA CHARITY LASSITER had the following children:

   i. **BERTHA[4] ADDERTON** was born in 1887 in New Hope, Randolph, North Carolina. She died on 15 May 1917 in Randolph, North Carolina.[851] She is **buried in Strieby Church Cemetery**.

   ii. **LUCY ADDERTON** was born on 24 Sep 1891 in New Hope, Randolph, North Carolina.[852] She may have died in Jan 1985 in West Hempstead, Nassau, New

---

[851] North Carolina, Death Certificates, 1909-1975 [Database on-line]. *Ancestry.com.* Bertha Adderton, 15 May 1917.

[852] 1910 US Federal Census; Census Place: New Hope, Randolph, North Carolina; NARA Roll: T624_1128; Page: 1B; Enumeration District: 89; Image: 362. *Ancestry.com.* Indicates Lucy Adderton was born about 1888.

York.[853] She married **LOUIS REED**, 26 Feb 1906 in New York, New York.[854] He was born in 1880 in Virginia.[855]

iii. **COLLIER ADDERTON** was born April1890 in New Hope, Randolph, North Carolina.[856] He was ordered to report for military duty on 23 Aug 1918 and is recorded as reporting to Camp Green in Randolph, North Carolina, along with his cousin William James Lassiter.[857] No other information has been identified to date. He may have been a World War I casualty.

iv. **MAE ADDERTON** was born on Mar 1893 in New Hope, Randolph, North Carolina. She died in 01 Mar 1931 in New York, NY.[858] She married **CHARLES**

---

[853] U. S. Social Security Death Index, 1935-Current. [Database on-line]. *Ancestry.com*. Lucy Reed, Jan 1985.

[854] New York, New York, Marriage Indexes 1866-1937. [Database on-line]. *Ancestry.com*. Lucy Aderton and Lewis G. Reed.

[855] 1920 US Federal Census; Census Place: Manhattan Assembly District 19, New York, New York; NARA Roll: T625_1221; Page: 1A; Enumeration District: 1351; Image: 1069. *Ancestry.com*. Louis Reed, head.

[856] 1900 US Federal Census; Census Place: New Hope, Randolph, North Carolina; NARA Roll: 1213; Page: 2A; Enumeration District: 0090. FHL #1241213. *Ancestry.com*. Alex Adderton, head.

[857] U.S., Lists of Men Ordered to Report to Local Board for Military Duty, 1917–1918. [Database on-line]. *Ancestry.com*. Callier Adderton, 23 August 1918 to Camp Green, North Carolina.

[858] New York, New York City Municipal Deaths, 1795-1949, index [Database on-line]. *FamilySearch.* Chas Lane in entry for May Lane, 01 Mar 1931;

LANE.[859]

v. **ROTAN EARL ADDERTON** was born in 1899 in New Hope, Randolph, North Carolina.[860] He died on 05 Jul 1915 in Colven, Randolph, North Carolina.[861]

vi. **DONALD ADDERTON** was born on 02 Apr 1904 in New Hope, Randolph, North Carolina.[862] He died in Jan 1958 in New York, New York.[863] He married **LEORA (LNU)**.[864] He later married **VIOLA H.** She was born on 23 Apr 1917, in North

---

citing Deaths: Manhattan, New York, New York, United States, New York Municipal Archives, New York.

[859] New York, New York City Municipal Deaths, 1795-1949, index [Database on-line]. *FamilySearch.* Chas Lane in entry for May Lane, 01 Mar 1931; citing Deaths: Manhattan, New York, New York, United States, New York Municipal Archives, New York;

[860] 1900 US Federal Census; Census Place: New Hope, Randolph, North Carolina; NARA Roll: 1213; FHL #1241213; Page: 2A; Enumeration District: 0090; *Ancestry.com.* Alex Adderton, head; Rotan E, age 1.

[861] North Carolina, Death Certificates, 1909-1975 [Database on-line]. *Ancestry.com.* Earl Adderton, 05 Jul 1915.

[862] 1910 US Federal Census; Census Place: New Hope, Randolph, North Carolina; NARA Roll: T624_1128; Page: 1B; Enumeration District: 0087; FHL #1375141.*Ancestry.com.* Alexander Aderton, head; Donnald Aderton, age 9.

[863] U.S. National Cemetery Interment Control Forms, 1928-1962, [Database on-line]. *Ancestry.com.* Donald Adderton.

[864] 1930 US Federal Census; Census Place: Manhattan, New York, New York; NARA Roll: 1573; Page: 4A; Enumeration District: 0903; Image: 134.0; FHL #2341308. *Ancestry.com.* Donel Adderton, head.

Carolina. She died in2 Oct 2008.[865]

12. **ULYSSES WINSTON[3] LASSITER** (COLIER PHILLIPS[2], MILES[1]) was born on 30 Dec 1869 in Lassiter Mill, New Hope, Randolph, North Carolina. He died on 26 Nov 1937 in Lassiter Mill, New Hope, Randolph, North Carolina. He married **ORA CLARA KEARNS**, daughter of **CLARKSON KEARNS** and **ABIGAIL HEAD** on 08 Sep 1892 in Asheboro, Randolph, North Carolina. She was born on 29 Apr 1874 in New Hope, Randolph, North Carolina. She died on 12 Sep 1951 in Lassiter Mill, New Hope, Randolph, North Carolina. They are **both buried in Strieby Church Cemetery**. *[See Entry Above]*
    a. ULYSSES WINSTON LASSITER and ORA CLARA KEARNS had the following children:

Figure 106: John Carol Bright and Mabel Claire Lassiter. Photo courtesy of Roz Covington.

i. **MABEL CLAIRE[4] LASSITER** was born in Mar 1893 in Lassiter Mill, New Hope,

[865] U.S. Veterans Gravesites, ca.1775-2006 [Database on-line]. *Ancestry.com.* Viola H. Adderton.

Randolph, North Carolina.[866] She died on 03 Nov 1970 in Denton, Davidson, North Carolina.[867] She married **JOHN CAROL BRIGHT**, son of **JEMIMA BRIGHT,** on 05 Apr 1913 in Asheboro, Randolph, North Carolina.[868] He was born on 10 Sep 1887in Randolph County, North Carolina[869] and died Mar 1981 in Asheboro, Randolph County, North Carolina.[870]

---

[866] 1900 US Federal Census; Census Place: New Hope, Randolph, North Carolina; NARA Roll: 1213; Page: 1B; Enumeration District: 0090; FHL #1241213. *Ancestry.com.* Winson Lassiter, head.

[867] North Carolina, Death Certificates, 1909-1975 [Database on-line]. *Ancestry.com.* Mabel Claire Lassiter birth date: Mar 1893 birth place: New Hope, Randolph, North Carolina, USA residence place: Farmer Community, Randolph, North Carolina death date: 3 Nov 1970 death place: Denton, Davidson, North Carolina.

[868] North Carolina, Marriage Records, 1741-2011 [Database on-line]. *Ancestry.com.* Carrol Bright and Mable Lassiter, 05 Apr 1913.

[869] U.S. World War I Draft Registration Cards, 1917-1918 [Database on-line]. *Ancestry.com.* John Carrell Bright, born 10 Sep 1887.

[870] U.S. Social Security Death Index, 1935-Current, [Database on-line] *Ancestry.com.* John Bright, born 10 Sep 1887, died Mar 1981.

Figure 107: Vella Lassiter, 1982. Photo by Margo Lee Williams.

ii. **NOVELLA ANNA "VELLA" LASSITER** was born on 04 Sep 1894 in Lassiter Mill, New Hope, Randolph, North Carolina.[871] She died on 02 Jan 1994 in Asheboro, Randolph, North Carolina.[872] She is **buried in Strieby Church Cemetery**.

---

[871] 1900 U.S. Federal Census; Census Place: New Hope, Randolph, North Carolina; NARA Roll: 1213; Page: 1B; Enumeration District: 0090; FHL #1241213.*Ancestry.com.* Winson Lassiter, head.

[872] North Carolina, Death Indexes, 1908-2004, [Database on-line]. *Ancestry.com*. Novella Anna Lassiter, 2 Jan 1994.

Figure 108: William James Lassiter. Photo by Margo Lee Williams, 1982.

iii. **WILLIAM JAMES LASSITER** was born on 26 Apr 1896 in Lassiter Mill, New Hope, Randolph, North Carolina.[873] He died on 08 Mar 1995 in Asheboro, Randolph, North Carolina.[874] He is **buried in Strieby Church**

[873] 1900; Census Place: New Hope, Randolph, North Carolina; NARA Roll: 1213; Page: 1B; Enumeration District: 0090; FHL #1241213.*Ancestry.com*. Winson Lassiter, head. *See also*: U.S., World War I Draft Registration Cards, 1917-1918, [Database on-line]. *Ancestry.com*. William James Lassiter, birth date: 26 April 1896.

[874] North Carolina, Death Indexes, 1908-2004 [Database on-line]. *Ancestry.com*. William J. Lassiter death date: 8 Mar 1995 death place: Winston-Salem, Forsyth, North Carolina, USA.

Cemetery.

Figure 109: Charles Colon Lassiter & Esther Adlene Robinson. Photo courtesy Patrice Lassiter Bryant.

iv. **CHARLES COLON LASSITER** was born in 16 Apr 1898 in Lassiter Mill, New Hope, Randolph, North Carolina.[875] He died in 24 Feb 1973 in Winston-Salem, Forsyth, North Carolina.[876] He married **ESTHER ADLENE ROBINSON.**[877] **She was t**he daughter of

---

[875] 1900 US Federal Census; Census Place: New Hope, Randolph, North Carolina; NARA Roll: 1213; Page: 1B; Enumeration District: 0090; FHL #1241213.*Ancestry.com.* Winson Lassiter, head.

[876] North Carolina, Death Certificates, 1909-1975 [Database on-line]. *Ancestry.com.* Charles C. Lassiter, Sr. 24 Feb 1973.

[877] North Carolina, Death Certificates, 1909-1975 [Database on-line]. *Ancestry.com.* Charles C. Lassiter, Sr. 24 Feb 1973. Esther Robinson, wife.

LEWIS HENRY ROBINSON and MATILDA BLACKER[878] and was born on 15 Aug 1905 in Evanston, IL.[879] She died in 18 Oct 1985 in Winston-Salem, Forsyth, North Carolina.[880]

Figure 110: George Ulysses "Grant" Lassiter. Photo courtesy of Patrice Lassiter Bryant.

---

[878] 1910 US Federal Census; Census Place: Goose Creek, Piatt, Illinois; Roll: T624_317; Page: 5B; Enumeration District: 0151; FHL microfilm: 1374330. *Ancestry.com*. Lewis H Robinson, head; Esther Robinson, age 5.

[879] Winnebago County, Illinois, Births, 1857-1937 [Database on-line]. *Ancestry.com.* Esther Robinson, 15 Aug 1905.

[880] North Carolina, Death Indexes, 1908-2004 [Database on-line]. *Ancestry.com.* Esther Adalene Lassiter, 16 Oct 1985.

v. **GEORGE ULYSSES "GRANT" LASSITER** was born on 18 Dec 1901 in Lassiter Mill, New Hope, Randolph, North Carolina.[881] He died after 25 Jan 1989 in Lassiter Mill, New Hope, Randolph, North Carolina.[882] He met and had a relationship with Randolph County native, **ETHEL MOZELLE WATKINS**. She was born on 28 Sep 1914 in Farmer, Randolph, North Carolina. She died on 03 Dec 2002 in Greensboro, Guilford, North Carolina.[883]

---

[881] U.S. WWII Draft Cards Young Men, 1940-1947 [Database on-line]. *Ancestry.com.* George Ulyses Lassiter, 18 Dec 1902, *See also*: 1910 U.S. Federal Census; Census Place: New Hope, Randolph, North Carolina, line 53; Roll: T624_1128; Page: 1B; Enumeration District: 0087; FHL #1375141. *Ancestry.com.* Ulyses Lassiter.

[882] U.S. Social Security Death Index, 1935-Current [Database on-line]. *Ancestry.com.* George U. Lassiter, Jan 1989.

[883] North Carolina, Death Indexes, 1908-2004, [Database on-line]. *Ancestry.com.* Ethel Watkins Dunn, 03 Dec 2002.

Figure 111: Sarah Juanita Smitherman.

He married (1) **SARAH JUANITA SMITHERMAN**, daughter of **CHARLES SMITHERMAN** and **MARY ANN HILL** on 20 Apr 1946 in Asheboro, Randolph, North Carolina.[884] She was born on 09 Jan 1901 in Strieby, Union, Randolph, North Carolina. She died on 29 Jul 1975 in Asheboro, Randolph, North Carolina.[885] He married (2) **DELORES BENNETT** on 01 Jun 1980 in

[884] North Carolina, Marriage Collection, 1741-2004 [Database on-line]. *Ancestry.com*. George A. Lassiter and Sarah Juanita Smitherman, 20 Apr 1946.
[885] North Carolina, Death Certificates, 1909-1975 [Database on-line]. *Ancestry.com*. Sarah Smitherman Lassiter, 29 Jul 1975.

Asheboro, Randolph, North Carolina.[886] Both **he and SARAH SMITHERMAN are buried in Strieby Church Cemetery**.

Figure 112: Lovell Marion Lassiter & Ira W. Gray. Photo courtesy of Patrice Lassiter Bryant.

vi. **LOVELL MARION LASSITER** was born on 22 Jul 1904 in Lassiter Mill, New Hope, Randolph, North Carolina.[887] She

[886] North Carolina, Marriage Collection, 1741-2004 [Database on-line]. *Ancestry.com*. George Ulysses Lassiter and Delores Hynes Bennett, 1 Jun 1980.

[887] 1910 U.S. Census; Census Place: New Hope, Randolph, North Carolina, line 54; Roll: T624_1128; Page: 1B; Enumeration District: 0087; FHL #1375141.*Ancestry.com*.Lovel Lassiter.

died on 21 Sep 1981 in Long Branch, Monmouth, New Jersey.[888] She married **IRA W. GRAY**, the son of **IRA GRAY** and **DAISY WATKINS**, 28 Dec 1934 in New York City.[889] He was born on 02 Feb 1907 in High Point, Guilford, North Carolina. He died on 07 Mar 1982 in Atlantic City, New Jersey.[890]

KATHERINE "KATE" MARTITIA LILLY BERNICE LASSITER was born on 23 Nov 1906 in Lassiter Mill, New Hope, Randolph, North Carolina.[891] She died on 22 Nov 2006 in Asheboro, Randolph, North Carolina.[892]

---

[888] U.S., Social Security Death Index, 1935-Current [Database on-line]. *Ancestry.com*. Lovell Gray, Oct 1981 [*sic*].

[889] New York, New York City Marriage Records, 1866-1938 [Database on-line]. Marriage: Manhattan, New York, New York, United States, New York City Municipal Archives, New York; FHL microfilm. Index, *FamilySearch.* Ira Walter Gray and Lovell Marion Lassiter, 28 Dec 1934.

[890] U.S. Find A Grave Index, 1700s-Current [Database on-line]. *Ancestry.com*. Ira W. Gray, Strieby Congregational U. C. C. Cemetery, Asheboro, North Carolina.

[891] 1910 US Federal Census; Census Place: New Hope, Randolph, North Carolina, NARA Roll: T624_1128; Page: 1B; Enumeration District: 0087; FHL #1375141. *Ancestry.com*. Kate Lassiter, line 55.

[892] U.S. Social Security Death Index, 1935-Current [Database on-line]. *Ancestry.com*. Katherine T. Jones, 23 Nov 1907 [sic], 22 Nov 1906.

Figure 113: George "Ikie" Jones & Katherine "Kate" Lassiter. Photo courtesy of Patrice Lassiter Bryant.

She married (1) **JAMES TRENT** in the 1940s, but they divorced.[893] She married (2) **GEORGE JONES**, son of **GEORGE JONES and MATTIE,** on 21 Jan 1965 in Westfield, New Jersey. He was born on 03 Aug 1904 in Norlina, North Carolina. He died on 03 Feb 1994 in Lassiter Mill, New Hope, Randolph, North

[893] Per conversations with the author during many conversations between1982-2006. No more details were ever provided and no documentation has been identified to date.

Carolina.[894]Both **she and GEORGE JONES** are **buried in Strieby Church Cemetery**.

Figure 114: Clark Henry Lassiter. Photo courtesy Patrice Lassiter Bryant.

CLARK HENRY LASSITER was born on 04 Mar 1910 in Lassiter Mill, New Hope, Randolph, North Carolina.[895] He died on 26 Jun 2003 in Bronx, New

---

[894] North Carolina, Death Indexes, 1908-2004 [Database on-line]. *Ancestry.com* George Jones, 3 Feb 1994.
[895] 1910 U.S. Census; Census Place: New Hope, Randolph, North Carolina, NARA Roll: T624_1128; Page: 1B; Enumeration District: 0087; FHL #1375141. *Ancestry.com*. Clark Lassiter, line 56.

York.[896] He married (1) **GLADYS SNEAD**, daughter of **SIDNEY SNEAD** and **GEORGIANNA** on 23 Jan 1945 in New York, NY. She was born on 23 Nov 1907 in the Bronx, New York. She died on 13 Jul 1995 in New York, New York.[897] He married (2) **FAY RAY MOSES** on 27 Oct 2002 at Strieby Church, Randolph, North Carolina.[898]

---

[896] U.S. Social Security Death Index, 1935-Current [Database on-line]. *Ancestry.com.* Clark Lassiter, 26 Jun 2003.
[897] U.S. Social Security Death Index, 1935-Current [Database on-line]. *Ancestry.com*. Gladys Lassiter, 13 Jul 1995. The author's mother and cousin of Clark Lassiter, Margaret Lee Williams, attended Gladys' funeral.
[898] North Carolina, Marriage Collection, 1741-2004 [Database on-line]. *Ancestry.com*. Clark Lassiter and Fay Moses, 22 Oct 2002.

Figure 115: Fay Ray Moses.
Photo by Margo Lee Williams, 2005.

She died on 14 Sep 2013 in New York, New York.[899]

[899] Fay Ray. *The History Makers.* Retrieved from: http://www.thehistorymakers.com/biography/fay-ray-41 The author received a personal phone call at the time of Fay Ray's death.

Figure 116: Wade Josiah Lassiter.
Photo courtesy of Patrice Lassiter Bryant.

vii. **WADE JOSIAH LASSITER** was born on 21 Apr 1912 in Lassiter Mill, New Hope, Randolph, North Carolina.[900] He died on 25 Mar 1986 in Miami, Dade, FL.[901] He married **ANGELINA "ANGIE" HERNANDEZ** on 06 Jun 1964 in Stamford, Fairfield, Connecticut.[902] She was born in Cuba.

---

[900] 1920 US Federal Census; Census Place: New Hope, Randolph, North Carolina; NARA Roll: T625_1318; Page: 10A; Enumeration District: 109; Image: 1044.*Ancestry.com.* Winston Lassiter, head.
[901] U.S. Find A Grave Index, 1700s-Current [Database on-line]. *Ancestry.com.* Wade J. Lassiter, 21 Mar 1986. *See also*: U.S. Social Security Death Index, 1935-Current, [Database on-line]. *Ancestry.com.* Wade Lassiter, Mar 1986.
[902] Connecticut, Marriage Index, 1959-2001. [Database on-line]. *Ancestry.com.* Wade Lassiter and Angelina Hernandez, 06 Jun 1964.

WADE is buried in Strieby Church Cemetery.

Figure 117: Aveus "Ave" Lassiter. Photo by Margo Lee Williams, 2003.

viii. AVEUS WILHELMINA LASSITER was born on 04 Jul 1913 in Lassiter Mill, New Hope, Randolph, North Carolina.[903] She died on 19 Oct 2014 in Greensboro, Guilford, North Carolina,

---

[903] 1920 US Federal Census; Census Place: New Hope, Randolph, North Carolina; NARA Roll: T625_1318; Page: 10A; Enumeration District: 109; Image: 1044. *Ancestry.com*. Winston Lassiter, head, Avais, age 6.

USA.[904]

Figure 118: Clarence E. Edmondson. Photo courtesy Patrice Lassiter Bryant.

She married **CLARENCE EUGENE EDMONDSON**, son of **JOHN EDMONDSON and DAISY** on 18 Aug 1942 in Westport, Connecticut.[905] He

---

[904] United States Obituary Collection [Database on-line]. *Ancestry.com.* Aveus Lassiter Edmondson, 23 Oct 2014, Retrieved from: http://search.ancestry.com/cgi-bin/sse.dll?indiv=1&dbid=7545&h=322221757&ssrc=pt&tid=66453873&pid=36231768278&usePUB=true citing *The Courier-Tribune* (Asheboro, NC), 23 Oct 2014, Aveus Lassiter Edmondson. Retrieved 015) from: http://courier-tribune.com/obituaries/aveus-lassiter-edmondson The author attended Aveus Lassiter Edmondson's funeral.

[905] Date and place information told to the author by Aveus Lassiter Edmondson.

was born on 17 Dec 1909 in Mebane, Alamance, North Carolina.[906] He died on 21 Jul 1982 in Salisbury, Rowan, North Carolina.[907] They are **both buried in Strieby Church Cemetery.**

Figure 119: Leonard Fulmer Lassiter. Photo by Margo Lee Williams, 1982

ix. **LEONARD FULMER LASSITER** was born on 17 Jan 1915 in Lassiter Mill, New Hope, Randolph, North Carolina.[908] He

---

[906] North Carolina, Birth Indexes, 1800-2000 [Database on-line]. *Ancestry.com*. Clarence Eugene Edmondson, 17 Dec 1909.
[907] North Carolina, Death Indexes, 1908-2004 [Database on-line]. *Ancestry.com*. Clarence Eugene Edmondson, 21 Jul 1982.
[908] 1920 US Federal Census; Census Place: New Hope, Randolph, North Carolina; NARA Roll: T625_1318; Page: 10A; Enumeration District: 109;

died on 24 Jul 1989 in Greensboro, Guilford, North Carolina.[909] He married **DOROTHY JACKSON TILSON**.

Figure 120: Harold Cleon Lassiter. Photo by Margo Lee Williams, 2003.

x. **HAROLD CLEON LASSITER** was born on 30 Jun 1918 in Lassiter Mill, New Hope, Randolph, North Carolina.[910] He

---

Image: 1044. *Ancestry.com*. Winston Lassiter, head. *See also*: North Carolina, Birth Indexes, 1800-2000 [Database on-line]. *Ancestry.com*. Leonard Fulmer Lassiter, 17 Jan 1915

[909] North Carolina, Death Indexes, 1908-2004 [Database on-line]. *Ancestry.com*. Leonard Lassiter, 24 Jul 1989.

[910] 1920 US Federal Census; Census Place: New Hope, Randolph, North Carolina; NARA Roll: T625_1318; Page: 10A; Enumeration District: 109; Image: 1044. *Ancestry.com*. Winston Lassiter, head. ***See also***: North Carolina,

died on 01 Nov 2004 in Charlotte, Mecklenburg, North Carolina.[911] He married **HELEN PATRICIA GOODWIN** on 15 Jun 1954 in Randolph County, North Carolina.[912]

13. **ABIGAIL[3] LASSITER** (WILEY PHILLIPS[2], MILES[1]) was born in 1846 in Lassiter Mill, New Hope, Randolph, North Carolina. She died 27 April 1931, in Friendship, Guilford, North Carolina. She married **JESSE SMITH** 14 Feb 1869. He was born ABOUT 1840 in North Carolina. He apparently died between 1928 and 1931 in Guilford County, North Carolina, when he was last identified with Abbey [*sic*] (1928) and she was reportedly a widow (1931). [*See Entry Above*]
    a. JESSE SMITH and ABIGAIL LASSITER had the following children:
        i. **WILEY[4] SMITH**, born about 1867, Friendship, Guilford, North Carolina.[913]
        ii. **MARY SMITH**, born about 1869,

Birth Indexes, 1800-2000 [Database on-line]. *Ancestry.com*. Harold Cleon Lassiter, 30 Jun 1918.

[911] North Carolina, Death Indexes, 1908-2004 [Database on-line]. *Ancestry.com*. Harold C. Lassiter, 01 Nov 2004.

[912] North Carolina, Marriage Collection, 1741-2004 [Database on-line]. *Ancestry.com*. Harold Cleon Lassiter and Helen Patricia Goodwin, 15 Jun 1954.

[913] 1870 U.S. Federal Census; Census Place: Friendship, Guilford, North Carolina. NARA Roll: M593_1140; Page: 67B; Image: 366; FHL#552639. *Ancestry.com*. Jesse Smith, head; Willie [*sic*] Smith, age 3.

Friendship, Guilford, North Carolina.[914]

iii. **JOSEPHINE SMITH**, born about 1873, Friendship, Guilford, North Carolina.[915]

iv. **JULIUS OSCAR SMITH**, born about 11 Apr 1874 in GUILFORD College, Guilford, North Carolina and died 17 Jun 1953 in Greensboro, Guilford, North Carolina.[916] He married first **CATHERINE "KATY" HEADEN**, 26 April 1902, in Guilford County, North Carolina.[917]She apparently died between 1910 and 1916 when he married **ELLEN MARTIN (nee WATSON)**, daughter of **RUFUS WATSON**, 24 Dec 1916, also in Guilford County.[918] She was born about 1876 and died 12 June 1960, in Greensboro, Guilford, North Carolina.[919]

---

[914] 1870 U.S. Federal Census; Census Place: Friendship, Guilford, North Carolina. NARA Roll: M593_1140; Page: 67B; Image: 366; FHL #552639.*Ancestry.com*.Jesse Smith, head; Mary Smith, age 3/12.

[915] 1880 U. S. Federal Census; Census Place: Friendship, Guilford, North Carolina. NARA Roll: 965; FHL #1254965; Page: 267C; Enumeration District: 122; Image: 0783. *Ancestry.com*. Jesse Smith, head; Josephine Smith, age 9.

[916] North Carolina, Death Certificates, 1909-1975 [Database on-line]. *Ancestry.com*. Julius Arthur [*sic*] Smith, 17 Jun 1953.

[917] North Carolina, Marriage Records, 1741-2011 [Database on-line]. *Ancestry.com*. Julius O. Smith and Catherine Headen, 26 Apr 1902.

[918] North Carolina, Marriage Records, 1741-2011 [Database on-line]. *Ancestry.com*. Julius Smith and Ellen Martin, 24 Dec 1916.

[919] North Carolina, Death Certificates, 1909-1975 [Database on-line]. *Ancestry.com*. Ellen Smith, 12 Jun 1960.

v. **JENETTE SMITH**, born 1875, Friendship, Guilford, North Carolina.[920]

vi. **GERTRUDE SMITH**, born 1878, Friendship, Guilford, North Carolina.[921]

vii. **BERTHA SMITH**, born 1886, Deep River, Guilford, North Carolina.[922]

14. **NANCY JANE[3] LASSITER** (WILEY PHILLIPS[2], MILES[1]) was born in Feb 1848 in Lassiter Mill, New Hope, Randolph, North Carolina. She died after 1900, most likely in Randolph County, North Carolina. She married **THOMAS BRYANT** on 01 Oct 1868 in Asheboro, Randolph, North Carolina. He was born in Aug 1842 in North Carolina. He died after 1900 in Randolph County, North Carolina. [*See Entry Above*]

a. THOMAS BRYANT and NANCY JANE LASSITER had the following children:

i. **GEORGE W.[4] BRYANT** was born in 1870 in New Hope Academy, New Hope,

---

920 1880 U. S. Federal Census; Census Place: Friendship, Guilford, North Carolina. NARA Roll: 965; Family History Film: 1254965; Page: 267C; Enumeration District: 122; Image: 0783. *Ancestry.com*. Jesse Smith, head; Jenette Smith, age 5.

921 1880 U. S. Federal Census; Census Place: Friendship, Guilford, North Carolina. NARA Roll: 965; FHL #1254965; Page: 267C; Enumeration District: 122; Image: 0783. *Ancestry.com*. Jesse Smith, head, Gertrude Smith, age 2.

922 1900 US Federal Census; Census Place: Deep River, Guilford, North Carolina. NARA Roll: 1198; Page: 10B; Enumeration District: 0046; FHL #1241198. *Ancestry.com*. Jesse Smith, head; Bertha Smith, age 13.

Randolph, North Carolina.[923] He may be the **GEORGE BRYANT**, servant in the home of **JESSE BUNDY** also from North Carolina, living in Atlantic City, New Jersey.[924]

ii. **WILLIAM BRYANT** was born in 1876 in Science Hill, Cedar Grove, Randolph, North Carolina.[925]He married **R. C. W. BURNS**, 22 Dec 1909, in Staunton, Virginia.[926]

iii. **JOHN M. BRYANT** was born in Jul 1881 in Science Hill, Cedar Grove, Randolph, North Carolina.[927]

iv. **CHILD BRYANT** was born in Randolph County, North Carolina.[928]

---

[923] 1870 US Federal Census; Census Place: New Hope, Randolph, North Carolina. NARA Roll: M593_1156; Page: 398A; Image: 245; FHL#552655. *Ancestry.com*. Thomas Bryant, head; George W Bryant, age 2/12.

[924] 1900 US Federal Census; Census Place: Atlantic City Ward 3, Atlantic, New Jersey. NARA Roll: 953; Page: 10A; Enumeration District: 0009; FHL #1240953. *Ancestry.com*. Jesse Bundy, head; George Bryant, servant.

[925] 1880 US Federal Census; Census Place: Cedar Grove, Randolph, North Carolina 1880; Census Place: Cedar Grove, Randolph, North Carolina; Roll: 978; FHL #1254978; Page: 154B; Enumeration District: 220; Image: 0601. *Ancestry.com*. Thomas Bryant, head; William Bryant, age 4.

[926] Virginia, Select Marriages, 1785-1940 [Database on-line].*Ancestry.com*. William V. Bryant and R. C. Burns, 22 Dec 1909.

[927] 1900 US Federal Census; Census Place: Cedar Grove, Randolph, North Carolina. NARA Roll: T623_31077_4117840; Page: 4A; Enumeration District: 0082; FHL #1241212. *Ancestry.com*. Thomas Bryant, head; John M Bryant, age 18.

[928] 1900 US Federal Census; Census Place: Cedar Grove, Randolph, North Carolina. NARA Roll: T623_31077_4117840; Page: 4A; Enumeration

v. **CHILD BRYANT** was born in Randolph County, North Carolina.[929]

Figure 121: Julia Ann Lassiter & Mary Martha Sanders. Photo courtesy of Martha Brooks.

15. **JULIA ANN[3] LASSITER** (WILEY PHILLIPS[2], MILES[1]) was born in May 1852 in Lassiter Mill, New Hope,

---

District: 0082; FHL #1241212. *Ancestry.com.* Thomas Bryant, head. Number of children born: 5; Living, 3.

[929] 1900 US Federal Census; Census Place: Cedar Grove, Randolph, North Carolina. NARA Roll: T623_31077_4117840; Page: 4A; Enumeration District: 0082; FHL #1241212. *Ancestry.com.* Thomas Bryant, head. Number of children born: 5; Living, 3.

Randolph, North Carolina. She died on 31 Jan 1921 in Cedar Grove, Randolph, North Carolina. She married **HENRY B. W. SANDERS** on 18 Jan 1877 in Asheboro, Randolph, North Carolina. He was born in Sep 1853 in North Carolina. He died in 1900 in Cedar Grove, Randolph, North Carolina.*(See Entry Above)*

a. HENRY B. W. SANDERS and JULIA ANN LASSITER had the following children:

   i. **JULIUS S.[4] SANDERS** was born in 1877 in Union, Randolph, North Carolina, but no information about him after 1880 has been found.[930]

   ii. **MARY MARTHA SANDERS** was born on 09 Jul 1882 in Cedar Grove, Randolph, North Carolina. She died on 07 Aug 1950 in Randolph County, North Carolina.[931] She married **R. VANDER HINES** on 27 Mar 1900 in Asheboro, Randolph, North Carolina.[932] He was born in Nov 1872 in North Carolina.

   iii. **THOMAS FRED SANDERS** was born on 22 Aug 1885 in Cedar Grove, Randolph, North Carolina. He died on 16 Feb 1943 in High Point, Guilford,

---

[930] 1880 US Federal Census; Census Place: Union, Randolph, North Carolina; NARA Roll: 978; FHL #1254978; Page: 196C; Enumeration District: 224; Image: 0683. *Ancestry.com*. Henry Sanders, head; Julius Sanders, age 3.

[931] US Find A Grave Index, 1600s-Current, [Database on-line]. Martha Hines.

[932] North Carolina, Marriage Records, 1741-2011 [Database on-line]. *Ancestry.com*. R. V. Hines and Martha Sanders, 27 Mar 1900.

North Carolina.[933] He married **FRANKIE LOLA CHAMBERS**, daughter of **EMMANUEL** and **ARZELETTE CHAMBERS.**[934] She was born on 05 Jan 1901 in Randolph, North Carolina. She died on 03 May 1988 in High Point, Guilford, North Carolina.[935]

iv. **LULA J. SANDERS** was born in Feb 1887 in Cedar Grove, Randolph, North Carolina. She died 1976 in North Carolina.[936] She married **JONES H. GREEN**, son of **SAMUEL GREEN** and **MARY JANE** on 26 Jun 1904 in Asheboro, Randolph, North Carolina. He was born on 26 Oct 1864 in North Carolina. He died on 03 Sep 1951 in Randolph, North Carolina.[937]

---

[933] North Carolina, Death Certificates, 1909-1975 [Database on-line]. *Ancestry.com.* Thomas Fred Sanders, 16 Feb 1943.
[934] North Carolina, Marriage Records, 1741-2011 [Database on-line]. *Ancestry.com.* Thomas F Sanders and Frankie L. Chambers, 29 Nov 1937.
[935] North Carolina, Death Indexes, 1908-2004 [Database on-line]. *Ancestry.com.* Frankie Lola Sanders, 03 May 1988.
[936] North Carolina, Death Indexes, 1908-2004 [Database on-line]. *Ancestry.com.* Lulah Jane Green, 3 May 1976.
[937] U.S. Find A Grave Index, 1600s-Current [Database on-line]. *Ancestry.com.* Jones H. Green, 3 Sep 1951.

Figure 122: Mary Martha Sanders & Myrtle Sanders.
Photo courtesy of Martha Brooks.

v. **MYRTLE M. SANDERS** was born in 17 Mar 1888 in Cedar Grove, Randolph, North Carolina. She died in 16 Feb 1941 in Hillsboro, Orange, North Carolina.[938] She married (1) **WILLIAM M. BUMPERS** on 03 Oct 1920 in Asheboro,

[938] North Carolina, Death Certificates, 1909-1975 [Database on-line]. *Ancestry.com*. Myrtle Brooks, 16 Feb 1941.

Randolph, North Carolina.[939] She married (2) **WILLIE BROOKS**, son of **GEORGE BROOKS** and **HARRIET LEE** on 26 Jan 1933.[940] He was born in Roxboro, North Carolina. He died 18 Jan 1942, in Durham, North Carolina.[941]

vi. **HENRY PLATO SANDERS** was born in May 1895 in Cedar Grove, Randolph, North Carolina. He died on 20 Jun 1915 in Cedar Grove, Randolph, North Carolina.[942]

16. **ADDISON B.**[3] **LASSITER** (WILEY PHILLIPS[2], MILES[1]) was born in 1862 in Fayetteville, Cumberland, North Carolina. He died after 1930 in Union, Ocean, New Jersey. He married (1) **ADELAIDE FREEMAN**, daughter of **ISAAC FREEMAN** and **MARY STITH** on 22 Sep 1883 in Randolph County, North Carolina. She was born in 1866 in Trinity, Randolph, North Carolina. He married (2) **ANNIE** (LNU) in New Jersey, about 1895. He married (3) **HENRIETTA STANTON** in 1905, in Philadelphia, Pennsylvania. She was born in 1885 in Maryland. She died between 1920 and1930 in Philadelphia, Pennsylvania. [*See Entry Above*]

---

[939] North Carolina, Marriage Collection, 1741-2004 [Database on-line]. *Ancestry.com*. Myrtle Saunders and M. B. Bumpass, 3 Oct 1920.
[940] North Carolina, Marriage Records, 1741-2011 [Database on-line]. *Ancestry.com*. Willie Brooks and Myrtle Bumpass, 26 Jan 1933.
[941] North Carolina, Death Certificates, 1909-1975 [Database on-line]. *Ancestry.com*. Will Brooks, 18 Jan 1942.
[942] North Carolina, Death Certificates, 1909-1975 [Database on-line]. *Ancestry.com*. Plato H. Sanders, 20 Jun 1915.

a. ADDISON B. LASSITER and HENRIETTA STANTON had the following children:

i. **ALICE ELIZABETH[4] LASSITER** was born on 18 May 1906 in Philadelphia, Pennsylvania.[943] She died on 11 Nov 1910 in Philadelphia, Pennsylvania of pneumonia.[944]

ii. **ADDISON P LASSITER** was born about June 1909 in Philadelphia, Pennsylvania. He died a few days after his sister Alice on 22 Nov 1910 in Philadelphia, Pennsylvania, also from pneumonia.[945]

iii. **JULIA LASSITER** was born about 24 May 1911 and died 13 Jul 1912 in Philadelphia, Pennsylvania.[946]

iv. **HENRIETTA LASSITER** was born in 1912 in Pennsylvania.[947]

v. **ARETTA LASSITER** was born in 1913 in

---

[943] Pennsylvania, Birth Records, 1906-1908 [Database on-line]. *Ancestry.com.* Alice Elizabeth Lasitier [*sic*], 18 May 1906.

[944] Pennsylvania, Death Certificates, 1906-1944 [Database on-line].*Ancestry.com.* Alice Lasiter, 11 Nov 1910.

[945] Pennsylvania, Death Certificates, 1906-1944 [Database on-line]. *Ancestry.com.* Addison Lasiter, 22 Nov 1910.

[946] Philadelphia, Pennsylvania, Death Certificates Index, 1803-1915 [Database on-line]. *Ancestry.com.* Julia Lassiter, 13 Jul 1912.

[947] 1920 US Federal Census, Census Place: South Brownsville, Fayette, Pennsylvania; NARA Roll: T625_1570; Page: 7B; Enumeration District: 85; Image: 541. *Ancestry.com.* Addison Lasiter, head; Henrietta Lasiter, age 8.

Pennsylvania.[948]

17. **ELLEN[3] DUNSON** (NANCY PHILLIPS[2] LASSITER, MILES[1] LASSITER) was born on 08 Aug 1852 in New Hope, Randolph, North Carolina. She died on 12 Jun 1920 in Asheboro, Randolph, North Carolina. She married (1) **ANDERSON SMITHERMAN**, reported son of **NOAH SMITHERMAN** and **LUCINDA SMITHERMAN** on 23 Sep1865 in Asheboro, Randolph, North Carolina. He was born in Nov 1848 in Union, Randolph, North Carolina. He died in 1909 in Asheboro, Randolph, North Carolina. She married (2) **CHARLES MAYO** in 1896 in North Carolina. *[See Entry Above]*

    a. ANDERSON SMITHERMAN and ELLEN DUNSON had the following children:

Figure 123: Mary Louise Smitherman. Photo courtesy of Margo Lee Williams.

---

[948] 1920 US Federal Census, Census Place: South Brownsville, Fayette, Pennsylvania; NARA Roll: T625_1570; Page: 7B; Enumeration District: 85; Image: 541. *Ancestry.com*. Addison Lasiter, head; Aretta Lasiter, age 7.

i. **MARY LOUISE[4] SMITHERMAN** was born on 03 Jan 1868 in Union, Randolph, North Carolina.[949] She died on 11 Apr 1936 in Elizabeth, Union, New Jersey.[950] She married (1) **SAMUEL D. PHILLIPS**, son of **LEWIS PHILLIPS** and **MARGARET PEACOCK CALICOTTE** on 23 Jul 1885 in Asheboro, Randolph, North Carolina.[951] He was born on 26 Mar 1864 in Cedar Grove, Randolph, North Carolina. He died on 13 May 1944 in New York, Manhattan, New York.[952] She married (2) **JOHN H. FLOYD** on 31 Jul 1907 in Asheboro, Randolph, North Carolina.[953] He was born about 1870 in North Carolina. He died between 1917

---

[949] 1870 US Federal Census; Census Place: Union, Randolph, North Carolina; NARA Roll: M593_1156; Page: 506A; Image: 465; FHL #552655. *Ancestry.com*. Anderson Smitherman, head; Mary L. age 2.
[950] State of New Jersey, Bureau of Vital Statistics, Certificate and Record of Death. Certificate #436C. Mrs. Louise Ingram, 11 Apr 1936. *See also:* U.S. Find A Grave Index, 1700s-Current [Database on-line]. *Ancestry.com*. Louise Ingram, Apr 1936.
[951] North Carolina, Marriage Collection, 1741-2004 [Database on-line]. *Ancestry.com*. Louisa Smitherman and Samuel Phillips, 23 Jul 1885.
[952] New York, New York, Death Index, 1862-1948 [Database on-line]. *Ancestry.com*. Certificate #11500, Samuel Phillips, 13 May 1944.
[953] Randolph County, North Carolina Marriage Registers, Book 6:79. Randolph Room, Randolph County Regional Library (Microfilm Collection). Jno. H. Floyd and Louisa Philips, 31 Jul 1907. *See also:* North Carolina, Marriage Collection, 1741-2004 [Database on-line]. *Ancestry.com*. Jno. H. Floyd and Louisa Philips, 31 Jul 1907.

and 1918 in 152 N Dudley St. Greensboro, North Carolina. She married (3) **JOHN INGRAM** about 1923 in Asheboro, Randolph, North Carolina. He was born about 1870 in North Carolina. He died after 1925.[954]

ii. **EMORY W. SMITHERMAN** was born in 1873 in New Hope, Randolph, North Carolina. He died before 1890 in New Hope, Randolph, North Carolina.[955]

iii. **AMMA J. SMITHERMAN** was born in May 1877 in New Hope, Randolph, North Carolina. She died on 28 Sep 1929 in Asheboro, Randolph, North Carolina.[956] She married **GEORGE PHILLIPS**, son of **REUBEN PHILLIPS and MARY SCOTT** on 31 Dec 1892 in Asheboro, Randolph, North Carolina.[957] He was born in Apr 1875 in Cedar Grove, Randolph, North Carolina. He died on 22 Apr 1926 in Asheboro, Randolph, North

---

[954] U.S. City Directories, 1821-1989 [Database on-line]. *Ancestry.com*. John Ingram, Louisa Ingram, 1930 [Ingram, Louise (wid John), h 1076 William St.].

[955] 1880 US Federal Census; Census Place: New Hope, Randolph, North Carolina; NARA Roll: 978; FHL#1254978; Page: 185C; Enumeration District: 223; Image: 0661. *Ancestry.com*. Ande Smither[man], head; Emory W. Smither[man], age 7.

[956] North Carolina, Death Certificates, 1909-1975 [Database on-line]. *Ancestry.com*. Armay [Ammy] Phillips, 28 Sep 1929.

[957] North Carolina, Marriage Records, 1741-2011 [Database on-line]. *Ancestry.com*. Amma Smitherman and George Phillips, 31 Dec 1892.

Carolina.[958]

Figure 124: Roxanne "Roxie" Smitherman. Photo courtesy of Charleen Walker-Horton.

iv. **ROXANNA SMITHERMAN** was born in Sep 1878 in New Hope, Randolph, North Carolina.[959] She died on 15 Mar 1940 in Baltimore, Baltimore, Maryland.[960] She married (1) **WESLEY WADDELL**, son of **NATHAN WADDELL** and **MARY MARTHA STRICKLIN** on 09 Apr 1897 in

---

[958] North Carolina, Death Certificates, 1909-1975 [Database on-line]. *Ancestry.com*. George Phillip, 22 Apr 1926.

[959] 1880 US Federal Census; Census Place: New Hope, Randolph, North Carolina, NARA Roll: 978; Family History Film: 1254978; Page: 185C; Enumeration District: 223; Image: 0661. *Ancestry.com*. Ande Smither[man], head; Roxanna Smither[man], age 2.

[960] Baltimore City Health Department Certificate of Death, Certificate #F-67346. Roxie Wilburn, 15 Mar 1940. *See also*: U.S. Find A Grave Index, 1700s-Current [Database on-line]. *Ancestry.com*. Mrs. Roxanna Wilburn, 15 Mar 1940.

Asheboro, Randolph, North Carolina.[961] He was born in Jul 1863 in Browers, Randolph, North Carolina.[962] He died after 1930, most likely in Randolph County, North Carolina. Roxanna and Wesley divorced. She married (2) **WILLIAM H. WILBURN**, son of **JOHN WILBURN and MARTHA HARFORD** in 1910 in Baltimore, Maryland. He was born in 1878 in North Carolina. He died on 02 Jan 1931 in Baltimore, Baltimore, Maryland.[963]

18. **SARAH REBECCA[3] DUNSON** (NANCY PHILLIPS[2] LASSITER, MILES[1] LASSITER) was born in 1857in New Hope, Randolph, North Carolina. She died between 1881 and 1892 in New Hope, Randolph, North Carolina. She had a son but refused to name his father in court.[*See Entry Above*]

a. SARAH REBECCA DUNSON had the following child:

i. **WILLIE[4] DUNSON** was born in 1875 in Lassiter Mill, New Hope, Randolph,

---

961 North Carolina, Marriage Records, 1741-2011 [Database on-line]. *Ancestry.com*. Roxie Smitherman and Wesley Waddell, 9 Apr 1897.

962 1870 US Federal Census; Census Place: Browers, Randolph, North Carolina; NARA Roll: M593_1156; Page: 317A; Image: 83; FHL #552655 [Database on-line]. *Ancestry.com*. Nathan Waddell, head; Wesley Waddell, age 8.

963 Baltimore City Health Department Certificate of Death, Certificate #E-63968. William Wilburn, 02 Jan 1931.

North Carolina.[964] When or where he died is not known, but he was named in an 1892 petition to divide land.[965]

19. **M. ADELAIDE[3] DUNSON** (NANCY PHILLIPS[2] LASSITER, MILES[1] LASSITER) was born in 1861 in New Hope, Randolph, North Carolina. She died on 09 May 1929 in Concord, Randolph, North Carolina. She married **SOLOMON KEARNS**, son of **LINDSEY INGRAM** and **LYDIA "LETTIE" KEARNS** on 17 Apr 1890 in Asheboro, Randolph, North Carolina. He was born on 01 May 1853 in Farmer, Randolph, North Carolina. He died on 11 Sep 1942 in Thomasville, Davidson, North Carolina. *[See Entry Above]*
    a. SOLOMON KEARNS and M. ADELAIDE DUNSON had the following children:
        i. **SULA[4] KEARNS** was born on 03 Sep 1891 in Randolph County, North Carolina.[966] She died in Mar 1978 in White Plains, Westchester, New York.[967] She married **SELLS ELLER**, son of **WILLIAM**

---

[964] 1880 US Federal Census; Census Place: New Hope, Randolph, North Carolina; NARA Roll: 978; FHL#1254978; Page: 184A; Enumeration District: 223; Image: 0659. *Ancestry.com*. Nancy Dunson, head; Willie Dunson, age 5.

[965] Vidales. (2011). "William Dunston-1892," in Randolph County Estates: Diffee-Dumas. *The Genealogical Journal by the Randolph County Genealogical Society, Volume XXXV(2):*45-46.

[966] 1900 US Federal Census; Census Place: New Hope, Randolph, North Carolina; NARA Roll: 1213; Page: 3B; Enumeration District: 0090; FHL #1241213. *Ancestry.com*. Solomon Kearns, head; Sula Kearns, age 8.

[967] U.S. Social Security Death Index, 1935-2014 [Database on-line]. *Ancestry.com*. Sular Eller, Mar 1978.

ELLER and LUVENIA ELLER on 30 Nov 1916 in Randolph County, North Carolina.[968] He was born in 1890 in Midway, Davidson, North Carolina, USA. He died on 11 Nov 1947 in Thomasville, Davidson, North Carolina.[969]

ii. **MARY DIZY KEARNS** was born on 03 Aug 1893 in Randolph County, North Carolina.[970] She died on 11 Jun 1921 in Farmer, Concord, Randolph, North Carolina.[971]

20. **MARTHA ANN[3] DUNSON** (NANCY PHILLIPS[2] LASSITER, MILES[1] LASSITER) was born in 1864 in Lassiter Mill, New Hope, Randolph, North Carolina. She died between 1885-1886 in Lassiter Mill, New Hope, Randolph, North Carolina. She married **JULIUS HILL**, son of **EDWARD "NED" HILL** and **PRISCILLA MAHOCKLY** 24 Jan 1883, in Wadesboro, Anson County, North Carolina. He was born in Mar 1854 in Strieby, Union, Randolph, North Carolina. He died after 1930 in Strieby, Union, Randolph, North Carolina. [*See*

---

[968] North Carolina, Marriage Records, 1741-2011 [Database on-line]. *Ancestry.com*. Sells Eller and Sular Kearns [abstract reads "Teason"] 30 Nov 1916.

[969] North Carolina, Death Certificates, 1909-1975 [Database on-line] *Ancestry.com*. Sells Eller, 11 Nov 1947.

[970] 1900 US Federal Census; Census Place: New Hope, Randolph, North Carolina; NARA Roll: 1213; Page: 3B; Enumeration District: 0090; FHL #1241213 [Database on-line]. *Ancestry.com*. Solomon Kearns, head; Mary Kearns, age 6.

[971] North Carolina, Death Certificates, 1909-1975 [Database on-line]. *Ancestry.com*. Mary Dizy (abstract reads Dazy) Kearns, 11 Jun 1921.

Entry Above]

a. JULIUS HILL and MARTHA ANN DUNSON had the following child:

    i. **MAMIE^4 HILL** was born on 04 Mar 1884 in Lassiter Mill, New Hope, Randolph, North Carolina. She died on 23 Nov 1970 in Concord, Cabarrus, North Carolina.[972] She married **ARCH POOLE**, son of **BENJAMIN POOL** and **CHARLOTTE** on 27 Dec 1904 in Asheboro, Randolph, North Carolina.[973] He was born about 1879 in Montgomery County, North Carolina.

---

[972] North Carolina, Death Certificates, 1909-1975 [Database on-line]. *Ancestry.com*. Mamie Poole, 23 Nov 1970. (Certificate says her mother was Lizzie Hill, but Lizzie was Julius' second wife after Martha Dunson died. Lizzie raised Mamie.)

[973] North Carolina, Marriage Collection, 1741-2004 [Database on-line]. *Ancestry.com*. Mamie Hill and Arch Pool, 27 Dec 1904.

Figure 125: First cousins. (Top) Elinora (Phillips) Lee (1895-1918), daughter of Mary Louise Smitherman & (Bottom) Cleopatra (Waddell) Carter (1898-1953), daughter of Roxanne Smitherman. Photos courtesy of Margo Lee Williams & Charleen Walker-Horton.

Figure 126: Strieby Church Cemetery.
Photo by Margo Lee Williams, 1982

Strieby Church Cemetery

Listed here are those burials with headstones or other funeral home markers identifying who are in the graves. There are other alleged burials, primarily those who died in the early years when it was not common to place headstones. The Table here identifies the name of the deceased, the dates of birth and death, and the deceased's relationship to the core founding families of Ned and Priscilla Hill, of Strieby, or Colier and Kate Lassiter of Lassiter Mill or other early Strieby church families.

Figure 127: Left-Clarence Hayes Hill, Right- Julia Ritter Walden - Tombstones-Strieby Cemetery.

1. Blair, Marion R (Dr.) (b. 23 Jul 1931 - d. 19 Mar 2001) – Former Pastor	2.Cagle, Ross (b. 24 Jun 1909 - d. 7 Jun 1973) – Grandson of Anthony Davis (1900 census)	3.Carter, Faye Lassiter (b. 22 May 1926 - d. 13 May 2010) – granddaughter of Colier & Kate Lassiter	4.Edmondson, Clarence E (b. 17 Dec 1909 - d. 21 Jul 1982) – Husband of Aveus Lassiter Edmondson, granddaughter of Colier & Kate Lassiter
5.Epps, Marie Hill (b. 9 Sep 1928 - d. 2 Sep 2002) – 3rd Great Granddaughter of Ned & Priscilla Hill/Great Granddaughter of Colier	6.Everett, Edna Lassiter (b. 9 May 1900 - d. 24 Jun 1980) – Great Granddaughter of Colier & Kate Lassiter	7.Fisher, Coleen C (b. 10 Aug 1889 - d. 6 Nov 1906) – Great Great Granddaughter of Ned & Priscilla Hill	8.Fisher, William (b. 1861 - d. 16 Feb 1906) – Husband of Elizabeth Hill, great granddaughter of Ned & Priscilla Hill

Lassiter			
9.Franks, Faye Lassiter (b. 1 Dec 1926 - d. 12 Dec 1977) - Great Great Granddaughter of Colier & Kate Lassiter	10.Gray, Ira W (b. 2 Feb 1907 - d. 7 Mar 1982) - Husband of Lovell L. Gray, granddaughter of Colier & Kate Lassiter	11.Gray, Lovell L (b. 22 Jul 1902 - d. 21 Sep 1981) - Granddaughter of Colier & Kate Lassiter	12.Hill, Alton (b. 6 Mar 1923 - d. 27 Apr 1974) - 3rd Great Grandson of Ned & Priscilla Hill
13.Hill, Arthur H (b. 13 Sep 1887 - d. 13 Sep 1980) - Great Great Grandson of Ned & Priscilla Hill	14.Hill, Charles (b. 1918 - d. 1979) - Great Great Grandson of Ned & Priscilla Hill	15.Hill, Clarence Hayes (b. 26 May 1917 - d. 14 May 1958) - 3rd Great Grandson of Ned & Priscilla Hill	16.Hill, Lizzie (b. 1864 - d. 1936) - Wife of Arthur Hill; granddaughter of Colier & Kate Lassiter
17.Hill, Lizzie A (b. 17 Oct 1835 - d. 20Dec1888) - Wife of Barzilla "Zill" Hill, grandson of Ned & Priscilla Hill	18.Hill, C. J. Nettie (b. 15 Jul 1885 - d. 20 Dec 1888) - Daughter of Emsley Hill, granddaughter of Ned & Priscilla Hill	19.Hill, Priscilla (b. 1792 - d. 1911) 119 Years Old - Wife of Ned Hill	20.Hill, Zell H (b. 1864 - d. 1933) - grandson of Ned & Priscilla Hill
21. Jones, David (b. 21 Feb 1923 - d. 7 Jan 1924)	22. Jones, George H (b. 3 Aug 1904 - d. 3 Feb 1994) - husband of Kate L. Jones, granddaughter of Colier & Kate Lassiter	23. JONES, KATE L. (B. 1906 - D. 2006) - GRANDDAUGHTER OF COLIER & KATE LASSITER	24. Lacey, Bernice Bell (b. 1933 - d. 1979)

25. Lassiter, Amos P (Barzilla or Zill) (b. 4 Dec 1863 - d. 16 Dec 1930) - son of Colier & Kate Lassiter	26. Lassiter, Avon (b. 24 Aug 1933 - d. 28 May 1950) - Great Great Grandson of Colier & Kate Lassiter	27. Lassiter, Dwayne (b. 20 Nov 1963 - d. 1 Apr 2004) - Great Grandson of Colier & Kate Lassiter	28. Lassiter, Elbert John (b. 31 Mar 1937 - d. 2 Mar 1971) - Grandson of Colier & Kate Lassiter
29. Lassiter, Harriett J (b. 1 Feb 1862 - d. 1 Mar 1942) - Wife of Amos P Lassiter, son of Colier & Kate Lassiter	30. Lassiter, Harris S (b. 7 Feb 1889 - d. 31 Jan 1964) - Grandson of Colier & Kate Lassiter	31 .Lassiter, Katie (b. 7 Mar 1832 - d. 19 Dec 1906) - Wife of Colier Lassiter	32. Lassiter, Novella A (b. 4 Sep 1894 - d. 2 Jan 1994) - Granddaughter of Colier & Kate Lassiter
33. Lassiter, Ora (b. 29 Apr 1874 - d. 12 Sep 1951) - Wife of Ulysses W(inston) Lassiter, son of Colier & Kate Lassiter	34. Lassiter, Sarah Smitherman (b. 6 Sep 1896 - d. 29 Jul 1975) - Wife of Ulysses (George) Lassiter, grandson of Colier & Kate Lassiter	35. Lassiter, Ulysses (b. 18 Dec 1902 - d. 25 Jan 1989) - Grandson of Colier & Kate Lassiter	36. Lassiter, Ulysses W (b. 30 Dec 1871 - d. 26 Nov 1937) - Son of Colier & Kate Lassiter
37. Lassiter, Wade J (b. 21 Apr 1911 - d. 21 Mar 1986) - Grandson of Colier & Kate Lassiter	38. Lassiter, William J (b. 26 Apr 1896 - d. 8 Mar 1995) - Grandson of Colier & Kate Lassiter	39. Laughlin, Charles Harrison (b. 16 May 1916 - d. 26 Aug 1977) - Great Great Grandson of Ned & Priscilla Hill	40. Laughlin, Dwight E (b. 17 Jan 1949 - d. 18 Jan 1971) - Great Great Grandson of Colier & Kate Lassiter; Great Great Grandson of Ned & Priscilla Hill

41.Laughlin, Lester Madison (b. 27 Nov 1914 - d. 25 Jan 1998) – Husband of Ruth Lassiter, great granddaughter of Colier & Kate Lassiter	42 .Loflin, C Edward (b. 14 Oct 1913 - d. 23 Jul 1977) – 3rd Great Grandson of Ned & Priscilla Hill	43. Loflin, Rozina Hill (b. 10 Aug 1882 - d. 21 Nov 1943) –Great Granddaughter of Ned & Priscilla Hill	44 .Loflin, Thomas E (b. 10 Sep 1876 - d. 9 Jul 1927) – Husband of Rozina Hill Loflin, Great Granddaughter of Ned & Priscilla Hill
45. Loflin, William Emory (b. 3 Sep 1909 - d. 27 Jul 1927) – Great Great Grandson of Ned & Priscilla Hill	46. McLeod, Jerry (b. 1826 - d. 26 Apr 1908) –Husband of Tima S Waldon McLeod -- sister of Henry R Walden, daughter of Julia Ritter Walden	47. McLeod, Tima S Waldon (b. 8 Nov 1852 - d. 4 May 1908) – Sister of Henry R Walden; & Daughter of Julia Ritter Walden	48. McRae, Edgar, R(aymond) (b. 2 Jul 1918 - d. 21 Mar 2004) – Great Great Grandson of Ned & Priscilla Hill
49. McRae, Ivy W (b. 14 Feb 1912 - d. 24 May 1996) – Wife of Edgar R McRae; Niece of Henry R Walden	50. McRae, Jerald W (b. 4 Dec 1925 - d. 3 Jan 1974) – Great Great Grandson of Ned & Priscilla Hill	51. McRae, Lugena (b. Unknown - d. 1992) Great Great Granddaughter of Ned & Priscilla Hill	52. Potter, Lloyd W (b. 12 Apr 1912 - d. 27 Feb 1968) – Great Great Grandson of Ned & Priscilla Hill
53. Potter, Norma B (b. 6 Aug 1912 - d. 4 Sep 1965) – Wife of Lloyd Potter, Great Great Grandson of Ned & Priscilla Hill	54. Ratliff, Abbe M (b. 24 May 1929 - d. 30 Jun 2009) – Great Granddaughter of Colier & Kate Lassiter; Great Great Granddaughter	55. Redwine, Thanee (b. 1849 - d. 1922) – Daughter of Ned & Priscilla Hill	56. Smitherman, Bertis (b. 21 Jun 1884 - d. 9 Jan 1982) – Great Great Grandson of Ned & Priscilla Hill

	of Micajah & Harriet Cotton		
57. Smitherman, Harrison (b. 1 Jun 1894 - d. 14 Jun 1977) -- Great Great Grandson of Ned & Priscilla Hill	58. Smitherman, Mary (b. 1866 - d. 29 Jun 1931) – Great Granddaughter of Ned & Priscilla Hill	59. Smitherman, Roy (b. 20 Oct 1887 - d. 3 Sep 1889) -- Great Great Grandson of Ned & Priscilla Hill	60. Smitherman, Sallie M (b. 6 Mar 1898 - d. 27 Mar 1961) -- Great Great Granddaughter of Ned & Priscilla Hill
61. Smitherman, Winston (b. 1 Sep1894 - d. 24 Jul 1980) -- Great Great Grandson of Ned & Priscilla Hill	62. Speed, Alice Lassiter (b. 1 Apr 1898 - d. 16 Nov 1986) – Granddaughter of Colier & Kate Lassiter;	63. Spruill, Geraldine Finnie McMillion (b. 30 Sep 1944 - d. 5 Nov 2006)	64. Walden, Julia (b. 1820 - d. 15 Jan 1907) – Mother of Henry R Walden & Tima S Walden McLed
65. White, Delia Theodocia (b. 20 Oct 1898 - d. 14 Feb 1997) – Granddaughter of Ned & Priscilla Hill	66. Laughlin, Ruth L (b. 10 Mar 1922 – 24 Jun 2000) Great Granddaughter of Colier & Kate Lassiter	67. Walden, The Rev. Islay (b. ca 1844 – d. 2 Feb 1884) – Brother of Sarah Hill, wife of Emsley Hill; first Pastor and Postmaster	68. Walden, Eleanora W. (b. 1858 – d. 1892) – Wife of the Rev. Islay Walden, and Henry Ruffin Walden; first Principal and Teacher; Postmistress

Figure 128: Strieby Church Cemetery.
Photo by Margo Lee Williams, 2014.

Unmarked Graves in Strieby Church Cemetery

Following are the names of those buried at Strieby who, for the most part, do not have grave markers,[974] but whose names were identified from their death certificates, not tombstones. Therefore, some names in the cemetery listing are not included here. While death certificates in North Carolina can be found in on-line databases, they are not usually available after the mid to late 1970s. Since state and Social Security death indexes do not list burial

[974] Names without grave markers are indicated here with an "*".

information, many late 20th century burials cannot be confirmed if there is no known marker or community member with first-hand knowledge. Names included here rarely extend beyond the fourth generation from the two principal founding couples, Ned and Priscilla (Mahockley) Hill, along with Miles and Healy (Phillips) Lassiter. It should be remembered that even with the addition of the names listed here, there are many other burials. Burials can be presumed for earlier generations where no death certificates exist, but by virtue of their residence and their membership in these families, it can be assumed they are buried in Strieby Church Cemetery.

Only names, dates of death, and names of parents are listed here. For additional information, please see the genealogies in the previous sections.

Name	Date of Death	Father	Mother (Maiden Name)
Alexander Adderton*	01 Jun 1917	xxx	Jennie Adderton
Bertha Adderton*	15 May 1917	Alexander Adderton	Rhodemia Lassiter
Clara J Coble*	8 Feb 1922	Israel M Coble	Minerva Hill
Rodney Coble*	26 Jun 1917	Israel M Coble	Minerva Hill
Aller Eadie Davis*	16 Jul 1921	Joseph Eadie	Mary Jane Hill
Greeley Davis*	24 Jul 1918	William Davis	Jane Parker
James A. Davis*	21 Apr 1941	Anthony Davis	Annie Hearn/Crump
Lovie Potter Davis*	2 Feb 1952	Thomas Potter	Mary Jane Hill

Mary Jane Hill Eadie*	28 Nov 1923	Ned Hill	Priscilla Mahockley
Elizabeth Hill Fisher*	2 Oct 1933	John Bello	Bethana Hill
George Henley Jr.*	27 Mar 1962	George Henley Sr.	Metta Cotton
George Henley Sr.*	31 Dec 1943	Postell Henley	Bethana Martitia Lassiter
Metta Cotton Henley*	04 Feb 1930	Webster Cotton	Rosetta Short
Arthur Haze Hill	13 Sep 1980	Barzilla Harrison Hill	Elizabeth Hearn
Barzilla Harrison Hill	2 Dec 1933	Calvin Hill	Elizabeth Chandler
David Edward Hill*	27 Jun 1958	Carl Hill	Bertha McRae
Elizabeth J Davis Hill*	06 Mar 1940	Anthony Davis	Annie Crump
Elizabeth Hearn Hill	4 May 1936	Rollin Hearn	Rebecca Davis
Elizabeth Lassiter Hill	16 Dec 1962	Amos B. Lassiter	Harriett Phillips
Ernest Marvin Hill*	23 Mar 1970	Julius Hill	Elizabeth Davis
Ethel "Effie" Hill Mills*	10 Nov 1964	Julius Hill	Elizabeth Davis
James Martin Hill*	14 Jun 1965	Julius Hill	Elizabeth Davis
Lucretia Hill*	25 Jun 1918	Ulysses Grant Hill	Izetta Redwine
Steven/Stephen Hill*	17 Nov 1922	Edward Hill	Priscilla Mahockley
Thomas Winburn Hill*	9 Sep 1929	Jesse Potter Jr	Bethana Hill
Ulysses Grant Hill*	20 Aug 1925	Calvin Hill	Elizabeth Chandler
Unnamed Hill (f)*	30 Dec 1924	Carl Hill	Bertha McRae
Mary Elizabeth Fisher Holt*	11 Jan 1933	William Fisher	Elizabeth Hill
Barzillai (Amos B.) Lassiter	16 Dec 1930	Colier Lassiter	Katherine Polk
Harriett Phillips Lassiter	10 Mar 1942	Reuben Phillips	Mary Scott
Harris Stockton Lassiter	31 Jan 1964	Amos B. Lassiter	Harriett Phillips
Ora Clara Kearns Lassiter	12 Sep 1951	Clarkson Kearns	Abigail Head
Sarah J. Smitherman Lassiter	29 Jul 1975	Charlie Smitherman	Mary Ann Hill
Ulysses Winston Lassiter	26 Nov 1937	Colier Lassiter	Katherine Polk
Rozina Hill Laughlin	21 Nov 1943	xxx	Mary Louisa Hill
Thomas Edward Laughlin	8 Jul 1949	Chesley Laughlin	Sarah Ganaway
Emma Luther*	16 Apr 1952	Benjamin Luther	Bethana Hill
Delphina "Della" Potter McRae*	17 Mar 1944	Lege Wilson	Mary Jane Hill
Edward McRae	19 Feb 1919	John McRae	Delphina "Della" Potter
Geneva McRae*	21 Jun 1932	John McRae	Delphina "Della" Potter

Jerald W McRae	3 Jan 1974	John McRae	Delphina "Della" Potter
Unnamed Pool(f)*	15 Apt 1923	Arch Pool	Mamie Hill
Calvin Duckery Potter*	27 Jan 1940	Ira Potter	Charity Hill
Charity Hill Potter*	31 Mar 1921	Ned Hill	Priscilla Mahockley
Lloyd Watson Potter	27 Feb 1968	Calvin Dockery Potter	Elizabeth Eadie
Norma Bolding Potter	4 Sep 1965	William Bolding	Mary Byrd
Bethana "Thanie" Hill Redwine	29 Oct 1922	Ned Hill	Priscilla Mahockley
Harrison Smitherman	14 Jun 1977	Charlie Smitherman	Mary Ann Hill
Mary Ann Hill Smitherman	29 Jun 1931	Edmund Cranford	Sallie Hill
Sarah "Sallie" Smitherman	27 Mar 1961	Charlie Smitherman	Mary Ann Hill
Winston Smitherman	24 Jul 1980	Charlie Smitherman	Mary Ann Hill
Harry Speed*	06 Jul 1941	Alson Speed	Annie (Unknown)

Figure 129: Right side Strieby Church Bell-Narthex--Nave-Fellowship Hall. Photo by Margo Lee Williams, 2014.

Figure 130: Right side of Strieby Church with stained glass windows. Photo by Margo Lee Williams, 2014.

PART FIVE:

STRIEBY TODAY

Figure 131: Deacons & Trustees: L-R Standing-Jerry Laughlin, Oberia H. Hill, Lester Laughlin. L-R Seated-Kate L. Jones, Arthur Hill, Raymond McRae, 1972.

Figure 132: Old Strieby Church just before demolition, 1971.
Photo courtesy of Patrice Lassiter Bryant.

Change Comes to Strieby

The original Strieby Church building served the community well for nearly 90 years when, in 1969, it was condemned for large gatherings. As the community had changed and younger families moved away for new opportunities, the old church building was not being maintained adequately.

A "Fun for Fund Club" was established, spearheaded by Strieby graduate, Kate Lassiter Jones, then living in Westfield, New Jersey.

Figure 133: Kate Lassiter Jones, August 2006. Photo by Clyde Foust.

Katherine Martitia Lilly Bernice Lassiter (1906-2006) was the daughter of Ulysses Winston and Ora (Kearns) Lassiter and grew up in the Lassiter Mill community. Kate attended Strieby School before going on to Columbian Heights High School in Winston-Salem. She attended Brick Junior College, in Enfield, now the Franklinton Conference Center of the United Church of Christ. During summers she earned money for tuition by going on church sponsored missions to Georgia, Texas, and Louisiana. She eventually earned college degrees from Schauffler College (loosely affiliated with the Congregational Church and now part of Oberlin University) in Cleveland, Ohio, and Columbia University in New York. Kate was by all measures a Strieby success story and Strieby remained near and dear to her heart throughout her life. “”How can I turn my back on such a towering symbol in my life and see it sag and decay and cease to be?”[975]

Figure 134: Katherine "Kate" Lassiter, Left- ca. 1940, Right-Ca. WWII

The Fun for Fund Club would reach out to community members and former community members and Strieby grads living in North Carolina and elsewhere. Two years later, they would be able to break ground. By

[975] Jones, 1972, p. 13.

1972, the old church would be gone and a new Strieby Church building would be dedicated.

Figure 135: New Strieby Church. Photo by Margo Lee Williams, 1982.

Souvenir Journal

for

The Dedication of the New Church Building

STRIEBY CONGREGATIONAL UNITED CHURCH OF CHRIST

Strieby, North Carolina

Sunday, December 24, 1972

Figure 136: Souvenir Journal from Dedication of the New Strieby Church Building, 1972.

Kate was deeply proud of this accomplishment, as much as any other in her life. She was not finished, however. Next, she set her sights on stained glass windows which were installed in the mid-1980s, including the central window of a Jesus who was not the standard, blonde, blue-eyed image so common at the time. This Jesus was swarthy, with dark hair. She was again very proud that Strieby would make a visible statement for a non-white Jesus. In the 1980s this was still a revolutionary move. She was even instrumental in having the road named "Strieby Church Road," replacing the State Route designation.

Figure 137: Strieby Church with stained glass windows. Photo by Margo Lee Williams, 2014.

Kate remained active in the life of Strieby throughout her life, playing piano, planning programs, being ordained a deaconess, and as a trustee. Recognizing that there was a dwindling congregation as younger generations moved away in search of education and jobs, she once said that she hoped the building could possibly be used as a senior center or some other creative use. She was always looking toward the future. So it seems fitting that the church and school she loved so dearly, and whose history she worked tirelessly to preserve and share, should become a recognized cultural heritage site.

Figure 138: Authur Hill Home. Photo by Margo Lee Williams, 1982

As for the community of Strieby residents, the last full time African American residents and descendants of the original community members were Arthur Haze Hill (Bulla, 1977),[976] whose home still stands across the road from Strieby Church and Cemetery, and Bertis Smitherman, whose former home faces High Pine Church Road. Both Arthur Hill and Bertis Smitherman were great grandsons of Ned and Priscilla (Mahockly) Hill. Arthur Hill died 13 September 1980,[977] and Bertis Smitherman died 9 January 1982.[978] They were both buried in Strieby Church Cemetery.

Figure 139: Looking through the woods at Arthur Hill's cabin. Photo by Margo Lee Williams, 2014.

---

[976] Bulla, 1977.

[977] North Carolina Death Indexes, [Database on-line]. *Ancestry.com*. Arthur Haze Hill, 13 Sep 1980.

[978] North Carolina Death Indexes, [Database on-line]. *Ancestry.com*. Birtis Smitherman, 9 Jan 1982.

Figure 140: Jerry Laughlin & Elbert Lassiter, Jr. Deacons & Trustees. Photo by Margo Lee Williams, 2014.

A New Day Dawns

That was not the end of the Strieby story. Although the school is gone now, Strieby Church continues to hold occasional services and bible study in the new church building, built in 1972. Recently, services have been led by the Rev. Winston Lassiter, his wife, the Rev. Tanya (Le'Gette) Lassiter, along with daughters, Mia and Amber. Currently, Elbert Lassiter Jr. and his wife, Rose (Anderson) Lassiter lead bible study and prayers, along with his brother Reggie Lassiter and cousin, Jerry Laughlin and his wife Jackcine (Simmons) Laughlin. Elbert, Reggie, and Jerry grew up attending Strieby Church. Elbert, Reggie, Jerry, and Winston are descendants of Colier Lassiter, son of Miles Lassiter. Jerry is also a descendant of Ned and Priscilla Hill.

The most important service Strieby Church still holds is its annual Homecoming-Revival on the fourth Sunday in August. In recent years a Friends and Family Day has been held on the Saturday before. It is a time when descendants of the Hill, Lassiter, associated families, and friends, gather to share fellowship, family stories, and make new memories.

Finally, as we have seen, Strieby descendants continue to bury their loved ones in the cemetery, next to their ancestors. Thus, they keep alive the promise that was, and is still, *Strieby*.

Thus the change came, leaving a precious few, strong in their religious convictions and determined in this effort, that Strieby Congregational United Church of Christ will never die. That she will stand through the ages, as long as the years of her past, as a historical, religious and educational landmark, reaching out through her children of many generations, to all mankind.

Kate Lassiter Jones,
24 December 1972[979]

Figure 141: George Jones Memorial Bench & Bird Bath Photo by Margo Lee Williams, 2014.

[979] Jones, 1972, p. 2.

Figure 142: Strieby Church, School & Cemetery Cultural Heritage Marker ca. 1880. Photo courtesy of Elbert Lassiter, Jr.

A Cultural Heritage Site

The cultural impact of Strieby was recognized by the Randolph County Historic Landmark Preservation Commission (HLPC), on 23 September 2014.[980] By gathering and presenting much of this history to the Commission at their monthly meeting, the community has been able to preserve and lift up this history for the world to see. The Commission agreed that Strieby Church, School and Cemetery property was an important Cultural

[980] HLPC, 2014a & b; Penkava, 2014; Walker, 2014; Williams, 2014; & Williams, 2015.

Heritage Site in Randolph County. In addition to issuing a proclamation, the history and pictures were uploaded to the HLPC website and copies preserved in their files. The final honor was the placing of a sign at Strieby Church providing visible testimony for all who venture down Strieby Church Road that Strieby Church, School, and Cemetery have been an important part of the historical and cultural heritage of Randolph County.

Randolph County Historic Landmark Preservation Commission

Resolution of Recognition

WHEREAS, The Randolph County Historic Landmark Preservation Commission desires to recognize those Cultural Heritage Sites that provide a tangible link to the past, with the people and events that have made significant contributions to Randolph County history, and thus shaped our present; and

WHEREAS, in 1880, former Randolph County slave the Rev. Islay Walden, founded the First Congregational Church of Randolph County, as well as a school to serve free people of color in an area called Hill Town in Union Township, Randolph County, which was renamed in 1884, due to Rev. Walden's effort to obtain a U.S. Post Office, as Strieby Congregational Church and School, and

WHEREAS, the impact of Strieby School continued well into the 20th Century, producing teachers, doctors, nurses, ministers, and others for the African American community of Southwestern Randolph County and beyond, and

WHEREAS, the new Strieby Church, constructed in 1972, continues to serve the community, holding special services led by a descendent of one of the founding families, and descendants of the founding families continue to be buried in the cemetery.

NOW, THEREFORE, BE IT RESOLVED, that official recognition as a Randolph County ***Cultural Heritage Site*** is given to:

STRIEBY CONGREGATIONAL CHURCH, SCHOOL, & CEMETERY, Ca. 1880

BE IT FURTHER RESOLVED, that this Resolution is approved by the Historic Landmark Preservation Commission and recorded in its minutes, with appropriate history and photographs placed on the Commission's historical website, and a suitable copy of the Resolution presented to the recipient.

Approved this 23rd Day of September, 2014.

Resolution Number 2014-01

Figure 143: Randolph County Historic Landmark Preservation Commision "Resolution of Recognition" approving Strieby Church, School & Cemetery as a Cultural Heritage Site, 23rd September, 2014.

Past Ministers at Strieby

The Rev. Islay Walden - Founding Minister
The Rev. Zachariah Simmons
The Rev. Henry Stratton
The Rev. O. W. Hawkins
The Rev. H. W. Brown
The Rev. Henry Dillard
The Rev. Carl Campbell
The Rev. E. Christian
The Rev. Perfect DeBerry
The Rev. A. Anderson
The Rev. E. B. Cozart
The Rev. Frank Wooley
The Rev. H. Smith
The Rev. O. F. Barnhill
The Rev. John McCoy
The Rev. D. L. Poe
The Rev. J. H. Hooker
The Rev. Bernard Ingram
The Rev. Dr. Marion Blair
The Rev. Ronald Coleman
The Rev. Robert Jones
The Revs. Winston & Tanya (Le'Gette) Lassiter

Figure 144: Gathering at Strieby, possible funeral.
Photo courtesy of Patrice Lassiter Bryant.

A Final Tribute

And finally, may we pay tribute to our parents, our grandparents, and great grandparents, for their insight and guidelines, which introduced us to strong religious principles, basic education, and the realities of personal adjustment.

Kate Lassiter Jones,
4 December 1972[981]

[981] Jones, 1972, p. 14.

**Figure 145: Leaving Strieby Church, headed back to High Pine Church Road.
Photo by Margo Lee Williams, 2014.**

Sources

Abigail, Colier, & Kate Lassiter to Jenny Lassiter. *Randolph County, North Carolina Deed Book 56*:430. FHL #0470244.

Addison & Cornelia Lassiter to H.W. Hubbard. (1880). *Randolph County, North Carolina Deed Book 42*:199.

American Antiquarian Society and Newsbank. (2004). Personal: Islay Walden, in *Patriot* (1873, 18 July), *IV*:1. Retrieved (5 June 2016) from: http://www.genealogybank.com/doc/newspapers/image/v2%3A12A5AB52CC49F908%40GB3NEWS-12AAA277C421F2AB%402405358-12A84F89068AF82D%400-138EBC1FF292B544%40Personal?search_terms=Walden%7CIslay

American Antiquarian Society and Newsbank. (2004). Personal and Literary: Islay Walden, in *Rockford Journal* (1873 26 July), 6. Retrieved (5 June 2016) from: http://www.genealogybank.com/doc/newspapers/image/v2%3A130FB81A1E9520B4%40GB3NEWS-132FCF81169E4AEC%402405366-132E28D90B086AB4%405-1330024BCDA42448%40?search_terms=Walden%7CIslay

American Antiquarian Society and Newsbank. (2004). Local News: Howard University—Normal Class, in *Evening Star* (1876, 16 June), 5. Retrieved (5 June 2016) from: http://www.genealogybank.com/doc/newspapers/image/v2%3A13D5DA85AE05A305%40GB3NEWS-13E363964C9D9188%402406422-13E0BC6679613198%404-13E4774D9EC39470%40?search_terms=Walden%7CIslay

American Antiquarian Society and Newsbank. (2014). Personal and Literary: Islay Walden, in *Goodhue County Republican* (1873, 24 July), 2. Retrieved (5 June 2016) from: http://www.genealogybank.com/doc/newspapers/image/v2%3A14B7A84E827D59CC%40GB3NEWS-14FC94838A9FDD28%402405364-14FC7B442F00AB48%401-14FD3A69B984DE68%40?search_terms=Walden%7CIslay

American Missionary Association (AMA). (1880) Self Help: North Carolina. *Annual Report of the American Missionary Association, Volumes 30-39*, *34*:68. Retrieved from: http://books.google.com/books?id=i38sAAAAYAAJ&pg=RA

6-PA58&lpg=RA6-PA58&dq=The+American+Missionary+Rev+Islay+Walden&source=bl&ots=t5CBVGIC0V&sig=Q7Rbug0QstAm9cE8fB9PRuewKC4&hl=en&sa=X&ei=-s75UeejBrT_4AOtw4DYAw&sqi=2&ved=0CEEQ6AEwBQ#v=onepage&q=The%20American%20Missionary%20Rev%20Islay%20Walden&f=false

American Missionary Association (AMA). (1880). Conferences: North Carolina Conference. *Annual Report of the American Missionary Association, Volumes 30-39, 34*:72. Retrieved from: http://books.google.com/books?id=i38sAAAAYAAJ&pg=RA6-PA58&lpg=RA6-PA58&dq=The+American+Missionary+Rev+Islay+Walden&source=bl&ots=t5CBVGIC0V&sig=Q7Rbug0QstAm9cE8fB9PRuewKC4&hl=en&sa=X&ei=-s75UeejBrT_4AOtw4DYAw&sqi=2&ved=0CEEQ6AEwBQ#v=onepage&q=The%20American%20Missionary%20Rev%20Islay%20Walden&f=false

American Missionary Association (AMA). (1881). Conferences: North Carolina Conference. *Annual Report of the American Missionary Association, Volumes 30-39, 35*:94. Retrieved from: http://books.google.com/books?id=i38sAAAAYAAJ&pg=RA6-PA58&lpg=RA6-PA58&dq=The+American+Missionary+Rev+Islay+Walden&source=bl&ots=t5CBVGIC0V&sig=Q7Rbug0QstAm9cE8fB9PRuewKC4&hl=en&sa=X&ei=-s75UeejBrT_4AOtw4DYAw&sqi=2&ved=0CEEQ6AEwBQ#v=onepage&q=The%20American%20Missionary%20Rev%20Islay%20Walden&f=false%20Missionary%20Rev%20Islay%20Walden&f=false

American Missionary Association (AMA). (1881) Anniversary Reports: North Carolina. *The American Missionary, 35*(7):211. Retrieved from: http://books.google.com/books?id=VW7OAAAAMAAJ&pg=PA211&lpg=PA211&dq=The+American+Missionary+Rev+Islay+Walden+obituary&source=bl&ots=Sn4QMYLZOJ&sig=9qh3NShoITJ6uWj1fqhh4VyqLX4&hl=en&sa=X&ei=scD5UfQR8YXJAb-kgYgL&ved=0CDYQ6AEwAg#v=onepage&q=The%20American%20Missionary%20Rev%20Islay%20Walden%20obituary&f=false

American Missionary Association (AMA). (1882). Common Schools: Lassiter's Mills, North Carolina. *Annual Report of the American Missionary Association, Volumes 30-39*, *36*:58. Retrieved from: http://books.google.com/books?id=i38sAAAAYAAJ&pg=RA6-PA58&lpg=RA6-PA58&dq=The+American+Missionary+Rev+Islay+Walden&source=bl&ots=t5CBVGIC0V&sig=Q7Rbug0QstAm9cE8fB9PRuewKC4&hl=en&sa=X&ei=-s75UeejBrT_4AOtw4DYAw&sqi=2&ved=0CEEQ6AEwBQ#v=onepage&q=The%20American%20Missionary%20Rev%20Islay%20Walden&f=false

American Missionary Association (AMA). (1883). Common Schools: Lassiter's Mills, North Carolina. *Annual Report of the American Missionary Association, Volumes 30-39*, *37*:65. Retrieved from: http://books.google.com/books?id=i38sAAAAYAAJ&pg=RA6-PA58&lpg=RA6-PA58&dq=The+American+Missionary+Rev+Islay+Walden&source=bl&ots=t5CBVGIC0V&sig=Q7Rbug0QstAm9cE8fB9PRuewKC4&hl=en&sa=X&ei=-s75UeejBrT_4AOtw4DYAw&sqi=2&ved=0CEEQ6AEwBQ#v=onepage&q=The%20American%20Missionary%20Rev%20Islay%20Walden&f=false

American Missionary Association (AMA). (1884). The Field: North Carolina. *The American Missionary, 38:*45. Retrieved from: http://books.google.com/books?id=RNPNAAAAMAAJ&pg=PA45&lpg=PA45&dq=Alfred+Islay+Walden&source=bl&ots=Hq8NNZBUbk&sig=AlFwnTCtsBgmnUmDG5W8Psyn98U&hl=en&sa=X&ei=Fpj4UbTfNovW9ATinIHoCA&ved=0CDAQ6AEwATgU#v=onepage&q&f=false

American Missionary Association (AMA). (1884). Items from the Field. *The American Missionary, Volume 38:*51. Retrieved from: http://books.google.com/books?id=4q0PAAAAIAAJ&pg=PA51&lpg=PA51&dq=Islay+Walden+postmaster+strieby+NORTH CAROLINA+post+office&source=bl&ots=TMTNv3WHDR&sig=FdCQ6AHtRKBp5yWbJZawOh6gKZQ&hl=en&sa=X&ei=sPwKUt7ROqLiyAHv5YDoBw&ved=0CCsQ6AEwAA#v=onepage&q=Islay%20Walden%20postmaster%20strieby%20North Carolina%20post%20office&f=false

American Missionary Association (AMA). (1884). Common Schools: Lassiter's Mills, North Carolina. *Annual Report of the*

American Missionary Association, Volumes 30-39, Volume 38:52. Retrieved from: http://books.google.com/books?id=i38sAAAAYAAJ&pg=RA6-PA58&lpg=RA6-PA58&dq=The+American+Missionary+Rev+Islay+Walden&source=bl&ots=t5CBVGIC0V&sig=Q7Rbug0QstAm9cE8fB9PRuewKC4&hl=en&sa=X&ei=-s75UeejBrT_4AOtw4DYAw&sqi=2&ved=0CEEQ6AEwBQ#v=onepage&q=The%20American%20Missionary%20Rev%20Islay%20Walden&f=false

American Missionary Association (AMA). (1892). Obituary: Mrs. Henry R. Walden. *The American Missionary, 46*(3):91. Retrieved from: http://books.google.com/books?id=KT8QAAAAYAAJ&q=Mrs.+Henry+R+Walden#v=snippet&q=Mrs.%20Henry%20R%20Walden&f=false

American Missionary Association. (1895). Report. *The American Missionary*. Volume 49, Number 5. Retrieved from: https://books.google.com/books?id=DgrPAAAAMAAJ&pg=PA359&lpg=PA359&dq=American+Missionary+Association+1893&source=bl&ots=fXVDurgPnP&sig=SdaqqeT2ZppxUDwKU6GpWKImtQM&hl=en&sa=X&ved=0ahUKEwjxyen7jdXJAhXCeSYKHXFlA80Q6AEINTAF#v=onepage&q=American%20Missionary%20Association%201893&f=false

Anderson Smitherman et al v. Solomon Kearns, et Ux, Final Decree, *Deed Book 248*:156. FHL #0470851.

Auman, D. &Auman, W. (1976). *Seagrove Area* (Village Printing Company). Retrieved from: https://archive.org/stream/seagrovearea00auma/seagrovearea00auma_djvu.txt

Bruce, D. D. (2013). Reconstruction Era (Appendix). *The Concise Oxford Companion to African American Literature*. (Oxford: Oxford University Press). Retrieved from: https://books.google.com/books?id=-9XtCY7cijMC&pg=PA464&lpg=PA464&dq=North+Carolina+Victorian+writers+Islay+Walden&source=bl&ots=3Dw5RKnAHu&sig=MmvHr7O5s_yCKOK-rAA1bByIyXA&hl=en&sa=X&ei=yJvzVJeKI4WGyASV-4LYDA&ved=0CB4Q6AEwAA#v=onepage&q=North%20Carolina%20Victorian%20writers%20Islay%20Walden&f=false

Bruce, D. D. (1992). *Black American Writing from the Nadir: The Evolution of a Literary Tradition 1877-1915* (Baton Rouge: Louisiana State University Press). Retrieved from:

http://books.google.com/books?id=R33hb83ltdwC&pg=PA23&lpg=PA23&dq=islay+walden+invisible+poets&source=bl&ots=sVsYdDJsWo&sig=suyoae_jdLi8fmTSLY76jn0MFs8&hl=en&sa=X&ei=YboCUqOBOKesiAKK24GwCw&ved=0CD8Q6AEwAw#v=onepage&q=islay%20walden%20invisible%20poets&f=false

Bruggink, D. J. and Baker, K. N. (2004). John Bergen and Islay Walden. *By Grace Alone: Stories of the Reformed Church in America* (Grand Rapids/Cambridge: Wm. B. Erdmanns Publishing). Retrieved from: https://books.google.com/books?id=tU4A1wkm0I4C&pg=PA103&lpg=PA103&dq=Islay+Walden+Howard+University&source=bl&ots=l6h5woZRXw&sig=XsA055-h-cOPGlZGk4qemCQ9vGc&hl=en&sa=X&ei=2vjsVLmFNY26ogSK_IKICQ&ved=0CDkQ6AEwBTgK#v=onepage&q=Islay%20Walden%20Howard%20University&f=false

Brumm, J. H., editor. (2000). The Experience of Black People in the Reformed Church in America. *Equipping the Saints: The Synod of New York, 1800-2000.* Retrieved from: http://books.google.com/books?id=rjgdN2oQxy4C&pg=PA75&lpg=PA75&dq=The+American+Missionary+Rev+Islay+Walden+obituary&source=bl&ots=mH7xlSg_sc&sig=8xHjYolpuDnnS6nUwOYbezwt0do&hl=en&sa=X&ei=rsn5UaW3CNTe4AP9q4HIAg&ved=0CDoQ6AEwAzgK#v=onepage&q=The%20American%20Missionary%20Rev%20Islay%20Walden%20obituary&f=false

Bulla, R. L. (September 20, 1977). At 90, He's the Last Resident of Streiby [*sic*]. *Asheboro Courier Tribune.* Copy provided by Christine Hill, granddaughter of Arthur Hill.

Cadbury, H. (1936). Negro Membership in the Society of Friends, Part Three (Miles Lassiter). *Journal of Negro History*, *21*:180-209. Retrieved from: http://www.qhpress.org/quakerpages/qwhp/hcjnh3.htm

Calyer Phillips, Bastardy Bond, May Term 1851, *Minutes of the Court of Common Pleas and Quarter Sessions.* FHL #0019652 or #0470212

Cemetery Census. (2010). *Randolph County North Carolina Cemeteries: 116 Strieby United Church of Christ.* Retrieved from: http://cemeterycensus.com/North Carolina/rand/cem116.htm

Chase, W. C., ed. (17 September 1898). Flotsam and Jetsam: Islay Walden… *The Washington Bee,* 4. Retrieved from: https://www.newspapers.com/image/46290383/?terms=Islay%2BWalden

Colier Lassiter to Samuel Hill (Tr), *Randolph County Deed Book 30*:15. FHL #0470234.

Colier and Katie Lassiter to Board of Education, *Randolph County Deed Book 38*:288. FHL #0470237.

Davis, W. A., ed. (6 August 1878). State News: Islay Walden… *The Torchlight,* 2. Retrieved from: https://www.newspapers.com/image/67576267/?terms=Islay%2BWalden

DeBoer, C. M. (2015). Blacks and the American Missionary Association. *Hidden Histories in the United Church of Christ, Volume I.* Retrieved from: http://www.ucc.org/about-us_hidden-histories_blacks-and-the-american

Delegates to the Constitutional Congress, North Carolina, Lassiter Mills District. Calvin Lassiter. *Bureau of Refugees, Freedmen and Abandoned Lands*. NARA #M843, Roll 32:107.

Dodson, N. B. (2 September 1911). Select Society for Research. *The Pittsburgh Courier,* 4. Retrieved from: https://www.newspapers.com/image/33455594/?terms=Islay%2BWalden

Dodson, N. B. (21 October 1911). Select Society for Research. *The Lexington Standard*, 1. Retrieved from: https://www.newspapers.com/image/144012734/?terms=Islay%2BWalden

Emsley and Susan Lassiter, et al, to Calier Phillips, *Randolph County Deed Book 29*:495. FHL #0470233.

Estate of Ezekiel Lassiter, *Randolph County Will Book 7*: (Sarah and Ezekiel) Inventory, 303; (Sarah) Account, 331; (Ezekiel) Account, 332; (Sarah and Ezekiel) Final Distribution of the Estate,406. FHL #0019643.

Estate of Healy Phillips or Lassiter, *Randolph County Will Book 10*:190-192. FHL #0019645.

Estate of Islay Walden. (1884). *North Carolina, Estate Files, 1663-1979*, index and images: Randolph County. Retrieved from: https://familysearch.org/pal:/MM9.3.1/TH-1942-35515-9366-66?cc=1911121&wc=93P6-8G2:183652401,183410401,1066674205

Evening Post. (2 July 1879). An Interesting Ordination. (New York, NY). Retrieved from: http://fultonhistory.com/newspaper%2010/New%20York%20NY%20Evening%20Post/New%20York%20NY%20Evening%20Post%201879%20Grayscale/New%20York%20NY%20Evening%20Post%201879%20Grayscale%20-%200613.pdf

Feinsilver, E. (1999). Reidsville teacher was early civil rights protester. *Greensboro News & Record,* A1.

Flick, D. P. & Hamilton, T. R. (2008). Strieby Congregational U.C.C. *Churches Related: Forty year history of churches and related ministries, 1965-2005, United Church of Christ* (Salisbury, North Carolina: Western North Carolina Association of the Southern Conference of the United Church of Christ), 194-195. (The church address is incorrectly recorded therein).

Foner, E. (2015). *A Short History of Reconstruction, Updated Edition.* (Harper Perennial Modern Classics). [Kindle Version].

Friedlander, B. (8 October 2009). The Birth of Poetry. *American Poetry in the Age of Whitman and Dickenson.* Retrieved (4 March 2016) from: https://ampoarchive.wordpress.com/2009/10/08/birth-of-poetry/#comments

Garner, H.L. (2011). *From Slavery to Strieby: Rev Alfred Islay Walden, 1843-1884.* (Lulu Publishing: www.lulu.com).

General Council. (1884). North Carolina: Lassiter's Mill. *The Year Book of the Congregational Christian Churches of the United States,* 176. Retrieved from: http://books.google.com/books?id=jhpKAAAAMAAJ&pg=PA176&lpg=PA176&dq=Alfred+Islay+Walden&source=bl&ots=nnmMvWTbcx&sig=-0uZH-GYXv6XT0N287XmhTeBaFA&hl=en&sa=X&ei=WZ34UYy2JoKg9QSzsYCIBQ&ved=0CDAQ6AEwATge#v=onepage&q=Alfred%20Islay%20Walden&f=false

Gershenhorn, J. (2010) A Courageous Voice for Black Freedom: Louis Austin and the Carolina Times in Depression-Era North Carolina. *North Carolina Historical Review*, Vol. 87 (1):85.

Grant, M. (2011). Strieby: Never Heard of It. *Asheboro Magazine, 1*, 11: 56-58. Retrieved from: http://issuu.com/ashemag/docs/ashemag_06_11_issuu

Hammond, L. and Cranford, C. L. (1982). *Farmer: Yesterday and Today: Families, individuals, churches, and schools* Denny, Z., ed. (Wooten Printing).

Hampton Institute. (1893). *Twenty-Two Year's Work of the Hampton Normal and Agricultural Institute at Hampton, Virginia.* (Hampton, Virginia: Normal School Press).

Hinshaw, W.W. (1991). Miles Lassiter (Back Creek Monthly Meeting). *Encyclopedia of American Quaker Genealogy, Volume 1, North Carolina* (Baltimore: Genealogical Publishing Company) I: 723.

Historic Landmark Preservation Commission (HLPC). (2012). Randolph High School Cultural Heritage Site. (2012). *Randolph County, North Carolina Historic Landmark Preservation Commission.*

Retrieved from: http://www.co.randolph.North Carolina.us/hlpc/RandolphHighSchool.htm

Historic Landmark Preservation Commission (HLPC). (2014a). Meeting Minutes, September 23, 2014. *Randolph County, North Carolina Historic Landmark Preservation Commission.* Retrieved from: http://www.co.randolph.nc.us/hlpc/minutes/hlpc_minutes_140923.pdf

Historic Landmark Preservation Commission (HLPC). (2014b). Strieby Church Cultural Heritage Site. *Randolph County, North Carolina Historic Landmark Preservation Commission.* Retrieved from: http://www.co.randolph.North Carolina.us/hlpc/StriebyChurch.htm

Hollyday, J. (2005). *On the Heels of Freedom: The American Missionary Association's Bold Campaign to Educate Minds, Open Hearts, and Heal the Soul of a Divided Nation* (New York: The Crossroad Publishing Company).

Howard University. (1896). Howard University Normal Department Class of 1876: Islay Walden Deceased. *Alumni Catalogue of Howard University with List of Incorporators, Trustees, and Other Employees, 1867-1896* (Washington DC: Union Alumni Association). 44. Retrieved (6 March 2016) from: https://archive.org/stream/alumnicatalogueo00howa/alumnicatalogueo00howa_djvu.txt

Jackson, B. (2000). Islay Walden. *Dictionary of North Carolina Biography,* William S. Powell, editor, *Volume 6*:109 (Chapel Hill: University of North Carolina Press). Retrieved from: http://books.google.com/books?id=y7UBnqTz3vsC&pg=PA108&lpg=PA108&dq=Islay+Walden+North Carolina+biography&source=bl&ots=9RWl-UqHo6&sig=kq-AUBxG_5VH3aiDgnquf4fizt0&hl=en&sa=X&ei=_I4CUuPLFeyQyQHxwIHYDQ&sqi=2&ved=0CD0Q6AEwAw#v=onepage&q=Islay%20Walden%20North Carolina%20biography&f=false

Jackson, B. (1994). Islay Walden. *NCpedia.* Retrieved from: http://NCpedia.org/biography/walden-islay

Jackson, B. (1984). Black Victorian Writers of North Carolina. *Victorians Institute Journal, Volumes 12*:55. Retrieved from: https://books.google.com/books?id=bC06AQAAMAAJ&q=Islay+Walden&dq=Islay+Walden&hl=en&sa=X&ei=UQHtVPyMJ4nYoASU0YDICg&ved=0CCUQ6AEwADgU

Jarrett, G. A. (2007). *Deans and Truants: Race and Realism in African American Literature,* 43 (Philadelphia: University of

Pennsylvania Press). Retrieved from: http://books.google.com/books?id=nYwaqm5dV0YC&pg=PA43&lpg=PA43&dq=Islay+Walden++african+american+poets&source=bl&ots=EQwEL-4jBF&sig=Iiqnpbo_vM2pfGv8IN1eVg5R1Z0&hl=en&sa=X&ei=qLYCUsCOOM7bqQHlsoGQCw&sqi=2&ved=0CEwQ6AEwBg#v=onepage&q=Islay%20Walden%20%20african%20american%20poets&f=false

Jarrett, G. A. (2006). Introduction. *African American Literature beyond Race: An alternative reader* (New York: New York University Press). Retrieved from: http://www.nyupress.org/webchapters/0814742874intro.pdf

Jesse Morgan to Miles Lassiter (1815). *Randolph County, North Carolina Deed Book 13*:402. (FHL #0019635 or #0470228).

Jones, K. L. (1993). Novella Anna Lassiter (361). *The Heritage of Randolph County, North Carolina,* 343-344.

Jones, K. L. (1972). History of the Strieby Congregational United Church of Christ. *Souvenir Journal for The Dedication of the New Church Building: Strieby Congregational United Church of Christ.* (Strieby, NC: Strieby Congregational United Church of Christ), 1-2.

Jones, M. D. (1987). The American Missionary Association and the Beaufort, North Carolina School Controversy, 1866-67. *Phylon (1960-2002), 48,* 2: 103-111. Retrieved from: http://www.jstor.org/discover/10.2307/274774?uid=3739960&uid=2129&uid=2134&uid=2&uid=70&uid=4&uid=3739256&sid=21103443109731

Kilcup, K. L. and Sorby, A. (2013) *Over the River and through the Wood: An Anthology of Nineteenth Century Children's Poetry.* (Baltimore: Johns Hopkins University Press).

Larsen, K., editor. (2012). *The Cambridge Companion to Nineteenth-Century American Poetry.* (New York: Cambridge University Press).

Letter from Jonathan Worth. (21 January 1851).Written for "Calier Phillips or Lassiter," on the division of the estate of Helia Phillips. (Personal Possession).

Letter from Lillian H. Thornburg to Mrs. Worth. (19 March 1941). Randolph Room, Randolph County Library, Asheboro, North Carolina.

Letters of Administration and order to sell slaves. (February 1840). Sarah Lassiter and Ezekiel Lassiter. *Minutes of the Court of Common Pleas and Quarter Sessions,* FHL #0019652 or #0470211.

Margo, R. A. (1990). Race and Schooling in the South: A review of the evidence. *Race and Schooling in the South, 1880-1950: An Economic History.* (Chicago: University of Chicago Press). Retrieved from: http://www.nber.org/chapter/c8792

McDaniel, D. and Julye, V. (2009). *Fit for Freedom, Not for Friendship: Quakers, African Americans, and the Myth of Racial Justice* (Philadelphia: Quaker Press).

Miles Lassiter Obituary. (22 June 1850). *Friends Review iii*:700.

Minutes of Back Creek Monthly Meeting, (March 1845, April 1845, June 1845, January 1849, & March 1849). *Friends Historical Collection.* (Greensboro, North Carolina: Guilford College).

Morrison, B. (2009). A Brief Synopsis of the History of Uwharrie Friends Meeting. *Science Hill Friends Meeting,* 1-4. Randolph Room, Randolph County Library.

National Council. (1885). Vital Statistics. *The Congregational Yearbook, 1885.* (Boston: Congregational Publishing Society) *Volume 7*:37. Retrieved from: http://books.google.com/books?id=P2EsAAAAYAAJ&pg=PA37&lpg=PA37&dq=Rev+Islay+Walden+dead&source=bl&ots=prv6-qO9lF&sig=SorB8F7lqjZYgj8MGiVtq02GKm0&hl=en&sa=X&ei=MR4LUpyeMojs9ATFm4HwCA&ved=0CC8Q6AEwAjgK#v=onepage&q=Rev%20Islay%20Walden%20dead&f=false

NBTS Anti-Racism Transformation Team. (February 25, 2016). *Slavery, Justice and New Brunswick Theological Seminary*. Retrieved (March 4, 2016) from: http://www.nbts.edu/slavery-justice-and-new-brunswick-theological-seminary/

NBTS E-Story. (n. d.). Alfred Islay Walden. *New Brunswick Theological Seminary.* Retrieved from: http://www.nbts.edu/newsite/estory.cfm?storynum=154

Newby, T. (1916). "Reminiscences of a Pioneer Hoosier Settlement in Central Indiana." Reprinted, arranged and illustrated by Thomas E. Q. Williams(2006).Retrieved from: http://hancaocknews.com/reminiscences_of_a_pioneer.htm

New Jersey, Marriages, 1678-1985. [Database on-line]. *FamilySearch.* Alfred I. Walden and Elenor W. Farmer, 18 May 1881, Retrieved from: https://familysearch.org/pal:/MM9.1.1/FZPL-QY7

North Carolina Advisory Committee to the United States Commission on Civil Rights. (1959-62). Education. *Equal Protection of the Laws in North Carolina.*99-124. Retrieved from: https://www.law.umaryland.edu/marshall/usccr/documents/cr12n81c.pdf

North Carolina Counties Map. Retrieved from: http://quickfacts.census.gov/qfd/img/counties/stout37.gif

North Carolina, Death Certificates, 1909-1976 [Database on-line]. *Ancestry.com.* Henry Ruffin Walden, died: 20 Jan 1951. Retrieved from: http://interactive.ancestry.com/1121/S123_363-2726/675132?backurl=http://person.ancestry.com/tree/66453873/person/36493560403/facts/citation/223242362753/edit/record

North Carolina Literary Map. (n. d.). Walden, Alfred Islay. Retrieved (4 March 2016) from: http://library.uncg.edu/dp/nclitmap/details.aspx?typ=auth&id=1754

Penkava, L., editor. (7 October 2014). Strieby Church named cultural heritage site. *The Randolph Guide.* Retrieved from: http://www.randolphguide.com/news/local_news/article_ab8b5180-4e36-11e4-9cd2-8b547d0b5025.html

Randolph Report. (1964). Lassiter's Mill, now quiet, still stands imposingly tall. *The Randolph Guide,* E2 (Randolph Room, Randolph County Library).

Reformed Church in America. (1877). *Minutes of General Synod: Directory and financial reports. Appendix 1, Volume 13*: 689. Retrieved from: https://books.google.com/books?id=V3s0AQAAMAAJ&pg=PA607&lpg=PA607&dq=new+brunswick+reformed+seminary+and+Rev.+Islay+Walden&source=bl&ots=Lv5GBs_B7C&sig=n21fOJF1t_tnGCRmBSv1cRogQ28&hl=en&sa=X&ei=c2jnVJaUM4ivogSgqYGIDw&ved=0CCsQ6AEwAw#v=onepage&q=new%20brunswick%20reformed%20seminary%20and%20Rev.%20Islay%20Walden&f=false

Richardson, J.M. & Jones, M.D. (2009). *Education for Liberation: The American Missionary Association and African Americans, 1890 to the Civil Rights Movement* (Tuscaloosa: University of Alabama Press).

Road Orders, (August 1807). Miles Lassiter. *Minutes of the Court of Common Pleas and Quarter Sessions.* FHL #0019650 or #0470209.

Roy, J. E. (1879). The Freedmen. *The American Missionary.* Volume 33(11):334-335. Retrieved from: http://ebooks.library.cornell.edu/cgi/t/text/pageviewer-idx?c=amis;cc=amis;rgn=full%20text;idno=amis0033-11;didno=amis0033-11;view=image;seq=359;node=amis0033-11%3A1;page=root;size=100

Sarah Lassiter and Miles Lassiter to Henry Newby (1826). *Randolph County Deed Book 17*:256. FHL#0019636 or #0470229.

Sherman, J. (1992). Alfred Islay Walden. *African-American Poetry of the Nineteenth Century: An Anthology* (Champaign, Illinois: University of Illinois Press). Retrieved from: http://books.google.com/books?id=pXEoic5_3YcC&q=Alfred+Islay+Walden#v=snippet&q=Alfred%20Islay%20Walden&f=false

Sherman, J. (1984). Alfred Islay Walden. *African-American Poetry: An Anthology, 1773-1927* (Champaign, Illinois: University of Illinois Press).

Sherman, J. (1974). Alfred Islay Walden. *Invisible poets; Afro-Americans of the nineteenth century*, 104-111 (Champaign, Illinois: University of Illinois Press).

Simmons-Henry, L., Henry, P., & Speas, C. (1990). *The Heritage of Blacks in North Carolina* (Raleigh: The North Carolina African American Heritage Foundation). Retrieved from: https://books.google.com/books?ei=uvnsVKfUGsazoQTSxoGYAQ&id=oR8NAQAAMAAJ&dq=Islay+Walden+Philadelphia+PA&focus=searchwithinvolume&q=Alfred+Islay+Walden+

State *v* Colier P. Lassiter. (Spring Term 1857). *Minutes of the Superior Court*. FHL #0470215.

The Brooklyn Daily Eagle. (8 August 1873). Personal: Walden (Brooklyn, NY), 4. Retrieved from: https://www.newspapers.com/image/50390354/?terms=Islay%2BWalden

The Carolina Times. (18 August 1939). Bus Case Hotly Contested in Randolph Court. (Raleigh, North Carolina.), 6. Retrieved from: http://library.digitalNorth Carolina.org/cgi-bin/showfile.exe?CISOROOT=/newspapers&CISOPTR=16757&CISOMODE=print

The Carolina Times. (18 August 1939). Wins Important Case. (Raleigh, North Carolina), 3. Retrieved from: http://library.digitalNorth Carolina.org/cgi-bin/showfile.exe?CISOROOT=/newspapers&CISOPTR=16757&CISOMODE=print

The Daily Times. (4 December 1878). Anniversary of Students' Mission. (New Brunswick, NJ), 3. Retrieved from: *FamilySearch.org.*

The Daily Times. (24 March 1879). City Matters. (New Brunswick, NJ), 3. Retrieved from: *FamilySearch.org.*

The Daily Times. (30 June 1879). City Matters. (New Brunswick, NJ), 3. Retrieved from: *FamilySearch.org.*

The Daily Times. (28 June 1879). Ordained. (New Brunswick, NJ), 3. Retrieved from: *FamilySearch.org.*

The Daily Times. (21 December 1879). Panorama and Concert. (New Brunswick, NJ), 3. Retrieved from: *FamilySearch.org.*

The Daily Times. (3 January 1879 & 4 January 1879). Shoes for the Poor. (New Brunswick, NJ), 3. Retrieved from: *FamilySearch.org.*

The Daily Times. (29 March 29 1879). Students' Mission. (New Brunswick, NJ), 3. Retrieved from: *FamilySearch.org.*

The Daily Times. (28 December 1878). Where There's a Will, There's a Way: Panorama and Concert. (New Brunswick, NJ), 3. Retrieved from: *FamilySearch.org.*

The National Republican. (15 June 1876). Howard University (Washington, DC), 4. Retrieved from: https://www.newspapers.com/image/71138199/?terms=Islay%2BWalden

The North State (1 August 1878). Islay Walden… (Greensboro, NC), 2. Retrieved from: https://www.newspapers.com/image/63457165/?terms=Islay%2BWalden

The Poetry Foundation. (2013). Alfred Islay Walden, 1847-1884. Retrieved from: http://www.poetryfoundation.org/bio/alfred-islay-walden

Tombstone: "Katie, wife of Calier Lassiter,7 Mar 1832 - 19 Dec 1906 " *Strieby Congregational United Church of Christ Cemetery*, Strieby Church Road, Strieby, Union Township, Randolph County, North Carolina. Retrieved from: http://cemeterycensus.com/North Carolina/rand/cem116.htm

Tombstone: "PRISCILLA HILL, 1792 - 1911. GONE BUT NOT FORGOTTEN."Strieby Congregational United Church of Christ Cemetery, Strieby Church Road, Union Township, Randolph County, North Carolina. Find A Grave Memorial #83483930. Retrieved from: http://www.findagrave.com/cgi-bin/fg.cgi?page=gr&GSln=Hill&GSiman=1&GScid=2433562&GRid=83483930&

Vidales, C. (2011). Randolph County Estates, Dunbar-Duty: William Dunston. *The Genealogical Journal by the Randolph County Genealogical Society,* Volume XXXV(2): 45-46.

Walden, H. R. (1891). Missionary Work at Strieby, N.C., *The American Missionary*, *45*(3):166-169. Retrieved from: https://books.google.com/books?id=89TNAAAAMAAJ&pg=PA313&lpg=PA313&dq=American+Missionary+Association+1891&source=bl&ots=PnnnV79lyt&sig=9ckaymUJ0SsumnjsQIJd56BCOlI&hl=en&sa=X&ved=0ahUKEwiJ5pyFpdrJAhVCSSYKHZv4BvAQ6AEIPzAI#v=onepage&q=American%20Missionary%20Association%201891&f=false

Walden, H. R. (1893). Teaching the young. *The American Missionary, 47*(10):318-319. Retrieved from: https://play.google.com/books/reader?printsec=frontcover&output=reader&id=bNXNAAAAMAAJ&pg=GBS.PA318

Walden, I. (1873, Reprint 2012). Introduction. *Walden's Miscellaneous Poems: Which the author desires to dedicate to the cause of education and humanity* (Hong Kong: Forgotten Books Classic Reprint). See also: http://books.google.com/books?id=5c8gAAAAMAAJ&pg=PA9&lpg=PA9&dq=Alfred+Islay+Walden%27s+Miscellaneous+Poems&source=bl&ots=KGqTqUaWZz&sig=kEQFcF0iQ9wL0rHidCbiLw822X4&hl=en&sa=X&ei=Z5X4UeXuBYTo9ATsuYCgCw&ved=0CEEQ6AEwBA#v=onepage&q=Alfred%20Islay%20Walden%27s%20Miscellaneous%20Poems&f=false

Walden, I. (1877). *Sacred Poems with a Sketch of His Life*. (New Brunswick, N. J.: Terhune & Van Anglen's Press; Reprint: Library of Congress).

Walden, I. (n.d.). Letter to Prof. David Demarest from Islay Walden (ca. 1845-1884) of the NBTS class of 1879, one of the first two African American graduates of the school. *Reformed Church in America: Following Christ in mission.* Retrieved (4 March 2016) from: http://www.nbts.edu/wp-content/uploads/2016/02/Alfred_Islay_Walden_Letter.pdf

Walden, I. (28 August 1879). What an Educated Colored Man Thinks of Goldsboro. *Goldsboro Messenger*. Retrieved (4 March 2016) from: https://www.newspapers.com/image/?spot=1664736&fcfToken=6e63503159727370755432 6f415755434c4f54664c6c306275493268754b425335736e392b52696945327a76714c754a4f3144354a6541566e5853776f346a45

Walker, J.D. (23 September 2014). Strieby Church, School, and Cemetery become latest Randolph County cultural heritage sites. *The Courier-Tribune*. Retrieved from: http://courier-tribune.com/news/strieby-church-school-and-cemetery-become-latest-randolph-county-cultural-heritage-sites#sthash.VDmhheCs.dpuf

Williams, M. L. (2011). *Miles Lassiter (circa 1777-1850). An Early African American Quaker from Lassiter Mill, Randolph County, North Carolina: My Research Journey to Home* (Palm Coast: Backintyme Publishing).

Williams, M. L. (2013). Vella Lassiter, 1937 Bus Suit. *The Miles Lassiter Family of Randolph County, North Carolina.* Retrieved from:

http://mileslassiter.tribalpages.com/tribe/browse?userid=mileslassiter&view=78&ver=352&storyid=49456.

Williams, M. L. (2014). *The History of Strieby Congregational Church and School, Union Township, Randolph County, North Carolina: Cultural Heritage Site Application.* Retrieved from: http://www.co.randolph.nc.us/hlpc/downloads/Strieby_Church_and_School_History.pdf

Williams, M. L. (February, 2015). Once upon a Time in Hill Town. *Thrive*. (Asheboro, NC: *The Courier-Tribune*).

Census Records

1830 US Federal Census, Randolph County, North Carolina, National Archives and Records Administration, (NARA,) M19-125.

1850 US Federal Census, free schedule, Randolph County, North Carolina, NARA #M432-641, and Family History Library (FHL) #444654, item 2.

1860 US Federal Census, free schedule, Randolph County, North Carolina, NARA #M653-910.

1870 US Federal Census, Randolph County, North Carolina, NARA #M593-1156; FHL #552655.

1880 US Federal Census, population schedule, Randolph County, North Carolina, NARA #T9-978.

1900 US Federal Census, Randolph County, North Carolina, NARA #T623-1213; FHL #1241213.

1910 US Federal Census, Randolph County, North Carolina, NARA #T624-1128; FHL #1375141.

1920 US Federal Census, Randolph County, North Carolina, NARA #T625-1318.

1940 US Federal Census, Randolph County, North Carolina NARA #T627_2962.

Figure 146: Back at the corner of Strieby Church Road and High Pine Church Road. Photo by Margo Lee Williams, 2014.

Index

M

O

P

60201652R00248

Made in the USA
Charleston, SC
27 August 2016